# Triumph

# Over

# Destiny

Peladija Woodson-Diers

All rights reserved. Except as permitted under the U.S. Copyright Act of 1976, no
part of this publication may be reproduced, distributed, or transmitted in any form
or by any means, or stored in a database or retrieval system, without the prior
written permission of the publisher.
Published by Peladija Woodson-Diers
901 North Frederick
Oelwein, Iowa 50662
Visit the website at www.triumphoverdestiny.com

Library of Congress Cataloging-in-Publication Data is available

First Edition; November 2014

ISBN 978-0-578-14183-1



Printed in the United States of America

*This book is dedicated to my parents Djura and Karoline Stefanovic whose story I have always felt compelled to share.*

*To my sisters Ingeborg, Krsmanija, Anneliese, and the entire Brase family.*

*I also dedicate this book to the many people along the way who were instrumental in my*

*parent's and sisters' lives and who aided in their survival.*

*War strips away humanity,*
*it breaks your faith,*
*unfairly steals away your ability to grieve,*
*and creates a numbness in your soul*
*that for me was everlasting.*

-Karoline Stefanovic

*What lies behind us and what*
*lies before us are tiny matters*
*compared to what lies within us.*
-Ralph Waldo Emerson

## Triumph Over Destiny

Prologue

When I was growing up, I heard many stories based in local folklore so I was quite superstitious by the time I reached adulthood. The concept of destiny in many of these stories often seemed confusing and frustrating. Also to be considered is the question of why God chooses to give us the destinies he does. As an adult, at times, I find it difficult to make sense of it all and question why certain events have happened.

My mother was a true believer in destiny. She told me destiny would play a significant role in my life even if I tried to wish it away. Her prophetic words had an important impact on my life. She was the person I looked up to, respected, and who most influenced my life. What I learned from her affects the way I make my own decisions and proceed with my life from day to day. Her beliefs and values have become part of me, make me think about and realize what's important in life, what is true and what is false; how superstition plays a role in our lives, and how we sometimes are unable to control our own destinies.

I ask myself, 'What is destiny?' Was it destiny that damaged Mother, and changed the way she looked for the rest of her life? If destiny is unavoidable, why are kind and compassionate people destined to experience terrible events? Why would God be cruel and make a person such as my mother suffer? She was a good and kind woman who never harmed anyone. Why was she being punished? Why was I? Why were my husband and my children? I have pondered what my life would have been like if circumstances had been different, if certain people had not crossed my path.

Some memories are so clear yet some of them are clouded by time and by the 72-years of my life that have already passed by. Some

1

recollections I can remember in full detail, others I've tried to forget because they are too painful. I told my children many times I needed to get all my thoughts and memories written down on paper so someday I could write a book about my life.

Not knowing how to start such a project, I forgot about it for many years. I had given up on the idea until my daughter, Peladija, began taping voice recordings of Djura and me in 1991. I have held these thoughts and feelings inside of me for over 70 years. While I sit here peacefully under this shade tree, I realize the time has come to record my story. My story of a life of happiness, pain, torment, and loss. I sincerely hope after reading my story, others will come away with a greater sense of urgency, genuine sincerity and determination to avoid future wars.

## Chapter 1

I was born in a small Austrian town called Knittlelfeld, Steiermark on November 3, 1922. Steiermark was a state within the borders of Austria. After the First World War, Europe and its people were still trying to recuperate from the death and the destruction that finally ended in 1918. I arrived during a period when the survivors were very conscious of the effects of the war; anxious and troubled about the future. Fear and uneasiness remained in the air as the death and devastation of World War I still haunted the minds of many.

My mother, Agnes Rink, wanted so very much to be a mother. The hopes and dreams of my mother marrying and having children came into doubt when she was 17-years-old. Following a botched dental procedure, the damage was obvious to anyone with the fortune of sight. Nerves damaged during the procedure left Mother with a permanent frown, resembling the facial paralysis of a stroke. Her hopes of ever having a family and being married someday weighed heavily on her mind. She was skeptical of finding anyone who would marry her. Her new sense of self-consciousness led her to look away or downward in hopes people wouldn't notice the damaged side of her face. Her asymmetrical smile avoided cameras and mirrors and led others to treat her as a poor soul to be pitied. Accepting her disfigurement was a challenge she faced throughout her lifetime. She intentionally placed few mirrors in her home and allowed very few pictures to be taken of herself.

Even with her disfigurement she eventually met my father, Valentine Rink, fell in love, and married. She had multiple miscarriages and began to question if motherhood was in her future. When she finally became pregnant with me at the age of 22, she was overjoyed as the pregnancy progressed. As most births in that day, she planned to deliver at home and rely on the sole help of a midwife. Apparently my stubborn

3

inclination to stay nestled in my mother's womb caused a lengthy labor. I finally relented in the early evening on a cool November day in 1922. I weighed a healthy 8 pounds, had shiny black hair, light brown eyes, and fair skin. I was named Karoline. Throughout my lifetime, I would receive numerous compliments on my rosy cheeks and flawless, radiant skin my mother had passed along to me. My father was 31-years-old when I was born and a very proud papa. When I was still very young, Mother told me that a child was the greatest gift God could ever give anyone and parents should be grateful for their little angels. Feeling as loved as a child could ever hope to be, she would tell me of her joy and delight when she had me. It was one of the most precious moments of her life.

Agnes was a kind woman, modest, and humble. She took enormous pride in her role as a daughter, wife, mother, and would eventually take pride in being a grandmother. She was not materialistic nor was she vain, she was however, compassionate, strong-willed and had a heart full of love for family, friends, nature, and the occasional stranger she encountered in need of help. Mother was a fairly tall woman at 5'7", was large breasted, with black, wavy hair, brown eyes, and had a fair, translucent complexion; a skin tone most women envied. She prayed daily and asked God for good health and happiness for her family, her friends and herself. She read to me every night from the Bible or a prayer book she had gotten from her grandmother.

**A rare photo of Agnes**

Mother was superstitious and a true believer in destiny. Her stories were permeated with superstition and folklore so it wasn't a surprise I had become quite superstitious by the time I reached adulthood. She told me destiny would play a significant role in my life even if I tried to wish it away. I often wondered what was destiny. Was it destiny that plagued my mother, and changed the way she looked for the rest of her life? If destiny is unavoidable, why does it target even the most kind and compassionate? What is God's purpose in tragedy and suffering?

My father, Valentin, a small-framed man, had curly, black hair and hazel eyes. He was mild mannered, yet very opinionated and felt strongly about his convictions. He wasn't much taller than my mother, was slender and agile, and relatively fit for his age. Both Father and Mother were quite limber. Every day they both climbed up the mountains to graze the livestock. I had to laugh at our guests who came to visit. They would get short winded from climbing a short distance up the mountain trail. My father made a nightly ritual of saying our prayers, tucked me into bed, and as he kissed me goodnight, his mustache tickled my nose.

My father started working for the railroad before I was born while my mother walked to a neighboring farm to do chores until my birth. Both incomes were needed to help pay the bills. After my birth, my father worked to provide our basic necessities.

**Valentin**

My maternal grandmother, Margarette, was also part of the family. She had come to live with us when I was just a baby and helped my mother with child rearing and household chores. Oma Margarette was born in Bleiberg and lived with us most of her life. She was never married and had to raise my mother by herself. I never knew who my maternal grandfather was and he was never talked about in the household. To this day I'm not sure who he was, and I don't know much about their relationship.

Oma Margarette's kind touch and soft smile made it easy for others to feel the gentleness and compassion generated from her lighthearted spirit. She was a kind, thoughtful and God-fearing woman. She believed all people should honor God, and be spiritually guided through life.

As a child, Oma Margarette told me stories, baked delicious goodies, took walks with me, and helped me say my bedtime prayers. Most children hoped and wished for a grandmother like Margarette. She helped contribute to many unforgettable stories and events my family and I experienced throughout the years.

Oma had given me a prayer book containing daily prayers in it for each given day of the year. My family read from it often. That prayer book would follow me into adulthood, be shared with my children, and spark memories, good and bad, of its journeys with me.

## Chapter 2

Knittelfeld was a quaint and picturesque village, with wide, brick-lined streets surrounding the town square.  Many of the houses and buildings stood at least two stories high.  They were made of brick and mortar with clay tile roof tops in overlapping rows.  Wooden shutters covered the windows, and as they swung outward to open like French doors, fresh, robust mountain air flowed through the opening.  Tall, skinny light poles lit up the town square at night.  Wooden fences surrounded farmsteads keeping the livestock from roaming freely throughout the hillsides.

Mountain ranges and scenic foothills surrounded the town.  The Alps were eternally spectacular and breathtaking.  From the mountain tops you could see farm houses nestled in hillsides which in the spring were surrounded by vibrant, green meadows.  It was a quiet place where you could view an entire village from the mountains, hear the sounds of the birds singing in chorus, and view meadow upon meadow of magnificent wild flowers.  If you lay on the plush multi-layered bed of deep, emerald grass, while getting lost in the blue sky, an indescribable connection formed.

You wouldn't be surprised to hear clanging bells that hung from the necks of the livestock as their owners herded them toward new pastures to graze.  Goats could be seen climbing up to the steepest parts of the mountain side and grazing openly throughout the foothills.  Bright yellow flowers lined the edge of the creek.  Pine trees whistled eerily at night, prompting thoughts of loneliness and seclusion.  Stories from Mother and Father were numerous and more often than not used the countryside outside my window as the setting.  I would listen with wonderment as they talked about the mountains and the animals that lived right next to us.  God had been gracious to bless us with this magnificent landscape.

Edelweiss, the national flower of Austria, grew abundantly everywhere and was widely used for medicinal purposes. It was traditionally used in folk medicine as a remedy for abdominal and respiratory illness. Picking them on numerous occasions as a child, I was unaware of the important role this little star shaped flower would play in the lives of my family.

We lived in Knittelfeld until the struggling economy began to impact employment opportunities. Gratefully, at the age of five, I was unaware of the financial struggles many were experiencing in the late 1920's. My family was no exception. In 1927 Father lost his job and we were forced to move to Bleiberg. He found work in the lead mines.

## Chapter 3

Bleiberg was a mining town and the literal translation for Bleiberg is "Lead Mountains." Blei meaning lead, and berg meaning mountain. The pay from working in the mines was barely enough to afford the rent for the small cottage where we lived. The cottage was close to the foothills near Bleiberg. Many families in the area were worried about how they were going to survive and where they would get their next meal. Times were hard. My one pair of shoes for the year were something to treasure and show off to my friends at school. Father fit metal clips to the heels of my shoes to prolong their durability. I liked the tickety-tap noise they made and I became an instant tap dancer when they hit hardwood floors. Wearing an apron in the house was another measure to extend the wear of my dresses. Although we had very little and were living in poverty, my lifestyle resembled those around me so I never felt underprivileged or impoverished.

When we moved to Bleiberg, it was like a new adventure for me; new neighbors, a different house, exquisite countryside to explore, and new friends to meet. Everything new sparked my interest and I was excited about living in a new region. It was easy to adjust to my new surroundings.

My parents, however, experienced a more difficult transition. The depressed economy was dragging down the mood and temperament of the Austrian people. My family hadn't yet become soured or resentful by the great depression. There would be events that would soon take place as our country was moving closer to war that would have a profound effect on the people of Austria. My family would not be spared.

It was inconceivable to the majority of the people in Austria, and to the whole world what the future had in store. Who could have ever imagined the vastness of the death and destruction that was yet to come to

Europe because Adolf Hitler came to power?  In the next ten years, my life, along with many others, would be forever altered.  The events being set in motion would change how I perceived the world and my own destiny.

In Bleiberg, life seemed nothing but normal to me.  My mother spent most of her time cooking, cleaning, washing clothes, and caring for me.  I watched her spinning her own yarn from the sheeps' wool after we had sheared the lambs.  She knitted us all long woolen socks, caps, and scarves that were welcome during the cold mountain winters.  My parents doted over me constantly.  I never had to help with household chores while I was young or do any housework unless I wanted to because my mother would do everything for me.  I had what most would consider, a carefree happy childhood.

Raising and feeding our farm animals, like the goats, geese and chickens on the homestead were part of our daily routine.  My father went up into the mountains to herd and graze our six goats as the weather permitted.  I would tag along with my father any time I was able to go with him.  When we got the chance we would pack a lunch to take with us and be gone for hours until the goats had their fill of vegetation.  We would sing while the goats grazed the mountain side.  Father was quite the yodeler and encouraged me to sing along.  Our voices bounced off the mountainous cliffs and echoed back, answering us.  Hearing the mirrored sounds of our voices amazed me.  Yodeled echoes were one of the great wonders of the Alps.  Sometimes I'd pretend I was a wealthy princess with an arm full of flowers walking back to my castle.  I'd imagine the goats were my white horses.  Father and I would sing along the way home and he taught me how to harmonize while we walked.

**Valentin in the foothills herding and grazing the goats.**

Winters near the Alps were bitter cold, deep with snow, and windy. We occasionally had avalanches and a rare earthquake. The winters were, however, a wonderful playground, especially if you were a child. As I grew,

I could fill my day sledding with a group of friends down the steep mountains and foothills on a hand crafted toboggan, or snow ski down a mountain slope. The vertical glide down the mountain was so steep it felt like you were racing down a hill going 150 miles per hour. There were horse drawn carriages that drove by the house in the snow overflowed with passengers in the bunk of the sled. It seemed as though we were never bored.

There was enough snow in the winter time to build snow forts the size of a castle or a snowman as big as a giant. Sometimes the older kids or an adult would pull our sleds behind their horse. We would circle around several blocks sliding behind the galloping animal and make a loop around the entire city of Bleiberg. If the horse rider took a corner at a fast enough speed we would roll off the sled laughing and screaming for the rider to stop. When the rider noticed, we'd be picked up and resume our race around town.

The landscape provided plentiful fun for children. From the many snow activities, to bicycle rides and hikes in the mountains, childhood adventures were countless. My restless dare-devil nature gave my mother plenty of reasons to worry.

## Chapter 4

During my childhood recovering from illnesses and injuries seemed a normal part of my life. Mother slathered my body with lard because it was considered a healing agent. She conjured up medicines from the herbs she gathered up in the mountains. Besides the mumps and measles, other common threats of the time were whooping cough (pertussis), smallpox, tuberculosis and the one that was most scary to me, polio. Without access to antibiotics, infections also could be very dangerous. It wasn't unheard of to learn about the death of a child in a family or several deaths in any single family from illnesses or injuries.

Given my sense of adventure, I had close calls that gave my parents reasons to worry about my well-being during my childhood. On my journey back home from a day playing outdoors with friends around age seven, I was viciously attacked by two wild dogs. I was taken to the hospital in Villach (ten miles from Bleiberg) by horse and wagon. My long dark curly black hair was shaved and staples sutured my gaping wounds in my scalp. Days after the attack my wounds became infected and I developed a high fever. Several days later, my fever broke bringing great relief to my family.

Around age 9, a game of dress-up with friends that included a walk down our staircase wearing Mother's heals led to a compound fracture on my right ankle. A lengthy surgery followed to repair the fracture with an even lengthier time to recuperate waiting for the bones to fuse back together. My poor mother, I could not even avoid serious injury in my own house.

Two years later, an adventure into the mountains on bicycles with my friend Cecilia led me to finally start thinking through some of my "great ideas." Both Cecilia and I decided we would hike up a trail in the mountains as far as we could to ensure our trip back down would be fast paced. A section of loose rock on our journey up the path forced us off our bicycles. Rather than consider the potential danger the loose rocks could pose for the return trip down, we decided to walk our bicycles through the rock and forge on up the mountain.

Needless to say, on the way back down, I lost control over the loose patch of rocks, and while gripping the handlebars as tight as I could, both the bicycle and I sailed through the air. After the crash, several of the metal spokes had penetrated through both my foot and ankle into the bone. The local physician was called to the house and cleansed my wounds.

A few weeks later I developed a high fever and had to be hospitalized. I underwent surgery to scrape the infection from my bone and was warned of the possibility of amputation or problems walking related to the distortion of my bone once scraped. It took me over a year to totally recuperate. A twisted disfigurement on the interior side of my ankle persisted. I was able to regain use of my leg and foot to the extent that my injuries went unnoticed by most.

Surviving in a world where a simple infection could lead to death led many to a renewed appreciation and greater strength when individuals or those they loved pulled through a life threatening illness. News of other children in the area contracting life threatening illnesses was a frequent reminder of the vulnerability of being a child. During the early 1900s there were many diseases and ailments that afflicted children. Some were life threatening and others like the mumps and measles meant we had to spend a week or two in bed confined to our rooms. The injuries and illnesses I endured as a child could not have begun to prepare me for what destiny had in store.

## Chapter 5

In 1935, at age 13, we moved to a new home in Bleiberg. Along with his full-time job in the lead mines, my father took on a second job as the groundskeeper for the Catholic Church and its adjacent cemetery. He was paid 40 dollars a year for taking care of the church grounds and digging the graves. Our family was also allowed to live in a large apartment house next to the church for free as part of the bartering agreement in return for his services. The lead mines where many of the townspeople worked were close by and it didn't take long for Father to get to work every day.

We lived in the three-story apartment house that was next to the church by ourselves for several years, and occupied both the first and second floors. The apartment house was very large and could have housed three families with each having their own separate living space on each level of the building. The third floor wasn't ever occupied because father used it primarily to store dead bodies and coffins. Occasionally when there were no bodies up there, the space was used for church meetings.

Eventually another family moved into our apartment building, occupying one of the floors. Both of our families used the same well for water. The well contained a deep, round, endless shaft several feet from the house. A wooden bucket on a long, thick rope was hung from a wooden crank in the middle of the rock-rimmed opening. My friends and I occasionally dropped a rock down the well to see if we could hear the rock splash when it hit the water. It was fun bringing water up from the well. The children that lived nearby and I would crank the rope that was attached to the bucket pulling the bucket to the surface. My family collected water at least once a day.

I would lean over the edge of the opening and look down the dark tunnel. Although I worried about losing my balance and falling in, I couldn't resist leaning over the side. My mother had told me a story once about a two-year-old boy who had climbed onto the side of the well and had fallen to his death. I always wondered if the story was true or if my mother just told me the story to scare me and keep me from playing around the opening. There was also an outside water pump a few feet away from the house that was close to the well where we could pump water for bathing, cooking and cleaning. We didn't have any type of indoor plumbing and shared the water pump and outdoor toilets as well.

Each apartment in the building had its own kitchen, and a small living room area. A potbellied stove dominated the middle of the living area. My parents had a 10 x 10 foot bedroom with enough space for two single beds and a small dresser. Next to the bedroom there was a small storage room. A communal smoke house was available for all the families to use downstairs. The aged wooden steps leading to the upstairs were noisy and rickety. They made strange, squeaky sounds with each step.

The interior of the house was old and had been damaged through the years. There were cracks in the ceilings and in the walls, and joint separations that had been caused by past earthquakes. The dwelling and grounds were daunting leading some to believe it was haunted by spirits. When wandering at night by myself to get a drink of water or a midnight snack I got spooked easily by the slightest noise. I'm sure most of it was my own imagination. If frightened, my mind raced and imagined bizarre happenings that may have transpired within the house or the confines of the church.

The protective 25-foot rock wall that stood as a barrier behind the house was made of rocks from the mountains. The rock was colored similar to the grave stones. Though it was gray and rough on the sides, the top was smooth and slick. The wall was about 20-feet from our house and approximately ten-feet from the back of the cemetery. The Alps circled the entire village. The town was nestled in the valley closed off by the towering mountain sides, which rose up to the heavens. A sidewalk ran in front of the house and the church. It wasn't unusual to see my father standing in the doorway of the church waiting on the priest or on one of the town's people requesting burial services.

The priest of the Catholic Church lived next door to us and I could see the cemetery through our pantry window. Many times I walked around the back of the house and through the cemetery when I went up into the mountains to play. The cemetery sat behind the tall stone wall that was built to prevent avalanches from engulfing our house and the church when the heavy snow came tumbling off the mountain. I helped my father dig graves if he needed it. Living near a cemetery was eerie at night seeing the outline and shadow of the gravestones in the moonlight.

Being the groundskeeper entailed many responsibilities. Father would have to keep the lawn trimmed and the grounds tidy. His role as the gravedigger proved strenuous. Trying to dig a six-foot hole in the earth of the Alps was a challenging and laborious task. With the ground in that area being very rocky, Father would come across slabs of solid rock while digging. Back then there were no motor driven contraptions to help make the job easier. Digging a grave began with father gathering his hand shovel, wheelbarrow, pick, and sledgehammer. It took hours to excavate a grave.

When he came across something significant while digging he picked out the findings and placed them on top of the ground at the edge of the grave. The findings included keepsakes of those previously buried as well as their remains. When father dug a new grave there was always a possibility that he may find someone else's skeletal remains. Burying a corpse in the same site where someone had been previously buried was acceptable and a traditional way for burial in most of Europe. When a person died they would initially be buried in an available location in a pine coffin. Then perhaps 15 to 20 years later another body might be buried in that same place. Before placing the new body in the space, my father first placed the old bones and the keepsakes back in the hole. He then scattered fresh dirt over the top of those items before burying the new body on top of the old.

While digging my father found gold wedding rings, bracelets, necklaces, small statues, watches, and tokens of all kinds that had been buried along with the deceased. Thieves preyed upon the graves searching for valuables that could be sold. Father talked about his disgust with people that stole from graves. He was always on guard and watched for suspicious people lurking about the cemetery at night. Because grave robberies were a frequent occurrence, he policed the cemetery every night. One evening while making his rounds of the cemetery, he encountered two men trying to steal gold fillings from the teeth of a dead body. He hollered at the men who then took off running and Father chased them out of the cemetery.

Sometimes my father let me help dig a grave and on occasion I rode in the wheelbarrow to and from the cemetery. It usually ended in a scolding for both of us when I returned home with my clothes tattered and covered with dirt. Sometimes I sat on the piled up dirt in the bucket of the wheelbarrow and he'd push me around until he found a dumping spot. It seemed as though there was always more dirt that came out of the hole than what we needed after the grave had been dug. For the next couple of years as I became old enough to help father, digging the graves kept us both busy.

During this time period in this area, bodies were not embalmed so after someone died their body had to be buried relatively quickly or they began to decompose after a few days. Most of the bodies that were brought to my father for burial did not have to be stored long and were usually buried within two to three days. The thought of dead bodies up on the third floor always gave me the creeps. I was reminded constantly of the presence of death. The cemetery made me feel like death waited just around the corner for me. I often paused over the granite grave stones marking the sites of children. As my fingers slowly lingered across the etched names, I pondered what their life could have been had fate not intervened so suddenly. Although I comfortably and easily wandered through the graveyard, I feared death. I shuttered at the thought of my body being placed deep in the cold ground, alone and decaying. I imagined the sadness my mother and father would endure if I died. I prayed that both my parents and I would be spared of an early death.

**Father standing in the doorway of the Catholic Church where he worked.**

## Chapter 6

Death was a regular occurrence at our house and it was common to have one of the town's people show up on our doorstep with a dead body. One morning in October I overheard the news of a neighbor's passing. I remember this particular neighbor as a slim woman with rosy cheeks who always appeared happy and greeted everyone with a big smile. When the neighborhood children played outdoors and passed her home, she waved us in and offered apples, pears, freshly picked berries or baked goods that she had wrapped up in her apron. After our sweet tooth had been satisfied, we sat and visited for a while. She told us short stories and then we were off to play.

Hearing of her death, I purposely watched out the window when her body arrived. The open-ended wagon carrying our friendly neighbor's body neared the house. The shape of her body showed through a worn, pale, blue blanket. I saw the indents and curves of her covered corpse. I felt a chill run down my spine as I caught sight of the outline of her figure underneath the blanket. Her toes lifted up the end of the blanket and the heels of her bare feet were visible. Strangely, one of my initial thoughts was to wonder why no one put stockings on her feet so they wouldn't get cold.

Two men and my father carried her body up the stairs. When they reached the third floor, the door closed abruptly. Hearing the door close, I quietly slipped to the base of the third floor staircase. I could hear muffled voices, but was only able to pick up bits and pieces of their conversation. A clunk could be heard as the weight of the wood gurney thumped against the table when they transferred her body onto the table. The two men left shortly thereafter while Father remained in the room.

The room was the largest in the house, and had few furnishings consisting of several hard, wooden chairs and a few tables. The table now holding our neighbor's body was specifically designed for preparing a body for burial. It was not a wide table, thinner and longer than most dining room tables, yet big enough to hold a body. I very slowly and gently moved up the stairs, halting with each creak in case Father heard and I needed to move quickly out of sight. I was relieved when I made it unnoticed to the door. I calmed my breathing and gently opened the door just enough so I could peek inside to see what was happening. I watched as Father prepared her body for burial. Peering into the room was like watching a scary film; it was both frightening and compelling to me.

I thought about her body being buried and going through the decomposition process. I had seen bodies decomposing at many stages. I was having a difficult time imagining this happening to someone I knew. I envisioned her being placed in the cold ground with bugs, worms, and maggots infesting her body. I prayed that I would not die in the winter. The thought of being cold and alone haunted me. My neighbor's death triggered many thoughts about my own mortality. My surroundings often fed these thoughts and fears. I often sought distractions to fend off my morbid thoughts so as not to consume my mind.

Facing the reality of death on a daily basis led me to think about what my future had in store. As a teenager, I at times desired to know what was to come. Looking back as an adult, I'm grateful that I was completely unaware of what was to come in the near future for myself and family. Had I known what I would be enduring, I believe it would have been difficult to function in life and find the will to survive future events. In spite of my beliefs, I tend to believe that our lives are governed more or less by our destiny. I don't know if I would have had enough faith in my own strengths and abilities to survive what was yet to come in my life. I do know, however, that people come and go in your life, change is inevitable, and life's circumstances can be extremely difficult. However, not until you have faced those complex moments in your life, will your true inner strength be known.

## Chapter 7

Fortunately, I was also exposed to fun and exciting activities living so close to the church. This house of worship became a refuge for those who needed shelter. It was also used by the town's people for all kinds of events and celebrations. I was, on occasion, in charge of ringing the church bell during special events like weddings, funerals and other important town gatherings. Knowing the whole town could hear the echoing chimes when I pulled down on the thick rope was thrilling. The sound that rang out was soothing and it played celestial music as it struck. I rang the bell when my father wasn't able to ring it himself. I looked forward to the days he was too busy knowing I could take my turn calling out to the town. The bell in Bleiberg was sounded for many reasons and on occasion would be rung as a warning sign alerting the town of impending danger like an avalanche or a fire.

Living in a three story building during the winter in Bleiberg generated new creative ways to enjoy the mounds of snow. At times we were trapped indoors for several days because of fierce blizzard conditions. After an incredible amount of snow had fallen, I went upstairs one day to find snow as high as the second story window. My imagination churned. There were three windows adjacent to one another on the wall. I opened the middle window looking out with amazement at the huge snow drift against the house. As soon as the snow was cleared from the front door and walkway I rounded up my friends.

Sleds in hand we climbed to the second floor. We opened the middle window and squeezed the sleds through it. I jumped on a sled while my friend pushed from behind. I flew down the drift and rolled off the sled as it slowed almost to a stop at the bottom. The snow was so deep I sank in up to my hips as I trudged back to the front door. My friends met me at the front door arguing about who was next. Mother was less thrilled as we tracked snow in the house and up to the second floor. Future snowstorms created drifts on both sides of the building enabling us to sled out of the window on the opposite side of the building as well. As the snow totals grew, traveling outside of Bleiberg became impossible. The snow at times isolated the town for months.

## Chapter 8

Despite the inclement weather, we trudged our way to school no matter the conditions outside. In 1935, I graduated from 6th grade which completed my schooling. Going to school was something I looked forward to everyday. I enjoyed the challenges of my studies and seeing my friends. Throughout my schooling, my class sizes had been small. I knew practically everyone in the entire school. My favorite subject, and the one I excelled in the most, was my writing class.

The teachers, though pleasant most of the time, could be very strict. If you would not or could not behave, you found yourself getting a hard whack across the back with a long, wooden ruler or stick. There was also the possibility of your fingers being firmly smacked. The teachers tolerated very little bad behavior. At times, the punishment drew blood or caused bruising. If a teacher determined a student was deserving of punishment, the student was told to place their hands palms down on their desk. Most punishments required whacks from the yardstick across the bare knuckles. Everyone knew not to let out a scream while being punished or face the grim possibility of further consequences for disturbing the rest of the class.

It wasn't uncommon to be punished in front of the entire class. The times I was punished at school, I didn't dare go home and tell my parents. If I had, I most likely would have been in further trouble. Punishment by teachers was rarely, if ever, questioned by parents.

The entire village, including our teachers, were free to discipline us. There always seemed to be a lot of eyes watching us. Spanking the children of others was considered acceptable. Running through one of my neighbor's gardens to get a wayward ball was a sure way to get yelled at, chased, and likely whacked if caught. Children were taught that being disrespectful to any adult was a sin and being impolite to an elder was never acceptable. I must admit that when trouble caught up with me, I probably deserved the punishment. Fortunately, my parents were not heavy handed disciplinarians.

In 1935 girls weren't expected nor were very many able to continue their education beyond the sixth grade. It was customary for women to take on domesticated roles after they graduated from grade school. Most children didn't get the opportunity to further their education unless they were academically gifted or had ample financial resources. Often children were expected to help supplement the family's income. Farm kids were considered assets to their family. As children reached their teens many began hard labor. Many worked in the lead mines of Bleiberg.

Although I desired pursuing a career in musical composition or writing, the financial situation of my family prevented this option. I spent little time fretting over the limitations placed on women during that time. I knew my parents worked hard for what they had and I was grateful for my life. I, however, continued to hope that someday I could go back to school.

Following my 6th grade graduation, both my parents and I understood the need for me to bring some income into the family. There weren't many job opportunities for an inexperienced 13-year-old in Bleiberg. I was disappointed to learn the only employer willing to hire me, had me working in the lead mines. It wasn't long before I found myself toiling in the tunnels, helping to excavate lead from the mountain as my father had done for some years. I was almost 14 when I started working in the mines. As can be imagined, this type of work was dirty and physically strenuous which wore on a person over time. The job involved frequent bending, lifting, pushing, and pulling of the overfilled carts loaded with chunks of lead. I hated the mines but tried not to complain to my parents knowing we needed the money.

Mother packed Father and me lunches every day. The days were long and we regularly worked 12 to 14 hour shifts, seven days a week. No matter the age of the employee, all were expected to work equally hard and all received only an occasional break.  Moving and sorting the chunks of lead seemed never ending.  The steel barrels after the lead was sorted were placed on wheels and rolled down a steel track to a shipping area where it was packed, then shipped and processed.

My mother hated that I worked in the mines.  She had hoped for a better future for me.  She already had witnessed the ill effects it had on many of the town's people.  I despised the smell, being filthy and the darkness we had to work in day after day.

The lead mines were the main source of employment in Bleiberg.  Many of the town's people worked there off and on at some point in their lives.  Women and children alike worked and toiled alongside the men in the dark, dirty and cold environment.  Bleiberg was not a town where young people flourished and thrived.  To me the mines were more like a death sentence.  I knew early in life that Bleiberg was not where I wanted to spend the rest of my life.  I didn't want to end up laboring in the dungeon-like tunnels.  I knew someday I would leave this town and find my own way in the world.  I swore I would not spend my life in the lead mines like so many here.

## Chapter 9

By 1937 Father was beginning to experience the effects of working in the mines for several years. He developed a chronic cough and congestion affected his breathing. His voice sounded raspy and hoarse. Sometimes Father wouldn't go to the mines if he was busy at the church. I overheard my mother and father talking one day. She expressed how concerned she was about his exposure to the dust in the mines and its probable impact on his health.

As time went on his symptoms grew worse. He began having spells that left him in a trance. A blank look would spread across his face as if he was in a daze and he was beginning to experience severe tremors in his hands. The tremors were so intense at times he could barely hold his coffee cup or a glass of water without spilling or dropping them to the floor. No one, at the time, could pinpoint for certain the cause. They did, however, speculate it was a result of working in the lead mines. His symptoms mimicked Parkinson's disease, although when I think back a better conclusion would have been lead poisoning. Mother and he had several discussions about how many others in our town had died with similar conditions in the past. I was very worried for my father.

One particular morning, Father had one of his seizures. Following this seizure his behavior was unlike anything I had ever seen before. He became frantic and raced toward the front door. Wild eyed and out of control, he yelled and screamed, saying crazy things that didn't make sense. He bolted out the front door into a cold day without a coat, hat or shoes. In disbelief, mother and I watched him run toward the stone wall behind the house. He yelled as if someone was after him and climbed up onto the 25-foot rock ledge. We were terrified he would fall. My mother and our neighbor chased after him desperate to catch him. Once he was up on top of the ledge he tiptoed along the edge and screamed he was going to jump off. He wouldn't let us near him.

My mother wasn't sure what was happening to him, but she knew they needed to do something quickly before he jumped from the ledge and killed himself. Mother and our neighbor tried their best to coax father down. He stood directly above us. His toes crowded up against the rock ledge. He swayed back and forth about to fall. He was totally incoherent; unaware of what he was doing. Mother and our neighbor continued to plead with him to come down off the wall. After what seemed like hours, my father finally listened, and agreed to come down. It was as if a light bulb had been switched back on in his head. The doctor had few answers and could never tell us for certain what caused my father's bizarre behavior. The doctor confirmed what we had suspected, father's psychosis might be related to lead poisoning.

After the incident, and with the knowledge that lead poisoning may be to blame, my mother felt driven to seek out home remedies she hoped would cure him. She made several trips up into the mountains to find herbs and flowers that were known to help, cure or minimize father's symptoms. Edelweiss was her favorite medicinal, mountain flower and it grew in abundance. She regularly gathered the flowering plant and had many uses for it. She dried the star shaped flower and made a special tea from the blossoms. Many of the people in town also believed the flower had compelling healing powers and could nurse sick individuals back to good health. She nourished my father with this therapeutic tea for several years. He recuperated from what very well may have been lead poisoning and although he worked in the mine for several more years, he did not have further incidences.

## Chapter 10

Working long hours in the lead mines took its toll physically. After a long day's work, I often welcomed the comfort of my bed. There wasn't much sleeping room in our house so Oma Margarette and I shared a small bedroom. Unfortunately my Oma Margarette's mind seemed to age at a faster rate than the rest of her. Many nights my sleep was disrupted by her failing mind.

When I was younger, we had a lot of fun at bedtime. We giggled, told stories and snuggled. As Oma Margarette gradually lost touch with reality she did and said many crazy and outlandish things. She became known in our household for her frequent sleep walking spells, memory loss, and her ability to function like she was awake when she was sound asleep.

I'd awake to find her tip-toeing quietly around the room as if she were looking for something or babbling incoherently. Her long, elegant, silver-white hair and full length, flowing, pure white nightgown projected a ghostly presence. She gave me quite a fright on many occasions.

Many mornings Oma would wake up with dirt-stained feet. She was known to roam about the cemetery at night when she slipped outside unnoticed. We suspected some of the stories circulating around town of a ghost in the cemetery were actually Oma Margarette lurking about at night.

I woke early each morning for work. I complained often to Mother that Oma Margarette kept me up many nights. Mother told me to be patient, Oma was old and her condition was deteriorating, and I should try to ignore her strange behaviors.

## Chapter 11

Working in the lead mines, caring for the church grounds, and keeping an eye on Oma Margarette kept my family very busy. We soon learned our lives were to become even more occupied. In the fall close to my 15th birthday, my mother found out she was pregnant. I was ecstatic to hear the news. Mother was as shocked as the rest of the family as she had given up hope of having another child. I had long dreamed of having a sibling.

As Mother's belly swelled, so did my anticipation of the baby's arrival. In February of 1938 my little sister Elfriede (Friede) was born. I loved holding her and kissing her precious, delicate cheeks. I also developed a new appreciation for my mother as I watched her tenderly and gently, care for my sister. I imagined her interacting with me in a similar fashion when I was an infant.

During this joyous time for my family we were also forced to be mindful of the political changes in Austria and the rest of the world. Father talked about Hitler's failed attempts to unify Germany and Austria. It was evident the pursuit for unification continued. As Nazi propaganda intensified in Austria, my father Valentin argued politics at the drop of a hat. He hated the Nazis and was vocal about his views at home, at work, and in the community.

Sundays seemed to bring out the fight in Valentin as though he was too busy the rest of the week to get worked up about politics. On Sundays he would start contemplating and considering Austria's and the world's affairs. He would sit at the table, smoke his pipe, and listen to the radio to catch up on the current happenings in the world. Austria's economy was poor and current politics that seemed to take advantage of Austria's vulnerable state would infuriate him. It wasn't unusual for him to begin raising his voice in disapproval. He complained about the state of affairs in the country, and ranted about the arrogance of the Nazis.

On March 12th, 1938, Hitler's troops invaded Austria. I was 15-years-old at the time of the Anschluss (the annexation of Austria into Nazi Germany). My father's frustration with the political environment after the Anschluss grew and he remained vocal about his views. This type of behavior by my father was not taken lightly by the local authorities and always left my mother in fear of retaliation from the government for his outspoken opinions.

After Hitler and his henchmen took over Austria, he desperately needed to gain the confidence, trust and support of the Austrian people. Hitler thought by organizing specific gatherings, making appearances in front of large crowds, using Nazi propaganda and charisma, he would gain followers that would join the Nazi party and support his politics. Hitler, along with some of his key military confidants, made a trip to Bleiberg following the Anschluss. They planned for a large assembly to present economic strategies to boost the European economy and to gain support to work toward the collective cause of building a super economy. He wanted to gain the loyalty of the Austrian people in hopes it would give him an advantage in gaining control of several countries in Eastern Europe. It didn't take long for the news to spread that Hitler was in Bleiberg and he was going to give a speech at the local school. The town's people were told attendance was a requirement. Many feared retribution from the Nazi soldiers if they did not show.

Hearing of the assembly, I was curious as to what Hitler would have to say and how the people would react to his comments. I wondered about all the talk that was taking place in town and was surprised at the excitement the upcoming assembly generated. The well-known infamous three, Hitler, Goring, and Hess, were coming to the same school I once attended, to give speeches that evening. No one in town was sure what would be talked about or what this meant for the Austrian people. Several of us local girls had gotten together earlier that day and couldn't help but gossip a bit about the upcoming event. We didn't know much about politics nor did we know much about Hitler or his ideology and thought it might be interesting to attend.

My father was furious when he heard I was going and didn't understand why I would want to waste my time going to listen to anyone that was affiliated with the Nazis. He tried his best to talk me out of attending. He criticized and made disparaging remarks about Hitler, his politics, and the Nazi Party. Father told me he didn't trust Hitler's intentions nor did he feel these men had anything constructive or beneficial to offer the Austrian people. He strongly objected to the concept that Germans were the supreme race and did not seem intimidated by the requirement to attend. Father was well aware of Hitler's use of violence and fear to gain conformity, however, he refused to abandon his beliefs despite the consequences. These included possible arrest or even worse being murdered for speaking out against German principles and politics.

The school where the assembly was held was several blocks from our house. Our plan was to walk to school and get there before all the good seating was taken, hoping to get an up-close look of the speakers. Several other girls I knew from school planned on going because of the great deal of curiosity and enthusiasm the Nazi threesome had created.

We arrived about a half-hour before the assembly began. I saw most of the town's people had shown up for fear they would be harassed or arrested if they didn't participate. I felt the nervous anticipation that emanated throughout the room. Many of the Austrian people were leery of the Nazi Party. Most guarded their feelings about the Party and their personal political philosophies.

As we entered the school grounds several uniformed SS soldiers stood by the entrance at the school gate. I'd never seen that many uniformed individuals in one place before. They had swastikas sewn on their dark uniforms. Their total attire was neat and orderly with every detail fixed, trimmed, and tidy. Their cuffs and collars exact, stiff and inflexible holding their shape and form, not a single wrinkle noticeable on their uniforms. The jackets and matching pants had been carefully pressed, lines and creases ironed precisely, tailored to fit perfectly. The bottom of their pant cuffs touched the tops of their freshly shined boots. The men had a disciplined look in their clear eyes, with caps worn at a tilt and not one hair out of place.

We entered a room that closely resembled an old gymnasium. My friends and I met at the entry. The men at the door ushered us to the front of the room where they seated us in the front row. We were excited to be placed at the front. The assembly was well organized with tables and chairs strategically placed throughout the big room. Several SS soldiers were seating people as they arrived. A table was set up in the middle of the floor of the assembly room. Many of us in the room had a close view of the speakers.

Several large banners hung on the walls around the room. All of them had the symbol of the swastika. One banner was larger than the rest. It could be viewed from every angle of the room. It was a photo of the German flag with numerous other photos showing prosperous people, towns and villages with words printed on the posters that read "Heil mein Fuhrer" (Hail my Leader) and "Sieg Heil" (Hail Victory). The Nazi propaganda had already been posted for all to see with images showing unity, peace and prosperity.

We sat close to the head table within ten feet of the seats reserved for Hitler, Goring, and Hess. Once in our seats we were expected to stay sitting since no one was allowed to roam about the room. We could feel the excitement and apprehension culminating in the room. Some in the crowd appeared energized and were eagerly waiting to see the three powerful men. Some were restless and became impatient while they waited for Hitler, Goring and Hess. Several in the crowd were already cheering and waving German flags while others had disapproving and agitated looks on their faces. It was apparent they were not supporters of the Nazi Party. The people who appeared critical made me think of my father and the looks he had given me right before I walked out the door. Father's stern look of disappointment and disapproval was still fresh in my mind.

The room buzzed with conversation and I couldn't help but hear as the audience talked amongst themselves. They made both derogatory and supportive comments about the new leadership in Austria. Some whispered not wanting anyone to hear them while others openly expressed their thoughts and opinions. Many discussions were taking place within the group about the promises Hitler had made in the past concerning the Austrian people and whether or not they thought he would be an upstanding, promising leader for Austria. There was a general feeling in the crowd of acceptance and approval for the Fuhrer. From the comments I heard, it seemed as though the majority of the crowd wanted to give Hitler a chance and hear what he had to say before they committed to supporting or opposing his ideology. Some in the crowd seemed to think he would be able to jump-start the economy and eliminate poverty, rescuing Austria and its people from an impoverished and weakened state.

My patience had begun to wear thin and it seemed like we waited hours for the three to enter the room and give their speeches. Hitler, Goring, and Hess were not anywhere in sight so everyone continued to chatter about the problems of the country as we awaited their big entrance. There was a side door in the building and I assumed they would enter there so they wouldn't have to walk directly through the crowd. The audience was getting even more restless and became louder and louder.

Suddenly a SS officer loudly commanded everyone to be quiet and within seconds got the attention of the babbling crowd. Instantaneously silence filled the room. The armed officer spoke as though he held a position of authority.

After everyone had quieted down, he directed the audience to follow a specific protocol. He told everyone that when Hitler entered the room we must all stand up, raise our right hand above our head and with support and vigor yell, 'Heil Hitler' (Hail Hitler), 'Heil mein Fuhrer' (Hail my Leader). We were told to do this to show our obedience and support to the Nazi Party, Hitler, and his leadership. I found it interesting to watch how the crowd reacted when we were instructed to yell 'Heil Hitler'. Some individuals whispered, others declared they would refuse to say it, while some just sat quietly waiting for the presentation to begin.

Hitler had not yet shown his face to the group and I did not think most of the people in the room believed he was even in the building, although everyone was hoping to get a glimpse of someone important before the night was over. I got a bit fidgety myself and began to wonder if the three men would ever appear. We were told the guest speakers were about to enter and give their presentation to the audience.

## Chapter 12

Anticipation filled the air when suddenly I heard the door opening and glanced off to the side of the room. I saw the door at the side entrance of the building opening. Three uniformed men entered and walked through the crowd toward the middle of the room. Hitler entered first, Goring followed next and Hess followed in both their footsteps. They were led to a table that had been prepared for them by another uniformed officer. All three men seemed relaxed and had friendly smiles on their faces as they made eye contact with the gathered crowd.

When Hitler entered the room some appeared in shock, others stood motionless, while some cheered for him. They were filled with hope he had the power to eliminate their poverty. I watched the reactions of the crowd. I sat quietly and prayed no one was watching me. I was afraid because I had not participated as was expected and worried perhaps an SS soldier might arrest me and take me away for not saying 'Heil Hitler'.

The demeanor of the three men became more rigid once seated and their sudden lack of emotion made the people feel more intimidated. They sat in chairs with a table in front of them so they were facing the crowd. I remember Hitler sipped from his glass of water before standing up. He came around from the back side of the table so he was positioned directly in front of the crowd and walked to the podium that had been placed in the center of the room. He motioned for his comrades to come up and join him. I noticed Goring was a hefty man compared to the other two and his combed back hair was receding on his forehead. Hitler looked just like he did in his pictures; he was easily identified from his photographs that were widely publicized throughout Europe. Hitler was a medium built man with dark hair. He had the infamous mustache that was his trademark and became legendary after his demise. Hess did not make much of an impression on me as I remember very little about the man, the way he looked or what he said during the assembly. My focus was concentrated on Hitler and Goring.

When Hitler spoke he commanded attention from the crowd. He impressed us as very gracious and polite. He seemed to sincerely care about the Austrian people. He projected compassion and concern in his voice when he spoke. He told of promises and pledged he would make major improvements in Austria's economy. Hitler talked about providing more jobs for the locals, stating everyone would have enough to eat and a car. His goal was to improve the quality of life for all the people in Austria.

Hitler instructed us during the lecture that instead of using the greetings good morning, good afternoon or good night to our friends, family and neighbors, we should instead say, "Heil Hitler" when we greeted someone in passing or during any event we attended. He wanted us to replace 'Guten Obend', 'Guten Tag', and other well-known German greetings with the words 'Heil Hitler'. Supposedly this would show compliance, duty and respect for Austria's new leadership and the Nazi party.

I was shocked when I heard this and couldn't believe my father or mother would ever submit to such conformity or use those words when greeting anyone. Can you imagine, going up to your mother, sister, friend or neighbor and saying 'Heil Hitler' instead of saying, hello, good morning or good evening? This new greeting the Germans wanted to impose on us helped me realize the new political structure was ridged, dictatorial and was not the best for the Austrian people. Contemplating having to say 'Heil Hitler' to all I came in contact with as a greeting was ridiculous. I couldn't understand how anyone could impose such an outlandish notion on everyone.

I began to understand why my father felt the way he did about Hitler and realized why he refused to support this man, his politics, and his beliefs. I began to sense Hitler and the Nazi Party were ready to forcibly impose many questionable things upon the Austrian people. The phrase

'Heil Hitler' brought new meaning to what was in store for our country. As the assembly progressed, a sickening feeling had grown within me.

Hitler had brought renewed hope to some in the crowd and at first was able to rally the people, and gain local and neighborhood support through his promises and kind words. When he was finished speaking many of his supporters yelled 'Heil Hitler'. I stood there quietly instead and didn't say anything. I soon realized if I didn't follow the protocol, harm would come to me, for not saluting and yelling 'Heil Hitler'. I felt forced to mouth the words and raise my arm in the salute for fear of being arrested.

After Hitler, Goring and Hess completed their presentations, they came out into the crowd and made an effort to visit with the audience. Because my friends and I were only a short distance from the speaker's podium, we were approached first by the threesome. All three walked toward the audience in a single file, first Hitler, Goring and then Hess. I never dreamed they would ever consider talking to me or my friends, but their path came straight for us. I became noticeably more nervous as they came closer to me. I thought to myself, what would I say to these men? I hoped they would veer off into another direction and I wouldn't have to talk to them. My fingers twitched, I wrung my hands together, and broke out in a nervous sweat. The palms of my hands were clammy, and I began to tremble as they neared my seat where I stood waiting. I heard every click when the heels of their shoes connected with the auditorium floor as they drew nearer.

I envisioned my father being handcuffed and dragged off by the soldiers for harsh remarks he would have probably made during the discussion about how Hitler would reform Austria's economy and improve our standard of living. Thank God father hadn't been there because I can only image what might have happened if he had been present. Hitler walked straight toward me and the closer he got the more afraid I became. My heart sank. I felt paralyzed and wondered if I would be able to speak if he did come up to me. I tried to inch my way behind my friend but she wouldn't let me step behind her. Hitler was almost at arm's length. I prayed, don't stop in front of my chair, and please just keep walking! He didn't stop and came straight toward me. I was face to face with Hitler, Goring and Hess. Thoughts of my father's negative feelings and comments about the Nazis still filled my mind. I pictured my father's disappoint in me. I stood right next to these notorious men and regretted it was too late to move away or change seats. I certainly could not run out of the school building so I just stood there and hoped for the best.

Hitler turned toward me extended his right hand, motioning that he wanted to shake my hand. I hesitated for a moment and thought of my father and his certain disapproval. Still, out of fear I quickly reached out my right hand, and with a stern handshake Hitler greeted me with "Heil Hitler." An overwhelming sense of betrayal to my father crept from my stomach to my throat as his hand gripped mine. My entire body reacted to a feeling of powerlessness at the grim realization this man wished to yield unrestricted control over all in this crowd and anyone within reach. The emanating thirst for complete domination frightened me to the core. He thanked me for coming to the assembly. I don't recall what I answered in response only my intense feeling of nervousness. Following my handshake he methodically moved to greet the next person. I heard him repeat 'Heil Hitler' in his staunch, unwavering voice as he greeted one after the other and thanked them for coming. The words 'Heil Hitler' echoed throughout the gymnasium.

I was grateful my father was not in attendance as he surely would have had difficulty concealing his views. He would have likely been forcibly removed and taken to jail. Strangely, it seemed at the time, most people in that room saw Hitler as a pleasant, reasonable, well-mannered man. He appeared as though he genuinely wanted to help the people of Austria. I, on the other hand, having listened to my father, had grave doubts.

It was not possible for most in the room to fathom what devastation and annihilation Hitler and his followers would bring to the world in the next seven years.  Many of us in that room soon found out he was not the friendly, caring man he projected that night nor did he care about human life, humility, or the wellbeing of any of the world's inhabitants.  His delusional and insane thought processes as he developed his 'master race' soon were recognized by millions.

My father's assumptions were right about the Nazis.  I'm not sure how he was able to foresee Hitler's and the Nazi's intentions but his intuitions and gut feelings were correct.  It wouldn't be long until realization set in for everyone and the horrors of the Second World War started to be known across the earth.  Hitler's closest comrades were extremely loyal to the Nazi Party as were all three of these men I had met that evening.  These men I was forced to salute came to be considered among the most brutal, corrupt and organized killers in all of human history.

## Chapter 13

Despite the assembly, Father remained openly opinionated about his views. We all fell back into our day-to-day lives. It was a bright, sunny July day and I was looking forward to writing another new song in my hardcover song book with my friend Irma. Father was busy working in the house as he made some repairs on the stairway while Mother was in the kitchen cooking supper. The aromas of ham and blueberry pie filled the house. The tantalizing scents made my mouth water and I looked forward to the call that supper was ready. The cat sat on the window sill basking in the light of the setting sun shining through the pantry window.

I heard Mother yelling at me, "Karoline come to the kitchen and help set the table for supper." As I walked toward the kitchen to help my mother someone pounded on our door. They must have been using their fists because the knocks were loud and forceful. It sounded as if someone was trying to break down the door. I heard several shoes scuffling around on the front porch. I stopped to listen for a second and then ran to answer the door. I thought it was probably someone who needed help in the neighborhood or the priest from next door needing my father for something.

Before I got to the front door it had already been pushed open a crack. I thought to myself that whoever was at the door must be very impatient if they couldn't wait for me to open it. I was within a few inches of reaching the handle when the door swung wide open with a boom. Startled from noise, I looked up as three Nazi soldiers pushed through the doorway. One of the men was tall, much taller than I, with dark hair and a mustache. Another man was a bit shorter with a huskier build, his eyes barely visible because his hat was low on his brow. The third man stood behind them and I did not get an impression of him at all. The men were wearing uniforms with calf-high leather boots that almost reached their knees, shiny black belts, and I specifically remember the swastika patches on their sleeves. They spoke to each other in German but used an unfamiliar dialect. Their eyes were as hard as granite and the expressions on their faces frightened me.

None of us in the house had heard them drive up or come to the front door until they knocked and burst into the entryway. The guards powered their way in with enough force they split the door frame holding the lock. Once they were in the house the door swung freely and stayed open. Everything happened so quickly they were inside the house before I knew it. I was instantly afraid. My father had told me terrible things about how the Nazis operated so I knew something was terribly wrong. My thoughts raced. I envisioned my family being harmed or even murdered if we did or said the wrong thing in their presence. I wanted to run away, but there was nowhere to go.

I stood in shock. I worried my father would walk into the room and become verbally confrontational. Father's many uncompromising actions toward the Party, his stubbornness and unwillingness to conform to Hitler's ideology and his derogatory comments about the Nazi Party ran through my head. I thought maybe they were here to arrest him, or worse kill him and perhaps the rest of us as well. Mother tried to tell Father to hold his tongue many times, but he had never listened.

The wind whisked through the door into the living room and it blew papers off the table where my father had been working earlier. The soldiers made their way into the room and surrounded me. They asked me who else was in the house, and specifically the whereabouts of my parents. Mother, Father, and Friede were all in other rooms. I assumed they had come for my father and wondered if I should tell them I was alone. I quickly realized they were likely to search the house and we'd be punished for my dishonesty. My breathing hastened, my heart pounded in my chest as I panicked.

"Mother, help, I need you!" I shrieked.

Reacting to my scream, one of the soldiers roughly grabbed my right arm. They had no intention of letting me go. My father was in the other room working, still unaware of what was going on. My mother heard my screams for help and rushed into the room. She was holding Friede who was now 5-months-old. When she saw the Nazi soldiers in our living room, and realized one of them had a hold of me, she cried out to my father, screaming for help, "Valentin come quickly, there are soldiers here and they have a hold of Karoline. Valentin, Kommen mach schnell, schnell! (Valentin come quickly, come quickly!)." The Nazi soldiers just looked at Mother as if she was of no consequence, and ignored her screams. One of them snickered as if he enjoyed seeing my mother consumed with fear, terrified I might be harmed. They were smug, amused and laughed as they continued to intimidate and terrorize us.

Friede sensing my mother's fear, began crying loudly. Her cries became more frantic which added to the already tense atmosphere. During all of the commotion it was difficult to try to say anything to any of the soldiers. It was difficult for mother and I to comprehend what was happening to us. Mother tried to regain some self-control and somehow in the confusion managed to sputter a few words. She asked one of the men why they had broken into our house and what they were doing in our home. The officer answered, "We are here to take your daughter."

Finally Father heard the commotion and sensed trouble. He came running down the stairs into the living room. Two of the men grabbed him by the arms as he entered. They held him back so he was unable to move and come to us. He struggled to get away from them but was unable to break their strong hold. The soldiers were armed with guns and said if we didn't cooperate we would be killed. My father continued to struggle with the two soldiers trying to get out of their hold. He wanted desperately to help us. The soldiers finally overpowered him.

Mother pleaded with the soldiers. "Please let go of my daughter, she is an innocent child who has done nothing wrong" she cried. Tears streamed down her face as she begged for their mercy. None of us understood what was happening or why they had come to take me. Friede screamed and cried so hard it was difficult for her to catch her breath. Mother held her tightly in one arm as she desperately grabbed at my other arm trying to pull me towards her. The man didn't release his grip and held my arm tighter. He told my mother to get back or someone would get hurt aiming his gun at my father. I couldn't believe this was really happening.

I was numb and in shock. It all felt like a bad dream but I could see the men right in front of me, in my living room. My father was in plain sight being held back by the guards. My mother still screamed hysterically and the baby's high pitched crying was unnerving. One of the soldiers spoke up as mother cried out. He ignored her pleas to release me. He shouted at her, "You need to be quiet. You have no say in this matter. Get back, and quiet yourself!" He told her she'd better calm down, be silent and threatened again if she didn't calm down someone would get hurt. Another soldier turned and looked at my mother with malice, drew his gun and pointed it toward my baby sister. I never forgot my baby sister's blood, curdling screams. Her little voice was getting raspy. I was afraid if she kept it up the Nazis would get angry and do something terrible to her.

My father began to weep out of desperation for our family's safety. He pleaded with the soldiers not to hurt his wife or his children. It was the first time I'd seen my father cry. The sight of his despair was heart wrenching. The soldiers had rendered him powerless. Mother continued to plead, "Please don't take my daughter. I only have two children, she is too young to leave her mother and family." Mother then cried, "She is only 15. What do you want with a 15-year-old girl?" My father attempted to bargain, "Take me instead. Please do not take my daughter! Take our money or any of our possessions." One soldier replied to my father's appeals in a stern voice that he was in control, I had no choice but to do what I was told or be killed.

My mother was not ready to give up. She shrieked, "Where will you take her? How long will she be gone?"

"We are taking her and that's all you need to know," the soldier sternly replied. Mother sank to the floor near us, the baby lay against her screaming in her arms. It was an agonizing sight.

My father kept a gun in the house somewhere and I wished we had it now. When Hitler took over Austria, it had become illegal for civilians to own weapons so Father had his hidden away in the house somewhere. Only military forces and the police had the legal right to bear arms. A civilian caught with a gun was punished with death. I'm not sure exactly where my father got his gun, but had heard talk he found it on a dead soldier several months ago. He told me never to tell anyone he had the gun or he would be shot.

Mother and Father had done all they could for me. As a last resort I pleaded with the soldiers myself, "I don't want to go with you, please don't make me go. I'm afraid to leave my family and my home. I will be no help to you." My comments were disregarded.

The officer in charge replied, "You have ten minutes to say your goodbyes to your family, get your things and we will be on our way! Now get ready there will be no more questions!" He warned me that I needed to get ready to leave without any arguments or any further questions. He was fully prepared to hurt and kill someone if I did not obey.

For a short moment everything seemed frozen. I felt immobile, unable to think straight. I focused on the grandfather clock in the corner of our living room as it ticked away the seconds. I could hear every sound it made. The stillness magnified the silence that surrounded me. The constant noise the clock made grew louder and clearer with every second that passed. I could hear every little noise, while watching the hands of the clock change position and strike the next minute. I could feel my heart pounding and was able to count every rhythmical beat within my chest. My eyes stayed fixed on the clock, and then something in my head clicked. I

46

was awakened from my haze, and the state of confusion paralyzing me. I realized I only had about six minutes left to say my final goodbyes to my family and my home.

The truth of what was taking place and what lay ahead of me was slowly becoming a reality. The soldier's intentions were known. It became very clear to me that I was to face the unknown and was being taken away from my home and family. I might never see my mother's kind face again, feel her gentle touch, hear her calling me to come in for supper or smell and taste her homemade blueberry pie. I turned my head to look over at my father in the corner of the living room as the tears ran down his cheeks. He looked beaten down, wore out, and surely felt the desperation of our situation.

I wondered if I would ever see this kind, devoted man again. My father had taught me so much about life, kindness, integrity, and compassion for others. I thought, "What about my baby sister, Friede? Would I get to see her grow up, be the big sister she'd need and that I wanted to be?" I loved helping my mother take care of Friede; I touched her tiny fingers and toes, and ran my fingers through that dark curly hair of hers. She had so much hair for a little baby. She looked like the doll I used to play with when I was a young girl. I wanted to be able to see her get older, laugh and play. I could make Friede break out in hilarious laughter by dancing around her, acting like a fool, or by making silly faces and noises when she was sitting in her highchair. I would miss her happiness and innocence. What a sweet baby she was and I didn't want to leave her.

I wished the clock would stop ticking; I didn't want the minutes to pass away knowing I would soon have to leave. There had never been a reason to wish for such a thing before. The unthinkable was about to happen, an event that changed the entire course of my life. The hands struck 8:30 pm, and the synchronized chimes began playing six notes as they always did every half-hour. Time was closing in on me and it was nearly time for me to leave my home with these menacing strangers. Right up until the last second I thought there was a chance the soldiers would change their minds and tell me I really didn't have to leave my home and go with them. I continued to go through the motions of trying to figure out what I should take with me if the guards really were to take me away. I still hoped this would all end up being a nightmare and everything would be normal tomorrow when I woke up. My instincts, however, told me I would probably never hear the grandfather clock strike the ninth hour.

I glanced at the adjoining wall close to where I was standing, and saw one of my favorite pictures. It was of the mountain side where I had once played and picked flowers for my mother. All at once I heard a soldier's voice telling me I could only take small items with me; ones I could carry and there better not be anything that would slow them down.

I began to think crazy thoughts. I planned an escape in my head. I thought maybe if I was lucky I might run across my father's gun while I was looking for my things. I thought to myself should I even touch the gun? Where would I hide the pistol if I happened to find it? Could I conceal it under my dress and be able to hide it so it wouldn't be noticeable to the soldiers? Would I really be able to shoot someone if I had to protect myself? Would I be brave enough to pull the trigger? It's amazing what one is willing to do if threatened or if your life is placed in danger. The thought of being all alone with three Nazi soldiers scared me to death. I was truly afraid for my safety and my life. My mother's words were embedded in my brain about the crimes against women during previous wars, and how cruel and inhuman some men could be to women. I couldn't get those thoughts of rape, murder and torture out of my head.

I knew none of my family could come with me and even though I was frightened, I didn't want my family to suffer and be persecuted by the Nazis anymore. They had already suffered enough and I didn't want them to have to endure any further anguish or torment. I would be all alone to face this ordeal, there would be no family or friends at my side when the time came to leave. I had no one to help, comfort or console me. The thought of being kidnapped and taken prisoner overwhelmed me. My throat was dry, my head began to pound and hurt so dreadfully I thought it would burst. The certainty of the situation was bleak, there was no way out, nowhere to escape and I was caught in a crisis I would never wish on my worst enemy. It became crystal clear I was truly alone and on my own the minute we walked out our front door.

Life is perplexing and unpredictable, and in a moment's time my life changed forever. At only 15, I had never even had a real boyfriend, and never experienced a heartfelt kiss. In just a few minutes, I would be taken away and held prisoner by these Nazi soldiers. I could have never imagined such a thing would happen to me or my family.

I hoped the few minutes I had left with my family would never pass, but the time had come for me to leave. One of the men followed me to my bedroom to guard me while I found a few small items they had given me permission to bring with me. I had no idea where they were going to take me once we left the house so it was difficult to choose what to bring. The soldier wouldn't let me out of his sight and followed my every move. I started looking through my dresser drawers and found an oval gold locket my mother had given me several years ago. It had great sentimental value and being somewhat superstitious, I hung it around my neck, hoping it would bring me good luck and help keep me safe after I was gone.

I turned and saw my old doll with the curly black locks mother had made me, sitting on the floor in the corner of my room. Even though I was too old to play with dolls, I longed to bring her with me. She made me feel safe when I held her, and the doll was a special link to my mother. Mother's love, kindness and loyalty was in every stitch she had sewn which was all the more reason to take her with me. I hadn't played with her for several years but liked having her in my room. She held good memories, had sentimental value and my mother had made her especially for me.

I only had ten minutes to pack my personal items and belongings and could only take items I could carry in a small bag. I had to figure out what items were most important and small enough to carry with me.  Ten minutes was not enough time to make those critical choices.

The bag I was allowed to take with me seemed so small.  There wasn't enough room to store all the memories, love and devotion my family had shown me during my 15 years of life.  How could I fit a lifetime of memories and my most precious mementos into one tiny bag?  I decided my curly-haired doll was going with me.  I thought if I took her, she would remind me of my home.

I continued to look around the house and spotted a small statue of Jesus, and placed him inside the small bag.  Two of the soldiers laughed when they saw me do this, mocking my choices.  They must have thought Jesus would be of no help or comfort to me after they whisked me away from my home.  I wanted to bring my hard cover song book.  The one my friend Irma and I created and used to compose new lyrics and songs.  I decided I didn't want to risk losing it and was afraid the Nazis might destroy it or eventually make me throw it away.

Suddenly a soldier yelled, "You have two minutes left then we'll go, be ready!"  I tried to stall them hoping to gain a few more precious moments with my family.  With only a few minutes remaining, I thought of pictures and wished I had more of my family and friends I could take with me.  We couldn't afford to take too many pictures of the family and I had few pictures of my mother.  I took a black and white photo of my family and placed it in a small compartment in my bag.

**Karoline's song book filled with songs her and her friend Irma wrote together**

I crammed a few more things into the bag including an apple and a few other snacks my mother helped me put in my sack. Her hands shook while she tried to help me get ready to leave. We looked at each other as her hand touched mine and I lost all control of my emotions. I didn't want to break down in front of my mother. She was already heartbroken, and couldn't stop weeping. I couldn't help her any longer, and the only thing I could do was try to reassure her I would be alright. The sadness in her eyes made me crumble and I couldn't stop myself from sobbing. I was crying so hard I stuttered when I tried to talk to her and it was hard to catch my breath.

No one knew what lay ahead for me and not knowing what the future would bring was the most challenging for all of us. I didn't know if my family would be safe after I left the house or if the Nazis would harm me after I was gone. I was forced to walk toward the door; they were ready to take me away. My mother was trying to clutch my hand when I walked by, still sobbing, not wanting to say goodbye. One of the soldiers barked one last order to my parents, "If anyone tries to follow us, your family will be killed." They took me out the front door and hurried me off into the darkness of the night, leaving my mother, father and little sister behind. The abductors took me away unwilling, crying and heartbroken.

## Chapter 14

The sky was filled with stars. I remember I saw a half moon at our backs as my home disappeared right before my eyes. Our shadows cast ahead of us are still clear in my mind. I asked several times where we were going but the men wouldn't divulge any information other than to say we were headed for the train station in Bleiberg. Our final destination was unknown. One of the soldiers told me we would make several stops before we reached our final destination. I wasn't told where exactly we were going. In his own strange way the soldier was perhaps trying to comfort me yet he was cold, distant and unwilling to share too much information. I didn't trust any of them and was suspicious for good reason. I had little experience dealing with grown men, feared for my life and was suspicious of their intentions.

No one had harmed me yet, although their lude stares made me feel uneasy. I tried to plan how I would fight them off if I had to protect myself. I had already made up my mind I would do whatever it took to keep them away from me even if it meant dying in the process. I'm sure I would have been overpowered yet death was my choice if given the opportunity. The Nazis spoke to me harshly, shoved me and ordered me to keep walking.

As we continued to walk, I realized we indeed were heading for the train station. I was surprised the truth had been revealed to me. There was little conversation among the soldiers along the way, only an occasional order from the ranking officer to step up the pace.

With all that was happening I found it impossible to rid myself of the agonizing thoughts and images of my mother's and father's heart wrenching sobs as I was forced into the night. They were distraught and helpless as I disappeared from their sight. I imagined how my parents felt at that moment and hoped I would catch a glimpse of them one last time before we were totally out of sight.  I imagined my father chasing after us, following in silence, hiding out behind bushes, quietly watching, and eventually sneaking up to come to my rescue.  The soldier's threat to kill my family lingered in my thoughts and squashed my hopes of any rescue.

I knew the area we were walking through well, but in the darkness of the night and with my heightened anxiety, everything looked so different.  As we grew closer I heard the whisper of voices.  It sounded like a crowd was gathered close by.  I could make out noises that sounded like shuffling feet and muffled voices; the voices were incoherent, garbled.  The voices and sounds seemed to blend together.  There was mixed chatter and I could hear a variety of tones and high pitched cries.

The train itself was now in sight and I could distinguish the boxcars on the railroad tracks.  I could see they were railcars that carried cargo and cattle in and out of Bleiberg.  Several were hitched together one car after the other sitting at an angle on the tracks so it was impossible to see the last railcar.  Painful cries and sorrowful weeping resonated from within the railcars, the distraught cries echoed toward me.  What I thought sounded like weeping became very clear.  I heard the howling cries of other women, sobbing, and grief stricken.

I recognized a few women from Bleiberg were, like me, being hurried along by soldiers.  They pushed us forward ordering us to move along faster.  We passed the first few boxcars which were filled with women I did not recognize.  I couldn't see much and wondered where they had been taken from.  Some were gasping for air having difficulty catching their breath, most likely from a long period of weeping.  I might have reacted the same, but I knew it would do me no good to call out for help or shed anymore tears.

We were ordered not to talk or cause any delays while we passed by the other cars.  As we neared the third boxcar, I was ordered by a soldier to step up into it.  It became my turn to enter the makeshift mobile prison cell.  A kindly older woman in the doorway held out her hand as I was ready to step up into the boxcar. She helped me up and through the sliding doors. I hadn't seen my friend Irma being herded into a boxcar. I wasn't sure if she had also been kidnapped along with the rest of us. I hoped she escaped the capture. I don't know how the Nazis chose their victims. I just knew I had become one of the unfortunate many that had been abducted.

The car was dark, dirty, and reeked of animal waste. Some straw had been spread out on the floor boards and most of the women sat motionless on the hard, dirty floor. I noticed a young woman in the corner of the car, curled up in a fetal position, despondent. Her clothes were soiled, and she looked utterly pitiful. It was easy to see she felt absolutely abandoned, alone, and forsaken. This reality mirrored what was happening to me. I easily envisioned myself huddled in the corner of a boxcar, cold, unclean, hungry and abandoned. The entirety of the situation had finally sunk in and I knew I was truly alone.

I moved toward the far end, found a small area and sat down. I was exhausted. I had no more tears left and knew it would do me no good to complain. I sat in a daze and watched the people around me. I hoped I could make a connection with some of the other women so I wouldn't feel so alone. One woman nervously paced back and forth. I understood from some of the others she had been on the train for hours. No one had answers as to where we were going, or if we were being shipped to the same area.

I couldn't get the thought of Mother weeping while she yanked on the sleeve of the soldier's uniform begging him not to take me away. The events of the last few hours replayed over and over in my head yet I was unable to rationalize my abduction. Was I being taken for the sole purpose of punishment? Or was I considered an asset? I quickly discredited being an asset. I was a 15-year-old girl who knew little of the world's affairs, the Nazi Party, or the collective strategies of war. I certainly wasn't someone who could be considered a spy, or a knowledgeable scientist that could create the next innovative weapon.

Every woman in the boxcars had their own story of horror to tell about their kidnappings. Many of the stories I heard were similar to mine, some more shocking and disturbing. I had been lucky I had not been raped and was unharmed. Some of the other women had not been so lucky. I guessed there were probably 20 to 30 women in each boxcar. I recognized a few of the women who had attended my school before I graduated. I didn't know most of the women on the train. It became obvious to us on the train the Nazis planned to make more stops along the way gathering up more women before we reached our final destination.

The horrifying effects of war began assaulting me on that day. I needed to learn how to survive on my own and wished I had more experience taking care of myself. I hoped I could prepare myself to deal wisely with the hardships that lay ahead of me. Fifteen years was not enough time to prepare for all of life's encounters especially when they included being ruthlessly abducted by Nazis, forced into a rank boxcar and transported to an unknown destination.

We were at the train station less than an hour when the order was given to make sure all the women were loaded onto the train. It had only been a couple hours since I was taken. We were told we would be leaving soon. I overheard soldiers mention the town of Klenkendorf. I knew Klenkendorf was in Germany, but I wasn't sure how far away Klenkendorf was from Bleiberg. I heard the steam engine along with an array of noises that sounded while the train was gearing up and getting ready to leave. The rhythmic pulse from the air pump that drove the steam-driven wheels, the hiss and the roar from the engine and the shrill blast as the steam escaped from the whistle on top of the train were sounds I never forgot. The metal wheels pulling, connected with the iron in the ground rails let off a loud screech. The train pushed forward. Looking between the cracks in the car, I bid farewell to Bleiberg and the life I once knew.

## Chapter 15

The train leveled off in speed and the ride became somewhat smoother. I nestled down in the corner of the car hoping to get some sleep. Reaching in my bag, I grabbed my doll and held her close. I must have drifted off for a time waking up somewhat disoriented to the screech of the braking train. I rubbed my eyes. It was still dark outside. I asked a lady next to me how long we had been traveling. She replied we hadn't been moving long, and was unsure of the time.

We neared the next train stop. I stood up and found it difficult to keep my balance. I positioned myself to prevent my body from being propelled forward into the others or thrown down on the hard floor. A thick cloud of hot, white steam gushed from the engine. Being trapped in the cars like a herd of cattle made me feel claustrophobic. Peering out of a crack, I recognized we were in Villach; the town I was brought to the few times when I needed to be hospitalized. Villach was near Klagenfurt approximately 12-miles from Bleiberg.

When the doors to the car opened, I saw ten more women gathered together and several Nazi soldiers around them. We stopped in Villach to pick up more women who were abducted from their homes. Their expressions became familiar, their faces drawn and the sadness in their eyes told stories of anguish. I tried my best to reach out to at least one of them like the kindly old women had for me when I entered the train. I hoped to give them a small ray of hope there was still a bit of compassion and kindness left in this world.

During the stop, some of the women asked to go to the bathroom. Their requests were ignored. The Nazis were in a rush to get the others they had taken prisoner aboard the train. I was able to reach out to one of the girls that needed a lift up into the boxcar. I smiled at her as I helped tug her upward through the double doors. She seemed about my age. She had the same look on her face as I did when I was forced to enter the prison car. Her eyes swollen and red from weeping. Within an hour the other women from Villach were loaded on the train and it again geared up moving toward our next stop.

As the train eased into a steady pace, I spoke with the girl I had helped onto the train. Her experience of capture was similar to mine. She was a timid girl, although approachable, and easy for me to strike up a conversation with once she was settled on the train. Hoping to make her feel less frightened, I told her of my experience. Anke was her name. We moved across to the other side of the car, and sat down in an area no one had claimed. I commented on her pretty, blue flowered dress. She thanked me and shared her mother had made it for her a few weeks ago. She was wearing black, high top shoes laced above her ankles. I had on a very similar pair of shoes. They worked so well for hiking up the Alps. If we were going to need to walk on foot, our high topped shoes would protect and save our feet from getting blisters. I thought about the times I complained about having to wear them with dresses, finding them too ugly to match. Now I felt blessed they were the shoes on my feet.

Some of the women on the train were complaining of being hungry. I, on the other hand, had no thoughts of food. While whispering with Anke, she told me her father had tried to resist when the Nazis took her. One of the soldiers butted her father in the head with his gun. He had been cut and was bleeding, as they dragged her out the door. She found her capture hard to talk about and had a difficult time opening up about the details. Anke was still in shock as she began to tell me her story, and she started to cry. Her dress had gotten soiled and dirty from the grime on the boxcar floor and this bothered her. It was nice to have someone to talk to. I felt like I was being some help to her by listening and hearing her story. Talking with her also made it easier for me.

We talked about our families, school, and our friends. We pondered what might happen to us while we were on the train. We thought about happier times and this lifted our spirits. I knew there was no way to escape so I tried to make the best of our situation. Anke and I leaned back against the rough cut lumber of the car carefully trying not to get wood splinters in our backs from the marred and weathered wood. We talked for some time before we eventually closed our eyes and tried to get some rest.

## Chapter 16

The train passed on through the starry night while we rested. Once again the train began to slow and the whistle blew. The shrill wailing sound became a forewarning of yet one more stop ahead, knowing we would be taking more women from their homes. We heard a whoosh sound as we came to a stop and as soon as Anke and I were able, we moved toward the door to see where we were. We looked at one another when we got to the door. Anke said, "I don't know how many more women we will be able to fit in this boxcar. How many more stops do you think we will make?" I didn't know the answer to that question and couldn't even venture to guess. Without warning and to our surprise, a Nazi soldier pulled open the doors. I looked outside realizing the train had stopped in Salzburg, Austria.

Salzburg lay about 130-miles or so from my hometown. I traveled there with my mother and father a few times in the past. Salzburg is on the western side of Austria and lies on the border between Germany and Austria. It is a large city, especially compared to Bleiberg. I kept track of our route and suspected we were headed for Germany. I wondered if Klenkendorf was really where we were going. I asked one of the guards if we were going to Klenkendorf, but he wouldn't acknowledge me. Then he abruptly replied, "Yes, we will be traveling through Germany." Anke looked to the left of the opening and yelled at me, "Karoline, I can see more women up there." She pointed to a building about a block or so from the train station. It looked like a small group, perhaps less than ten. It took them a few minutes to walk to the train station. I saw there were seven women in the group. Once they got to the train the newly captured women were loaded quickly into the cars. The whistling steam resumed.

We had traveled over 100-miles from Bleiberg, yet it seemed like we had gone much farther. Multiple stops had been made picking up more women and young girls along the way. Many of us had not eaten supper before we were taken. We were not offered food or drink which scared us. Everyone on the train appeared restless and our circumstances put everyone on edge. Some were at their emotional breaking point and I was surprised there wasn't more chaos and disorder among the women. It was difficult to get any rest. I was only able to drift off to sleep for a few moments at a time before waking. Being surrounded by unfamiliar noises, strange voices and the jerking and jolting of the train made it almost impossible to stay asleep. The sadness and relentless weeping that filled the car added to the bleakness of the situation and being locked together was becoming intolerable.

I was thankful that Anke and I had each other. Having someone to talk with made the journey easier. We had just met, though formed an immediate connection. We were afraid we would be separated at some point and hoped we could stay together.

The uncomfortable journey sped on. I didn't complain to anyone because it would have made no difference. Several women on the train were much worse off than I. One woman said she was five months pregnant. Another was much older than me. I guessed she was between 60 and 65-years-old. That poor old woman, she was close to Grandma Margarette's age and was forced to sit on the dirty, hard floor for hours. The Nazis wouldn't let her go to the bathroom when she complained of having problems.

As the train moved on I thought about jumping while the locomotive was moving. Realistically I knew at first I'd have to figure out how to get out of the car. If I was lucky, I might not get hurt but then I thought to myself what would I do next? The terrain was rough, making it more difficult to travel on foot even if I could accomplish such a task. Knowing the guards wouldn't hesitate to shoot me if I tried to flee scared me. Hour after hour passed. Anke began to fall victim to her worries and fears. I became worried when she seemed to lose touch with reality for several moments.  She began to ramble on and her speech was garbled and incoherent at times.  I was afraid she was going to do something drastic.  She started to babble about jumping off the train while it was moving.  She talked about a secret plan to distract the guards and make a get-a-way when the train came to a stop.

The crowded space surely added to her panic.  The car we were detained in measured approximately 10'x 30'.  She said she felt like the walls were closing in on her and she had to get out.  The dazed look in her eyes was unnerving.  I talked to her in a calm, quiet voice, almost a whisper, pleading with her, trying to distract her and change the focus of her thoughts.  I tried to make sense of our difficult situation by giving her facts.  We had no weapons, no water, no food or supplies, no maps to guide us through the terrain plus the fact the Nazis could certainly overpower us at any time made it ludicrous to think she could survive.  I talked about our families, our favorite music, and the happy times in our lives hoping she would come to her senses.  After much coaxing and persuasion she began to grasp what I was saying.

## Chapter 17

The train continued to travel northward through Germany. At the
next stop we were ordered to get out. When I jumped down to the ground,
I felt a sense of freedom. It was wonderful to actually see the sky and touch
the green bed of grass below my feet. I learned we had arrived in
Frankfurt, Germany. While off the train we were each given a drink of
water and a piece of dried bread that tasted old and stale. Everyone ate the
bread with no complaints. I began feeling the pangs of hunger and thirst.
They let us take a break to use the bathroom and we were allowed to stay
out of the car for nearly an hour.

At the shout to reload we were herded back onto the train like a
bunch of cattle; huddled together in groups and pushed hastily into the
boxcars. I was happy to have been out in the light and given some food and
water. The interior of the car was dark except for the light that shone
through the spaces between the planks. Anke and I again talked about our
lives. It amazed us both that we could laugh occasionally when
reminiscing, and for brief moments forget the seriousness of the situation.
A middle-aged woman suddenly yelled at Anke for placing her bag too
close to her. Anke quickly moved her bag away. We realized that everyone
was reacting to the fear and confusion in their own way. We tried to
occupy as little space as possible keeping to ourselves most of the time.

At our next stop we learned we had arrived in Bremen, Germany.
It had taken us a couple days to get there, yet I was still surprised how far
we had traveled. I had been transported nearly 1,126 kilometers (700
miles) from my family and my home in Austria. The commanding officer
announced in a stern voice, "Listen! Some of you will be taken to
Klenkendorf, others to Hannover, and some to Hamburg." He continued to
shout out more orders. I learned I would be traveling to Hannover which
was about 128 kilometers (80 miles) southeast of Bremen. We would be

making the 128 kilometers (80 miles) journey by wagon. Even though I was afraid of what might lie ahead for me in Hannover, I felt relieved there would be no more guessing. I knew where I was going, and how far away I was from my home.

We were separated into groups of ten, and loaded onto horse-drawn wagons. Anke and I were relieved we both ended up in the same wagon. The wagon ride was far from comfortable. We were crowded into one wooden wagon with a 6'x 12' bed. There was little space to sit comfortably or stretch, so most of us stood. The high wood sides attached to the wagon made it impossible to hang our feet over the edge and it was hard to see exactly where we were going. The road we traveled was bumpy and rough. We weren't allowed to get out and walk beside the wagon, I think it was because the guards thought some of us might try to escape if we were on foot. We traveled most of the day and during some of the evening.

While on the wagon we were again given water to drink, along with more stale, dry bread only this time it was in the shape of a hardened roll. It wasn't very filling and even as hungry as I felt it was still difficult to choke down. The awful taste it left in my mouth was terrible. While choking down the stale bread, I was told by one of the guards that once we reached Hannover we would be fed a meal. The guard who spoke to me about getting our next meal, was cordial, and addressed me in a polite manner. I was surprised by his pleasant manner and was very suspicious of his intentions.

By the time we arrived in Hannover it was close to 10:00 pm. We drove through the town until we reached a large warehouse on the outskirts of the city. The guards said we would have to sleep in the warehouse until we were routed to our work areas the following day. Work area? Hmmm... I wondered what that meant for both Anke and me. The news we would be working somewhere in Hannover helped me feel a bit more settled. I was relieved to learn we wouldn't be jailed or placed in a holding camp.

64

When we entered the warehouse I saw there were no beds to sleep in. A stack of blankets lay folded on a table. We were each issued a blanket of our own. I had my fill of sleeping on hard, cold, dirty surfaces. Happy to have the comfort of a blanket, Anke and I moved toward the middle of the room and spread them out. Exhausted from my travels, I was hoping sleep would come easy. Struggling to sleep, I lay awake on my blanket. I wondered where I was headed in the morning, what type of work was in store for me, and what were the people going to be like I'd be working for. I had made it this far and was lucky to be alive. I wasn't harmed and had made a friend who had become a valuable companion and ally.

I finally fell asleep and morning came far too fast. We were awakened by a guard yelling and ordering us to get up. It was almost 6:00 am. We were told we would be leaving soon for our work stations. I rubbed the sleep from my eyes, slipped on my shoes, and grabbed my small bag. I hid the locket my mother had given me in my pocket. We were allowed to splash a bit of water on our hands and faces from a bucket of water. It had been several days since I had a bath and I certainly needed one.

That morning they gave us our work details. Anke and I would be working for a large restaurant in Hannover owned by a local couple. The restaurant was not too far from the warehouse and we would be walking there. Anke and I were instructed to talk to the owner once we arrived to find out our duties for the day. I was thankful Anke and I would be together. I had helped my mother at home cook and clean some. My only experience working outside my home was in the lead mines. Restaurant work was unfamiliar to me and I was starting to feel nervous. With any luck I would learn the job quickly and stay out of trouble. Anke reassured me that she had worked in a local restaurant and the work wasn't too difficult.

Our group began our walk to town. The flood of unfamiliar sights and sounds fed my overwhelming feelings of discomfort. We walked a half-mile or so and came to a large restaurant. Anke and I were separated from the rest of the group by a guard who led us into the restaurant. The other women continued on to their assigned workplaces. Inside Anke and I were instructed to sit quietly and wait a moment while he fetched the owner. A few minutes later, the guard returned accompanied by the owner. The owner scanned us up and down, faced the guard exclaiming, "These two aren't suitable. They look too young and inexperienced. Have they any experience?"

Without emotion the guard replied, "These two were chosen for you, so make good use of their time."

Out of our hearing distance, the guard and owner continued their discussion. The guard returned to us a short time later with news that our work in the restaurant began that day. He would be back to talk to the owner and to check up on us later. He warned of the severe consequences that would result if we gave the owner any problems or tried to escape. He assured us we'd be found and killed. Both of us were too scared to attempt an escape; we did as we were told. We had no choice but to stay and work.

## Chapter 18

Anke and I were led upstairs by the owner. My memory is somewhat hazy when attempting to recollect his name, but I believe it was Friedrich. He showed us to our sleeping quarters. It was a tiny bedroom above the restaurant with one bed, a chair, and no window. Friedrich instructed us to leave our things in our room and hurry back downstairs and be ready to work. He wasn't a friendly sort so when he spoke, his tone was stern. He gave orders instead of making suggestions or requests. His voice was harsh, his gestures unwelcoming, and he did not smile. From that first encounter, I knew this man would be difficult to work with. Anke and I had become part of the abduction of thousands into Germany for the purpose of forced labor. Friedrich had the power to make us do anything he wanted. We were helpless and considered *Auslanders* (foreigners). We were looked upon as nothing more than unpaid forced laborers.

Friedrich told us to report to his wife and she would give us further instructions. We were taken to the kitchen where she was already cooking breakfast for some of their regular patrons. I timidly asked her what she wanted us to do. She scowled answering, "I would like to know your names, have you no manners?" After learning our names, she bellowed, "Karoline can't you see the dirty dishes? Start washing them! Anke, go out in the dining room and wipe down all the tables."

A few customers entered the restaurant and Friedrich's wife, Gertrude, left me in the kitchen while she waited on them. I worked throughout the day scrubbing dishes and floors. We were given one half-hour break during the work day. We were allowed to eat food specifically chosen for the help which included cheaper, more abundant foods. We were not allowed to eat many things the restaurant served its customers. Meat and dairy products were expensive so we were given soups, rice, potatoes or bread.  I never complained though.  It was much better than the dry, stale bread we had eaten during the long, fear filled train ride.

Anke and I worked until 10:30 pm our first night.  Our first day had been long and tiring.  We worked 15 hours that day and learned that was to be our usual shift with the possibility of longer hours if necessary.  If everything was done by 10:30 pm or so, we were allowed to go upstairs to our room.  Before we left the kitchen that evening Gertrude instructed us to report the next morning at the same time, 7:30 am.

I lay with Anke that night in our shared bed as she appeared to sleep peacefully.  I wondered how Mother and Father were handling what had happened.  I was grateful for Friede and hoped she'd be a loving distraction during my absence.  I worried about my parents more than I did about myself and was deeply saddened by thoughts of their pain.  Their grief-stricken faces filled my mind.

I tried not to cry as I lay there, but it was impossible to hold back my tears.  Tiny droplets fell slowly down my cheeks and soaked my pillow.  I struggled to be quiet so as not to wake Anke.  I never liked crying in front of other people, besides Anke had plenty of her own worries.  The tears I shed that night were more for my mother's and father's loss rather than my own.  I didn't want them to suffer anymore.  I made up my mind I would survive this ordeal one way or another and if not for myself, then for my family.  I finally fell asleep and awoke to reality.  Emotional fatigue blanketed both of us.  We dressed quickly and went to find Gertrude.

## Chapter 19

We reported for work early every morning, worked long hours, and retired upstairs to our room exhausted every night. This same routine went on for months. Friedrich and Gertrude continued to bark orders and were often critical of our work. Along with criticizing our work, I was ridiculed for speaking like an Auslander (foreigner). I was told I would never be able to wait on customers because I didn't know the language and spoke like a "Polack." They said I sounded uneducated and stupid which would give their establishment a bad name. On a number of occasions I was ridiculed in front of others and made to feel like an idiot.

I wanted to master the language so my time in Germany would be more tolerable. It was not easy for me to perfect the language and sound like a native who had been born and educated in Germany. I tried my best to learn their dialect. As I worked on the language, my hatred for Friedrich and Gertrude grew. I knew I was intelligent. They were both extremely bad mannered, smug and prejudiced. I tried hard to fend off their injurious slurs and remarks, though at times they hurt me deeply. Friedrich and Gertrude firmly believed Hitler's fascist ideology of the German people as the superior race. They treated both Anke and me with little regard and no respect. We were considered free slave labor and basically sub-human foreigners that had been brought by force into their country to work for and serve them.

After three months in Hanover, we were finally allowed to write letters home. I'm not sure why they didn't let us write home at first. I believe it was another way for the Nazis to show they had control over us. I sent letters off to my family at least once a month if not every other week. The letters I wrote to Mother and Father tended to be several pages long and I tried not to worry them.

Sadly in one of my early letters from home, I learned my dear Oma Margarette had passed away at the age of 78. She was buried near our home in Bleiberg. I thought about my family standing over her gravesite, and realized I would never see her again. I thought about her crazy antics as she lurked about during the night, which surprisingly brought a smile to my face. I truly missed my sweet, frail, kind Oma and never forgot the role she played in my life. Even though I had suffered a great loss, my circumstances were not altered in any way.

Since I arrived in Germany I had been mocked and treated badly, yet looking back I consider myself considerably luckier than most. I wasn't Jewish, Russian, Polish, or Yugoslavian. I wasn't starved, tortured or put to death in a concentration camp. I happened to be one of the survivors during WWII that was fortunate enough to be born of Austrian descent.

After six months or so of working in the restaurant, our work environment and relationship with Friedrich surprisingly began to improve. Friedrich became more cordial and we were even able to have a civil conversation. Gertrude, on the other hand, remained difficult to deal with. Perhaps Friedrich allowed himself to get to know me better as a person and realized I wasn't just a stupid, little girl. I was shocked and humbled when he offered to teach me the restaurant business. As encouragement he said after I became more proficient in the German language, I could start waiting on more of the customers. Perhaps even help Gertrude run the restaurant someday. He talked about his plan to teach me to cook some of the restaurant's most popular dishes.

Friedrich began to gain trust in me, made me feel respected, and treated me like a real human being. His acts of compassion made my future seem more hopeful. The hatred I had been feeling toward all German people began to soften. I was hopeful that most, like Friedrich, could also change their view of foreigners.

Despite all that was happening around me, I had similar thoughts and feelings like any other teenager would who was not directly experiencing the war. My life in Hannover was extremely boring and monotonous especially for a young girl of 16. I longed to do what all normal 16-year-old girls enjoyed. I wanted to meet my first real love, go to dances and parties, buy nice clothes, and wear pretty jewelry.

I daydreamed about someday finding my Prince Charming, being happily married, and having a family of my own. All of my dreams seemed very far out of reach if not downright impossible. Such fantasies during this time in my life were hard to imagine ever coming true. My life was not normal for a 16-year-old girl. My days amounted to going to work, heading to my room to write letters home followed by sleep.

While at work one day, I overheard a patron talking about local dances in Hannover. The thought of actually going to a dance excited me. After a few days, I worked up the courage to ask Friedrich about the dances. He told me he believed they were held once a month and were attended by many young people including German soldiers. My eyes brightened and without thinking, I asked if Anke and I could possibly leave work early one day so we could go. To my surprise and delight, he said "Yes." He offered to find a day that would work where both Anke and I could leave early.

Friedrich, and to my surprise, Gertrude became easier to talk to. I felt less like a prisoner. There were moments at work when I felt like they actually tried to help me. Gertrude became less suspicious of me and no longer questioned everything I did. I became a more trusted employee. They began to leave me on occasion to run the restaurant on my own. After receiving no pay for several months, they began to pay me a few dollars, (German Marks) a week. I bought a few things and saved enough money to go to the dance.

After I received permission from Friedrich to take that night off work, I couldn't wait to get together with Anke. We talked about the upcoming dance. It was wonderful to have something to look forward to again. It had been a long time since I felt happiness. That evening, Anke and I reacted as expected. Deliriously giddy. Despite being tired we jumped up and down as we anticipated a night full of fun. Anke and I planned to go to the dance hall the next Saturday. We talked of meeting some boys and dancing all evening.

The days passed slowly until Saturday finally arrived. It was hard to concentrate on work that day because all we could think about was the dance. Anke and I repeated our same old routine. We got up early, went down to work, but instead of working into the evening we would be going to a dance! It had been very busy in the restaurant that day so we weren't able to talk about our evening plans. The hours passed too slowly. Fortunately we were allowed off work early enough to have plenty of time to get ready and primp for the dance.

When our work was finally complete, Anke and I raced up to our room. We both were very excited and hardly believed we were truly going to a dance. This was the first time since we had been kidnapped from our homes we actually felt we would have some fun. I couldn't wait to share the news with my mother.

## Chapter 20

Anke and I were both able to buy dresses for the dance. Mine was a simple dress, but very pretty. Mother had always made my dresses. I was so excited because this was one of the few dresses I actually purchased. My dress was made of flowered material, it came to my knees, and had a sheer, shiny, light blue-green material that overlaid the top with a nylon-type cloth. It flowed at the bottom so when a boy twirled me around while we danced, it would whirl and flow freely.

I borrowed some earrings from Anke as I didn't have any. She only had clip-on earrings, but I didn't mind. A friend of mine pierced my ears when I was younger. She used a sewing needle and a potato placed behind my earlobe. I suppose the potato was used to prevent the needle from accidentally stabbing into my neck. I would have worn pierced earrings, but I didn't have enough money to buy both a dress and earrings. I found a teal ribbon that matched my dress, and pinned it at the side of my thick, naturally curly hair where my hair parted.

Without any mirror in our room, we relied on each other for opinions on how we looked and if any necessary adjustments were needed. Anke told me I looked pretty and that was good enough for me. We hadn't taken long to get dressed and in no time we were both ready to go. The dance was a few miles from the restaurant so we set off on foot. During the walk we talked about whether or not we'd be accepted by the others however most importantly we hoped a handsome someone would ask us to dance.

Our path brought us closer to the dance hall, and soon we heard music blaring and people laughing. The dance hall was in sight yet I worried about how I looked. My worries were replaced by sheer amazement at the number of people attending the dance. It seemed as though the entire town had shown up. The dance hall was crowded with young men and women including many young German soldiers in uniform. Wine, whiskey and beer were available to anyone in the ballroom. Anke and I had not drunk much alcohol before this other than an occasional glass of wine with our parents at dinner time. An occasional alcoholic beverage was not unusual for people under the age of 18. It was not uncommon for me to have an occasional glass of wine during dinner or during a family celebration. Both of us looked forward to sipping a new drink. Anke and I decided we would have a few drinks while we enjoyed the music.

We found a table and sat down, but happily before long we were dancing. Being able to forget the drudgery of our day-to-day boring labors was wonderful. I wished the evening would last forever. Most of the crowd at the dance was very social and helped us forget our earlier worries of not being accepted. I nudged Anke to dance with a boy who kept looking at her and was obviously interested. Her shyness relaxed and she was soon dancing with him. I was also approached by several boys including a few German soldiers to dance. Dancing was a freeing experience.

I decided to sit for a while after dancing to several songs and soak up the dance hall atmosphere. Anke continued to dance while I sat. We both feared the evening ending too soon. While I sat, I watched the crowd. I smiled at some of the flirting taking place. Couples held hands. I also observed much kissing on the dance floor. The dancers held each other so close it would have been impossible to pry them apart.

I gazed at a table across the room and noticed an attractive, young soldier sitting and laughing with his buddies. He was staring back at me at the same time. I looked down instantly when our eyes met. I did not want him to think I'd been watching him nor give him the impression I was too forward. When I looked away, I hoped he was still watching me. I looked toward him and found he hadn't taken his eyes off of me since our first glance. I secretly hoped he would come over to my table and ask me to dance. I nonchalantly looked around the room as though I was as relaxed as I could possibly be. I made a point to very slowly take a drink of my wine. Feeling his gaze upon me, I was certain he noticed that I nearly spilled my wine when I set my glass down.

Catching movement from his table out of the corner of my eye, I glanced in his direction. He was walking toward me. I hoped he wouldn't be sidetracked by one of the other beautiful girls. He was very handsome and I was sure they would have happily invited him to join them. He walked across the dance floor past the other girls. Every time I glanced in his direction, his eyes seemed to be keenly focused on me. He approached my table and politely asked if he could get me a drink. I smiled and accepted his offer. He was even more handsome up close! His charming half-smile beguiled me into wanting to know more about him. He asked if he could sit down with me for a while when he handed me my drink.

We began to talk. I learned his name was Hinrich Brase and he was 23-years-old. He was dressed in full German Luftwaffe (Air Force) uniform. I was shocked this tall, handsome, blond-haired man chose me over all the other beautiful women in the room. He had deep, blue eyes, a perfect physique and he didn't have one hair out of place. I was smitten with him immediately and wanted to know all about this man. The biggest problem I could see right away was the fact he was a German Soldier! Because he was German, I needed to be cautious. I wanted to find out as much as I could about him before divulging much information about myself.

My father despised the Nazis before I was forcibly taken, and I imagined he must think worse of them now. My experience with Nazi soldiers had definitely contributed to my opinions of the German people. Despite my ordeal, I was intrigued with this man. His heritage was not going to stop me from getting to know him. As this handsome soldier sat across from me and we spoke, I noticed he stood out from the other men in the room.

Hinrich made the first advance and politely asked me to dance. He held me close and we talked with ease. We danced many times throughout the rest of the night. He seemed somewhat mysterious and philosophical when we spoke about life in general. Hinrich came across as genuinely thoughtful when he spoke about his family and other cultures. He treated me with respect. He spoke highly of his family, and particularly of his mother, which I took as a good sign. It was obvious Hinrich was well-educated. He spoke the German language proficiently, without a single flaw. When I made a few mistakes with the dialect, he was kind and understanding. I learned about his fascination with architecture and how he had wanted so badly to be an architect. The draft ended his educational pursuits. He resentfully withdrew from his college courses and began training to be a pilot for the German Luftwaffe.

We talked for hours that night. I couldn't help but wonder what my father would have thought of Hinrich and even more shocking, of his daughter keeping company with a vile Nazi soldier. Hinrich explained to me that because of his position and rank he had to leave for combat duty the next day and would probably not be back in Germany for several months. I felt so disappointed knowing he would be leaving so soon. Toward the end of the night though, we exchanged addresses so we could write to each other while he was gone. We both wanted very much to stay in touch. We had found something very special that evening and didn't want our time together to end.

When the night ended Hinrich asked if he could see me again when he returned and said he felt it was important we stay in touch. At the end of the last song he had his hands lightly about my waist even though the music had stopped playing. He leaned down and kissed me very gently and sweetly on the lips. We said goodnight and then we had to part ways. I believed when we parted that we both hoped destiny would play a role in our lives and our paths would indeed cross again. I told him I would write to him faithfully until we met again. We both hoped for a chance to pick up where we left off and wished we had more time together.

During war time it was impossible to predict too far into the future and I learned to never take anything for granted. I was uncertain if I would ever see Hinrich again after we parted. Anke and I walked back to the restaurant reliving events of the evening. The warmth of Hinrich's lips lingered on mine and I still felt his gentle embrace. I dearly hoped we would be reunited.

The night had turned out wonderfully. I had met an intriguing gentleman and had a delightful time. I finally started dreaming about my future again; a moment I always remembered. Anke said she had a wonderful time also however she hadn't met anyone she was exceptionally interested in. The next day we would be back to the same old tedious routine including long work days and hearing increased concerns about the war. I didn't want to think about war and what may lay ahead of us as a result. I had just experienced one of the most wonderful nights of my life and didn't want to think about how bad things were becoming in the world.

## Chapter 21

As the months passed by the Nazi Party grew stronger. The war was intensifying and the invasion of Poland had taken place. Aerial and artillery bombardment on many fronts became more strategically planned and concentrated throughout all of Nazi occupied Europe. I couldn't help it, I worried about what lay ahead for me. War had a way of transforming once optimistic feelings into pessimism, which created excessive worry for my family, friends, and my homeland.

It was over four months since I last saw Hinrich. We had written each other many times since he left for duty and talked about being together once again. We had only one precious night together yet I already missed him dearly. I lived each day waiting for his letters. I hoped he would be able to come home soon. In his last letter he said he would be coming home in the next month and we would be together once more. Hinrich wrote that his military training was nearly over. He had become a full-fledged fighter pilot for the German Luftwaffe. Although to most of the German people, and the Nazi high command, this would be viewed as quite an accomplishment, Hinrich's dreams lay in learning to design structures and seeing them be built.

He had no choice whether or not to participate in the war effort. He was considered able-bodied and there was no way to avoid the draft. He was expected to fight for Germany and be proud of his service to the Fatherland and Hitler. Hinrich's feelings about the Nazi Party were similar to his father's beliefs. Neither of them agreed with what was going on in Germany during the war and certainly didn't agree with Hitler's fascist ideology or with the chaos that was taking place. Hinrich knew he would eventually be involved in bombings. As the war progressed the Germans began to draft anyone that could carry a weapon. Some were only 12 and 14-year-old boys while others they recruited were 60 and 70-year-old men who were afraid to refuse the Nazi Party. It made no difference what Hinrich wanted for his future. Fate would determine his destiny.

I learned so much about Hinrich through his letters I felt I'd known him for years. Hinrich wrote of his family including his two brothers, who were also drafted into the war within the same month. His older brother Klaus, Klaus's wife, Anne and their children lived with Hinrich's mother and father on their farm outside of Klenkendorf. His father's mentally challenged sister, Mata, also resided with them. Hinrich's younger brother, Johnon, had married Anne's sister Berta. Johnon and Berta, who was pregnant when he was drafted, had a house in town. Hinrich wrote his family was worried as they had not heard from Johnon since he had entered the war. Once Johnon was drafted into the army, he was never able to come back home for a visit, write his parents, or contact with his wife, which was very disturbing to the family.

Their father, Klaus Brase Sr., referred to as Opa Brase was also asked to join the German army and fight during the war even though at that time he was over 60-years-old. He refused to go even though he was informed he would be drafted if he refused to participate willingly. He told the army recruiters he had several issues with the Nazi party's forced acceptance of Hitler's ideology, and voiced his difficulty supporting the war in general. Opa Brase was the Mayor of Klenkendorf at the time, and managed somehow to find connections and allies that helped him avoid the draft. Opa Brase had some clout during that time, not only was he the mayor of Klenkendorf, his father, who was also named Klaus, had been the town's mayor before him.

There was some worry in the family for Mata's safety as Hitler's stance proclaimed mentally challenged persons a burden. Forced sterilizations had occurred to keep the handicapped out of society. It is unknown to me if Opa Brase's status or that of his father before him helped spare Mata or if her mental status was just unbeknownst to the Nazis.

Whatever the reasoning Mata was able to continue on living with the Brases.

Even though Hinrich and the rest of his family did not support Hitler's Nazi Party, they had no choice except to participate in the war. Hinrich and his brothers were all drafted and forced to fight as Nazis. If they had refused, they would have been jailed or executed. The entire family was afraid Opa Brase was going to be killed for speaking out against the party and for his unwillingness to participate in the war. His wife, Engle Brase, was the most afraid of all. She worried she would lose not only her three sons during the war but also her husband.

Below is a picture of Hinrich and his brothers, all of them were drafted and served in the German Service at the same time. From left to right, is Johnon, the youngest brother, Hinrich in the middle (Luftwaffe), and Klaus Jr. (Army) the eldest son, his father Klaus Brase and his mother Engle Brase.

## Chapter 22

Hinrich and I wrote heartfelt letters to each other. I waited impatiently for him. I felt both nervous and excited for his return. Once home on leave, Hinrich arranged for a nice dinner at the restaurant where I worked and planned for us to go to another dance. The day of our date finally arrived. I was flustered and wanted to look my best. Anke appeared to be as excited as I and offered to help me get ready to greet Hinrich. You would have thought I was preparing to be married. My heightened mood was obvious to everyone.

When at last I locked eyes with Hinrich as he walked through the door, he was certainly more handsome than I remembered. He immediately reached for my hand and told me how happy he was to see me again. He traced my cheek with his finger and kissed me as if he was afraid he'd lose me. When he looked down at me I was lost in his clear, blue eyes. Hinrich told me how beautiful I was as he held my hand. I was like a princess being whisked away by her Prince Charming and felt like a lovesick school girl about to swoon.

It was strange being in the restaurant for dinner having others wait on me. I was always the one in the kitchen cooking and cleaning. It troubled Hinrich that I had to work so hard when he was gone. He expressed concern for the agony I felt being so far from my mother and father. I was treated with more respect by people in general while out with Hinrich. Probably because he was a German soldier. He was so charismatic and openly showed his affection without hesitation. He seemed to want the world to share in our happiness.

Several times at the dance he reached for my hand and pulled me close for an embrace. When he held me in his arms I felt beautiful and he made me feel like I was the most important person in his life. We had so much fun that night meeting up with some of Hinrich's friends, yet it was strange how easily they accepted me. Hinrich and I spent as much time as we could together while he was on leave. Our time together was short as Hinrich had to report back to duty. He could have been home for a year and it wouldn't have been long enough for us. It was hard to say goodbye after only a few short weeks. Our reunion affirmed his declarations he had written in his letters. I knew he was truly a good man. He did his best to make me feel loved and let me know I was the only one for him.

During this time I was free to travel around Hannover unguarded. The Nazis now left me alone and my supervision was provided solely by Friedrich and Gertrude. I became more accepted by the locals because I dated a Luftwaffe officer.

In letters, Hinrich told me he hadn't been ordered to fly on a mission yet, but was told by his commanding officers he would before long. He became part of the dive bombers within the Luftwaffe. I was fearful because I knew he was in one of the most dangerous branches of the service; his life was at risk every time he took off. I tried to put these thoughts out of my mind. Often their assignments were tagged suicide missions and many pilots never returned home.

The war expanded as time went on with bombings having begun by both the Axis and Allied powers. I feared for both Hinrich and me, as neither one of us was prepared for what the war brought upon us. We were two simple people caught in situations the war had forced upon us. We had no choice but to figure out how to survive and stay together.

Our relationship strengthened and deepened regardless of the war happening around us. We clung to each other's letters as salvation from our situations. We were each other's promise for a better, brighter future. Time passed so quickly, before we knew it a year had flown by since we met. I still worked at the restaurant in Hannover and lived in our small apartment with Anke. Hinrich came home on leave for short periods of time and then returned to duty. His visits were never long enough and I thought about him constantly when he was gone. We grew closer as time passed and began to discuss marriage in our letters.

Hinrich said he worried about me while he was away and wanted to make sure I would be safe and taken care of if anything ever happened to him. After a year of courtship Hinrich felt it was time to introduce me to his parents. I was unsure how this first meeting would go and was afraid to meet his family. I was a foreigner and though Hinrich fully accepted me, I was uncertain if his family would do the same. He took me to meet his parents.

## Chapter 23

Hinrich came from a farm family in Germany. His parents and siblings had farmed 60 acres in the Klenkendorf area just at the edge of town for many years.

**Map below shows Klenkendorf**

During the 1940's his parent's farm was considered a large farm because most people in Germany were lucky if they owned a few acres. The house they lived in was simple, although considered large for a farm home. Hinrich told me he and his brothers helped his parents farm the land while they were growing up. The entire family worked hard to make ends meet and were able to raise their own produce and animals for sale. They also butchered their own meat.  Having enough to eat, a place to live, decent clothes to wear, and enough money to provide an education for your children were of great value and significance to anyone anywhere. Hinrich's family was fortunate to have these opportunities before the war began.

During the 1930's the Great Depression was a global crisis, the entire world had problems with a depressed economy and times were difficult for most people no matter where they lived.  The Brases were considered well off compared to many other families in Germany.

Hinrich had lived in Klenkendorf all of his life and was well known in the area.  It was easy for him to strike up conversations with others.  His eloquent speaking skills and charm captivated his listeners.  I, unfortunately, had the opposite experience as people often misunderstood what I was saying and reacted with disgust.  Fortunately, Hinrich never made me feel like a lesser individual than he.  He had faith that I would master the German language.

I pictured his family as being like Hinrich, caring and compassionate.  Instead when the day came to meet his family, it felt more like when I first met Friedrich and Gertrude.  I could tell I wasn't the kind of girl they had hoped for their son to marry.  His mother and father weren't pleased with the fact I didn't come from a good German family. Also I didn't have any money or resources to offer and contribute to the relationship.  I thought for the most part they disliked me initially because I was Austrian and didn't have true German blood running through my veins.  I wasn't as well educated as their son, which certainly annoyed them.  They definitely felt he could do better than to court someone like me.

Hinrich's mother, Engle Brase, who everyone called Oma Engle, showed her distaste in me more so than his father.  Later when I discussed this with Hinrich, he told me not to listen to them as he loved me and that was all that mattered.  He said it would take some time, but he was sure his parents would come around and be more accepting of me and our relationship once they knew me better. My love had grown for Hinrich so much I was willing to be ridiculed by his parents as long as we remained together. I countered the humiliation I felt from them with my father's pride in me and my mother's love for me. Dignity radiated within me, and I clung to this for comfort.

Unofficial word came that Hinrich's brother, Johnon, had died. The family's fear having not heard from Johnon had become realized. No one was ever sure what exactly had happened to him. They just knew he died and never returned home. How he died was based on speculation because his body was never found. They were told he died of pneumonia in a German prison camp because of his political dissention and anti-Hitler rhetoric. Others spoke of him having been tortured and killed by Russian soldiers. He was still a young man when word came of his death. He was perhaps 22-years-old and left a young wife with a one-year-old son behind. The news was heart wrenching for Hinrich and his family. Not having his remains to lay to rest afforded them no peace of mind.

After my initial meeting with Hinrich's parents each time Hinrich came home on leave we visited his family and spent most of our time in the country staying on the farm together. Getting along with his parents continued to prove difficult. It was hard to establish even the slightest bond with them in the beginning. Word of Johnon's death seemed to make Oma Engle even more resentful and hateful towards foreigners. When we were there I struggled with the negativity that pervaded the household and the clear feelings of disapproval I got from his mother. I tried to stay positive. I hoped to get through our family visits without any arguments, yet I sometimes found it impossible because of the rude things said to me.

In the early days both of his parents gave me the impression they hated me. His mother openly spouted her prejudices and intolerance of me. She either talked down to me or refused to acknowledge my presence. I was an Auslander, an outsider, and she never hesitated to let me know I wasn't an acceptable mate for her son. I understood, according to Oma Engle, my coloring was not correct. My black hair and my brown eyes were not favorable attributes in her eyes. Time I spent in Oma Engle's and Opa Brase's presence was difficult and always tense. Their rejection was blatant and so was their dissatisfaction with me. Everyone was uncomfortable and felt the uneasiness. No matter what I did or said, I was wrong. I found it impossible to live up to his mother's expectations of the woman she thought Hinrich should marry.

Our love endured even though Oma Engle was outraged we even dared speak of our intentions to marry. Life was certainly more difficult for me with Hinrich often gone. I had to deal with his parents on my own when I saw them. When Hinrich was not there to support me, my relationship with his parents was more volatile. They seemed to be a little more reserved with their comments toward me when he was around.

Hinrich was stationed in France after the Nazi occupation took place and was gone for months at a time. While he was gone, exchanging letters was the only way we had to express our love and affection for each other. As well as keeping track of how our lives were going. There was a large void in both our lives. The war made everything about our lives more complicated. The constant separation forced us to learn to have trust and faith in each other.

I tried to keep things in our relationship simple yet wanted to ensure Hinrich knew how I felt about him. Our feelings were often hard to describe through a simple handwritten letter. We yearned to be together. Neither of us wanted to worry the other so we were careful how we wrote about our feelings. I didn't want to trouble Hinrich too much so I often didn't burden him with my mistreatment from his family.

While he was away, Hinrich sent me elegant gifts from France. He was particular about how he wanted me to look. He always wanted me to look my best. On many occasions he bought me beautiful dresses and lovely shoes to match. When he came home on leave he wanted to see me wearing them and told me how beautiful I looked.  I found it so easy to love Hinrich.  He clearly expressed warmth, devotion and affection for me.

## Chapter 24

I waited impatiently for letters to arrive from Hinrich. Receiving word he was alive and well provided the continual reassurance I needed. I received a letter from Hinrich one day explaining he wasn't feeling well and as a result would be coming home on military leave. He wrote of the difficulty to gain approval to come home. After several requests, he said his commander finally approved his leave due to his health problems. I was elated to hear news of him returning home while at the same time was very concerned about his overall health.

Once Hinrich arrived home, I immediately asked him about his feelings of ill health. I was relieved to hear he would soon see a doctor to evaluate his symptoms. He complained of a nagging cough that never seemed to abate and recurring nausea. At times the sick feeling in his stomach made him violently ill and it took him days to improve. His sickness had started to interfere with his duties. He was concerned about his health, but he didn't appear overly worried.

During his two week leave, physicians completed a thorough examination and assessed his symptoms. It took him quite a while in the doctor's office and at the hospital for he had several medical tests done at both locations. After the doctors carefully evaluated his condition, they gave him a full release, and prescribed no treatment other than some medicine for his cough. The doctors foresaw no future medical issues related to his complaints. His test results revealed no major concerns for his overall health. The outcome was good and his prognosis was positive. I was relieved and happy to hear the great news. He received a clean bill of health from the doctors which meant he must return to full military duty with no restrictions. The Luftwaffe had no reason to extend his leave of absence. He was expected to return and be ready for active duty. Once again he departed, leaving me behind, obligated to serve in the Luftwaffe. Another goodbye, as difficult as the others.

With each passing day the separation between Hinrich and I grew harder to bare. The influences of war constantly interfered with our plans to marry and raise a family. Hinrich had become my confidant; I found it reassuring to confide in him. Our bond strengthened, even though we were apart more than we were together. Hinrich and I talked about marriage in almost every letter we exchanged.

His family continued to disapprove of our relationship. I wondered if they ever would approve of me. His mother persisted in seeing me as an outsider not worthy of her son. In his letters, Hinrich encouraged me to ignore their behavior. I saw this as an impossible task for I was expected to visit his family while he was gone. I was left to try and build a relationship with his family on my own. I wondered if their harsh views would soften when we were married. I waited to see what the future would bring.

While Hinrich was away, I continued to work at the restaurant every day. I wrote to my mother and father several times a month. I hoped father had begun to warm up to the idea I was in a relationship with a Luftwaffe pilot with the real possibility of marriage. Father had met many good people from Germany in his day, however he didn't trust the Nazis at all. I wasn't sure if he trusted my judgment, nonetheless I planned to continue my relationship with Hinrich. My abduction from our home had taken place less than two years prior. It had permanently tainted my father's perception of the Nazis for good reason.

I tried to explain to my father in the letters I sent home how Hinrich and I were both victims of the war, thrown into circumstances beyond our control. We would have never chosen this life for ourselves nor would we have chosen to play the roles we were now forced to assume. Neither one of us was willing nor did we want to be separated from our families and friends.

Hinrich never wanted war or to fly with the Luftwaffe. He was a well-mannered, peaceful man, young and full of hope with dreams of being an architect. I never wanted to be kidnapped, taken from my home and family, and forced to work and live in a country I had never seen. I know father struggled with the idea of me being involved with a Luftwaffe fighter pilot. I could barely believe it myself, but I believed things would be better once father actually got a chance to know Hinrich and perhaps meet him someday. He would then be able to judge for himself what type of man Hinrich really was. I hoped my father would see Hinrich in the same light I saw him. He was just like the rest of us, raised as a farm boy and had the same hopes and dreams we all have for ourselves and for our futures. Father and Hinrich were alike in many ways and I very much wanted my father to like him. The war had caused us all to be more suspicious than we had ever been before.

I had good news to report when I wrote to my mother and father. I learned that soon we might be able to cross the border into Austria, which meant I could visit my parents. It had been nearly two years since I was taken from my home and I had been unable to return to Austria. Visas were not made available to forced-labor victims such as myself. The border between Austria and Germany was heavily guarded by the military making it very dangerous if not impossible to cross. It was unsafe and very risky to try to sneak across the border and I didn't want to chance getting captured or killed.

Mail delivery had become one of the most important events in my life as every day I looked forward to getting a stamped envelope from Austria or France. The anticipation of opening a letter I knew was filled with love and affection from Hinrich or my family became the highlight of my week. The handwritten, black ink that filled the paper reassured me and helped keep things in some sort of perspective bringing me an element of hope and peace that someday we would all be together again.

## Chapter 25

In May of 1940 Hamburg suffered heavy bombing because their oil refineries were key targets. Bremen, Hamburg and Hannover were all in close proximity. Klenkendorf lay in the center of a triangle created by these metro centers. It was a terrifying time for all of us as the bombing got closer and closer to our city. Air raid sirens went off continuously as they became a common occurrence. We took cover in bomb shelters daily. I waited every day to hear from Hinrich and my worries grew that he might be killed as the war intensified.

With each letter I received from him, I experienced a sense of relief and stopped worrying for a brief moment. My feelings of uneasiness and anxiety grew. Hinrich sent a letter saying he would be home soon, but he could not stay long. He confided in me that he continued to feel sick and was never able to get rid of the constant cough. He had never experienced a cough like this before.

His commanders refused to allow him to stop flying so he could seek medical help. They had little sympathy for his complaints. His letter caused me grave concern yet my heart flooded with emotion when he went on to write that the only way he endured us being apart so long was due to my undoubted love for him. He knew I waited for his return and he looked to our future together. He went on to say he had something important to ask me when he returned home. I hugged the letter tight against my chest as tears trickled down my cheeks; tears of happiness this time. I knew what his words meant and they meant the world to me. When I showed the letter to Anke, I thought she might explode from the excitement she felt for me.

Two weeks whisked by quickly and I knew Hinrich would soon be home at the farm. I went there to meet him and we spent time together. I never looked forward to seeing his mother, but I couldn't wait to see

Hinrich.  I had an inkling about what he was going to ask me, making his homecoming all the more exciting.  I tried to put my best foot forward so I went to his mother's thinking I'd arrive earlier than Hinrich.  The lack of acceptance from his mother made me very nervous going over to the house to wait for him.  I wondered what she would say to me when she found out Hinrich and I had discussed marriage for the last six months.  With any luck maybe someday his mother and I would become friends and share happiness and friendship.

When I arrived at the farm I walked through the front door.  There stood Hinrich with open arms ready to greet me.  I had not realized he would get there first.  I ran into his arms, gave him a big hug and a long kiss.  We wanted some privacy so we took a walk by the stream that ran close to the house.  We sat down in the shady grass by a huge, old pine tree and talked about our future plans.  I asked him what was so important he wasn't able to ask me in his letters.  He teased me about my curiosity.  He gave me a gentle hug and a tender kiss, then in a quiet voice proposed to me, asking me for my hand in marriage.  I accepted without hesitation and with whole heartedness told him I couldn't wait for our life together as man and wife.

It was wonderful to have Hinrich home which gave us time to take several leisurely walks throughout the country side.  Walking was peaceful and provided Hinrich with plenty of fresh air he so desperately needed.  During one of our walks we came upon a band of Gypsies parked in a nearby field.

One of the women was a fortune teller.  She flashed shiny bracelets on her wrists, many jeweled rings sparkled on her fingers and a number of multicolored necklaces wove around her neck.  Over her hair was a turban head dress, fancy and colorful, while her long, black, flowing locks wisped in the breeze.  She gazed at us from under her turban with piercing, black eyes.  She intrigued us both, yet I was also hesitant to stop to visit with her.

My superstitious nature warned me this was not a good idea and I should not have my fortune told.  My curiosity, however, was greater than my fear and I decided I would listen to what she had to say even though I had my reservations.  Neither of us could resist having our fortunes told and although I was very leery of what we might hear, I went ahead anyway.

I almost made Hinrich go first then I decided I would instead.  Since I was quite superstitious I worried about her psychic abilities and what she may share with us about our futures.  I didn't want to hear anything bad.  When I told Hinrich having our fortune told frightened me, he just laughed out loud at me.  He told me I was being silly, and we were doing this for fun.  He said he didn't believe in any of this stuff and the predictions were made up fibs.  Gypsies had used fortune telling for centuries as a way to swindle people out of their money.  Their tribes were well known around Austria and Germany.  His jests made me feel a little better, but I was still somewhat fearful.

When we arrived the Gypsie woman invited us to enter her wagon where we sat down at a very small table.  It gave me the creeps sitting there in the tiny, dimly lit wagon, yet I remained.  I thought since Hinrich was there, he would protect me.  Perhaps he was right and her predictions would be nothing but gibberish.  After we were seated, the brightly-dressed woman's demeanor changed.  She became very serious.  She wanted us to believe in her magic and warned that what she told us would come true.  She also said she couldn't control the future that held our destinies.  She began to read my palm, touching me, and looking at her cards.  It was eerie.  Her intense, black eyes stared me in the face while she touched my hand and read my future.  She made me shutter.

The fortune teller predicted I would have a baby girl and face many hardships over the next few years.  She couldn't tell me exactly what those hardships would be, but she saw not only happiness in my future, but also sadness and despair.  The information she gave me was pretty general, so it was easy to take her words with a grain of salt.  I had had enough after a few minutes of her spoken prophecies and didn't care to hear anymore.

The whole time during the psychic's reading Hinrich grinned, not believing a word she said; hoping to make me laugh. He still wanted his fortune told and turned his head a few times as she spoke to him because of his obvious disbelief. He thought it was a bunch of hocus pocus, but his curiosity made him continue the reading. The voodoo-like atmosphere made me feel apprehensive, although I could tell Hinrich wasn't the least bit concerned with anything she told him.

The Gypsy woman began his fortune by relating nonspecific details pertaining to future happenings, some of pain and suffering. Then she foretold his death. Her expression became somber, she warned us the situation was grave and she saw an apparition of death. Dimness clouded the room when she spoke of death. Her dreadful stare directed at Hinrich made me want to leave. The fortune teller spoke of sadness and misery. Then she got a puzzled look on her face. She turned her head slowly, her eyes glaring, looking directly at Hinrich. She told him she had seen a vision so awful he might not want to continue. The prophecy she was about to foretell would cause fear and bring great harm to our family. Her body shook, her voice trembled. I saw she was dismayed by the vision she had just seen.

The fortune teller looked at Hinrich and told him he would die at a young age, and his death would be excruciating. Hearing these prophecies aloud made me want to go, yet Hinrich just sat there. Suddenly fear overwhelmed me and I was ready to leave right then. Hinrich smiled, not believing a word spoken, and asked her to continue. He told me later he had thought to himself, I'm a fighter pilot and I am at risk every day. This woman is just putting two-and-two together telling me I will die at a young age and yes it could happen. However, with the war going on I didn't want to hear the word death, much less hear someone predict the one I loved would die at a very young age. I knew she was making generalizations but I didn't like it. The sitting went on so I was forced to stay because Hinrich insisted we finish since we had already paid the woman.

The Gypsy woman was persistent and the reading seemed never-ending. She said Hinrich would endure much suffering, undergo a series of challenges that would test his strength and will. Also he would need to tolerate pain and agony from an affliction that had no cure. She waved her hands back and forth over her head as she spoke. She said he was destined to die, then blurted out the date November 7, 1944 but she gave no details of how or why. Frightened by the specific predictions she conjured up, I turned to Hinrich and motioned we leave now! I was frightened enough by what she said, I was ready to run out the door. I couldn't stand to hear another word of her babblings. Hinrich waited until she was finished, then we left. She watched us walk away from the wagon until we were out of sight.

Hinrich was not fazed by the visions she had conjured up, yet he could tell I was visibly upset. He tried to make me feel better by joking about her predictions, about how phony and ridiculous her apparitions seemed. He repeated he was well aware the Gypsies in the area had been telling fortunes to the villagers and farmers for many years. It was all about the money and their predictions were totally false. He was a non-believer when it came to their futuristic prophecies. I was glad to leave the Gypsy's wagon that day.

I decided I would never have my fortune read again. To this day I have never gone to another psychic and never will. The memory of what happened with Hinrich and the Gypsy fortune teller has stayed with me; a painful moment among so many in my life.

## Chapter 26

Times had become more difficult in Germany, however, we didn't want the war to stop us from planning our wedding. Over the next few days Hinrich, Oma Engle, and I discussed our wedding plans. I could tell his mother was very unhappy when she heard the news of our wedding, but she was trying to put up the best front she could while Hinrich was home. It was left to his mother and I to make sure everything was ready for the wedding. I included his mother in the process and let her make many of the decisions; I hoped things might be easier that way. We decided it made more sense to try and keep the wedding small since Hinrich was gone most of the time. I found it was neither affordable nor practical to plan anything other than a small wedding.

Most weddings that took place in small villages like Klenkendorf turned out quite large even if it wasn't the original plan. In this local culture it was almost expected that everyone in the town was welcomed to attend the celebration. Custom dictated that no one was ever turned away unless they happened to be an enemy of the family.

Fortunately, both Friedrich and Gertrude gave their blessings. I was still considered a forced laborer in the eyes of the Nazis. The restaurant owners could have easily made our planned nuptials more complicated by informing the Nazis. Gratefully they did not wish to interfere with my desire for a normal life.

Hinrich and I wanted our wedding planned quickly and agreed we would be married during his next expected leave from duty. We were optimistic about our future and the war ending. We planned our nuptials with the anticipation that nothing would interfere with our wedding day. Because it was wartime, plans could be easily canceled or disrupted so all we could do was set a date, hope for the best, and pray nothing happened to upset our big day.

Oma Engle and I worked together coordinating the wedding plans relatively quickly once we found out the date of Hinrich's next leave. Getting married was one of my life long dreams. As a young girl I had envisioned many different scenarios of what my dress would look like, what my husband would look like, and where I would live. Of course, images of combat had never entered my mind and now I found myself planning and working around the grim events of WWII.

After all that had happened, it was hard for me to believe I was actually engaged to be married. Being taken away from my home in Austria had changed many things I had thought at one time would be part of my destiny. I realized at least one of my childhood dreams was within grasp, and in the near future would come true. My dream of having my own home and family someday was in sight. I still feared for Hinrich's and my own safety every day. The turmoil of frequent bombings near our homes and Hinrich heading back into hostile zones made us live our lives day-by-day and moment-by-moment.

Our wedding approached. Hinrich was on his way home for leave while his family and I were in the midst of making the last preparations for our wedding celebration. My white wedding dress turned out beautifully. Oma Engle and Opa Brase helped me arrange and make plans for the entertainment and also helped with all the food. We would marry at the farm and had invited all the neighbors and longtime friends.

Prior to the war and before the depression, most of the town's people came and partook when a wedding took place. They knew they were welcome as soon as an event became public knowledge. Most people usually brought gifts or plates of food, but nothing was expected from anyone. The family who was having the wedding was expected to make and provide all the food and drinks.

Hinrich's mother, his aunts, his cousins and I had prepared the house, the food, and many other things for the upcoming festivities. We prepared for a large group of guests. If a large group showed up we wanted to make sure there was enough food and drinks for all. There would be dancing and music at the wedding. Also consistent with most of the weddings that took place in Klenkendorf, we anticipated the celebration lasting for two to three days. A constant flow of visitors were expected to come and leave throughout the week, congratulating us on our marriage. We needed to be ready to entertain them all.

I wished with all my heart my mother, father, and sister could have been part of my very special day. Neither they nor I were able to legally cross the border between Germany and Austria. I tried to convey to them through my letters how much I missed them and how badly I wanted them by my side when I married Hinrich. I knew it was impossible for my family to come to Germany. They would have risked their lives if they tried to cross the border.

It seemed to take forever for our wedding day to arrive yet the day finally came in 1940 towards the end of summer. The entire marriage ceremony was held outside. I was very thankful for the clear, warm, sunny day. It was a picture perfect day for a wedding. The blessing of good weather gave us one more reason to celebrate. I was so nervous knowing all eyes would be on me, but I knew Hinrich would be by my side and he was good at entertaining and being the center of attention.

All our hard work had paid off and everything looked wonderful. The tables were covered with the family's finest table cloths. After the ceremony they would be covered with luscious, home-grown fruits, scrumptious desserts and enough beer, whiskey and wine for all who chose to partake in the festivities. We also prepared a variety of meat dishes, vegetables, fancy cakes and tortes filled with whipped cream and layered high.

The local minister arrived at the farm. I was ready for the ceremony to begin and couldn't wait for the moment I would be standing before the minister alongside my husband. All the guests were seated. While I stood waiting for the signal to walk down the aisle and come before the minister, I heard music playing and the guests talking and laughing outside my door.  The clock struck 12:00 pm and I saw the attendant from the wedding party motion for me to walk down the path where I would greet my husband-to-be.

## Chapter 27

I acted on my cue and stepped out the front door. I was so happy yet at the same time saddened my family was not there to share my joyful day. Opa Brase walked me down the aisle. Hinrich waited beside the minister for me to join them. His eyes met mine as I walked toward him. I felt my full-length, long, white, wedding gown drag across the ground with every synchronized step I took. My dress was tightly fitted, long sleeved, with a sheer veil that hung to the floor. Aware of my nerves, Hinrich shot me the mesmerizing half-grin of his. He nodded his head at me to convey his admiration. I thought to myself how handsome and debonair he looked in his uniform. I couldn't wait to get through the crowd and stand next to him. I was ready to say my vows, become his wife and I didn't want to wait a moment longer.

The band played softly in the background. I never took my eyes off of Hinrich. Within moments I found myself next to him. I was so excited I didn't remember walking down the aisle once I joined him. Once face to face with the man I loved, I gazed into his eyes, hardly believing this was really happening to me. It was a dream come true. We joined hands and stood together, our eyes fixed on one another. Thoughts of love, of someday having our own home and family filled my head.

The crowd became quiet once I joined Hinrich. The music stopped. The minister read our marriage vows. As he read the vows I hung onto every word he said. I promised to become Hinrich's wife, repeated each of the words, and gave my word to love, honor and cherish Hinrich forever. That moment was enchanting, it was everything I had ever hoped for. I had forgotten about all the disappointments and sorrows that once troubled me. The only thing that was missing was seeing my parents and sister sitting in the front row smiling at me as I pledged my love for Hinrich.

The ceremony lasted less than an hour. Afterwards it was time to enjoy the music and take pleasure in the German cuisine prepared by all the women in the family. The men's only job was to take care of the drinks and mingle with the guests. It was time for some laughter, entertainment and for everyone who attended to meet the new Mr. and Mrs. Hinrich Brase.

**Below is a picture of the happily married couple Mr. and Mrs. Hinrich Brase; Hinrich was 26-years-old and Karoline almost 18, both young and very much in love.**

## Chapter 28

As predicted the marriage celebration continued for several days. I was exhausted from all the preparation efforts and excitement. Considering the times, everything had turned out wonderfully. In just a few short days after the wedding, Hinrich reported for duty. I was alone once more, but tried not to dwell on it. The plan was for me to live with Hinrich's family on the farm once we were married. Hinrich felt this was safer for me. Also it was the customary thing to do. In Germany, especially if the family owned land, the woman in most cases would live with the husband's parents and since Hinrich was gone that seemed the right thing to do.

I expected we would most likely live there or very close by after Hinrich was discharged from serving in the Luftwaffe. It was possible we would live in that area the rest of our lives. The thought of living with his family worried me. Oma Engle, even though helpful at times, continued to treat me like an outsider. I had hoped since we were now married she would show me a bit more respect. We had our good days, but I still felt the animosity and bitterness she directed towards me.

I had many reservations about moving in with Hinrich's parents. I didn't like the thought of being left alone on the farm with Opa Brase and Oma Engle, Anne and their children. Even so I knew this was what I needed to do. I decided to leave the small apartment where I lived with Anke and do what was customary for the times. Anke was saddened when I left, but she understood I had to do what was best for me. Times were hard and the economy poor, it made sense for me to band together with Hinrich's family. Hinrich and I would have much rather had our own place.

Often sons inherited the land, helped on the farm, and lived on or near the homestead after marriage. Usually the oldest son was expected to live and take over the homestead, as was the case with Hinrich's brother Klaus. Although that didn't necessarily hold true especially during wartime.

**Below is a picture of Opa and Oma Brase, Hinrich's brother, Klaus, Klaus's wife, Anne, and their children.**

I continued to work in Hannover at the restaurant until I learned I was pregnant. Hinrich and I were thrilled with the news. It was then I decided to leave my job and begin to help Oma Engle on the farm on a full-time basis. My chores on the farm consisted of helping with the cooking, cleaning, and housework. I did a few outside farm chores too. Most of my chores were not too strenuous and I mainly worked inside the house. I never stopped wishing for a place of our own yet I knew that wasn't about to happen anytime soon.

Several laborers were needed to handle all of the work at the Brase's farm. They were relied on more with Hinrich and Klaus Jr. gone with the war effort. With so much to do on the farm, there seemed to be farm hands coming and going all the time.  Sometimes they rotated war prisoners to work on German farms though it depended on each farmer's need.  Many times, however, if you were initially placed on a farm as a prisoner, it was possible you would stay on the same farm to work for several years.  The Brases had a couple of long-term farm hands that worked for the family prior to the war.  For reasons unknown to me, they were not drafted, but were allowed to stay on the farm.  The other men working on the farm were forced-laborers from the nearby prison camp.  I sympathized with these men as I had also been a forced-laborer.  I likely would have remained so if I had not met Hinrich.

At that time, of course, there was no modern equipment to help with the laborious farm work.  The tools we used to farm the land were basic garden hoes, rakes and shovels.  Work horses and oxen were used to till the fields.  Sixty-acres was a lot of ground to work by hand.  Working so hard made it easy to work up quite an appetite.  Oma Engle cooked large quantities to feed the family and workers every day.  She used a wood-burning cook stove to prepare food.  I helped her cook at times, but I mainly served the meals.  It was similar to working in the restaurant only there were fewer patrons to wait on.  The farm hands/workers were thankful and never complained about the food or the service we provided.

The farm hands lived on the farmstead, and were housed in another building on the property.  They all came in to eat at the main house every day, but had to sit at different tables in a different room.  The "help" was not allowed to mingle with the family.  They were considered underlings and there was a definite hierarchy in our household.  Everyone seemed to know their place including the forced-labor men.  If they got out of control, Opa Brase and Oma Engle handled the situation themselves most of the time.  Nazi guards checked in with Opa Brase occasionally to see how the workers were doing and disciplined them if necessary.  When a worker misbehaved, Oma Engle and Opa Brase quite firmly told them they needed to follow the rules or they wouldn't be working for them long.  If the forced-laborers were unable to do their jobs, they were taken back to the harsh prison camp where they lived behind wire fences, were treated cruelly, and literally had no freedom.

Oma Engle and Opa Brase had an abundance of blueberries they grew on the farm. They were plentiful and at our disposal for eating, baking and cooking such things as fresh blueberry pies, cakes, and other wonderful dishes. There was a profusion of flowering magnolia trees. Also a small wooded area with a stream flowing nearby. In the front yard grew evergreens measuring 50 to 60 feet high.

In Klenkendorf the soil reminded me of peat moss, spongy and springy. If floors were made of cement, they had to be redone every seven to ten years because of the consistency of the ground. The stress of the shifting ground caused cracks and crevices in the cement that required continual repair. The ground shifted like a sponge making it difficult to erect some construction projects. Many people cut the peat moss into squares, then stacked and dried it. They burned the squares to heat their homes.

## Chapter 29

As time went on, my relationship with Oma Engle didn't improve much. We seemed to be constantly in disagreement about something. If I disagreed or put up an argument I was most often on the losing end of the quarrel. I found it was easier to just shut up, sit back and listen to what she had to say. I didn't want to start any arguments and rarely responded to her negative comments because I didn't want to create any more hard feelings between us. I never gave up hope perhaps someday she would treat me like one of the family. Oma Engle wasn't ready to make any concessions or compromises when it came to our disagreements. As my mother-in-law and an elder, I was obligated to respect her and her wishes. It was her home, she made the rules and was in charge of making all the decisions.

I knew I must endure this situation until we found a place of our own. Hinrich advised me not to listen to her when she spouted off orders. That was easy for him to say, he wasn't around most of the time and it was his mother we were talking about. She was able to dictate what took place in her household and didn't hesitate to tell me how to do things. I just tried to go about my business and pay as little attention to her as possible.

Oma Engle on occasion showed her better side although those episodes were few and far between. She was a stubborn woman, hard headed, rude and very demanding. I thought she could have been a master drill sergeant if anyone had given her the opportunity. Initially when we met, acceptance was not anything she considered nor was tolerance for other cultures one of her positive traits. To accept an outsider into her family was a struggle for her and an idea that was hard for her to fathom. I remember feeling hurt and insulted when I first moved in with Opa Engle and Oma Brase. Every time she set the table for the family's supper, she didn't set a place for me. It was as if I didn't exist, and she didn't want to have to look at me.  I retrieved my own plate and sat by myself trying hard not to let her humiliation get to me.  I was surprised she let me eat the food she prepared.  Her passive and direct actions sent a loud and clear message to me even if she never uttered a word.

I felt like one of the forced-laborers as she blatantly tried to segregate and distance me from the rest of the family.  I was uncertain if we would ever resolve the differences between us or if she would ever consider me part of the family.  She complained about the way I dressed and ridiculed me as to why I dressed the way I did.  Thanks to Hinrich, I owned and wore nicer clothes and shoes than the rest of the family and chose to wear them when doing my housecleaning and farm chores.

Oma Engle told me it was silly of Hinrich to buy me fancy gifts as they were impractical and useless.  She told me looking showy on the farm while doing chores was ridiculous and it didn't make any sense at all.  Oma Engle insisted I wear old dresses like her and an apron to keep my dress from getting too soiled or torn.  Wooden shoes like she wore every day were also "recommended."  I was 18 and conscious about my looks.  I wasn't about to wear those ugly, wooden shoes.  Besides their hideous looks, they were the most uncomfortable shoes I had ever put on my feet.

I tried my best to be patient with her when she barked orders and insults at me.  Once I moved to the farm I had no one to confide in or talk to.  When I wrote Hinrich I couldn't help but complain about his mother.  She and the other in-laws got along and seemed to band together against me.  Hinrich was the only one that listened to me about how poorly his mother treated me.  As before, Hinrich encouraged me to be more assertive with her or just ignore her.

One day I worked up enough courage to hold my ground and let her know what I thought about some of her rude comments and irrational ideas.  I fired back at her when she was berating my dress.  I firmly told her I would never wear those old ugly dresses or revolting wooden shoes.  This was her house, but I had made up my mind she would not control the way I dressed.  Fortunately after that conversation, her comments about my attire lessened.  I was proud of myself that day.

By the time I was eight months pregnant I had gained over 20 pounds.  I was hopeful my baby would be born in the next month.  It was getting more difficult to find the energy to get my chores done.  I felt like an elephant waddling around the house when I served the hired hands.  Even though I was uncomfortable at times I was thrilled with my pregnancy.  I, like my mother, loved children and couldn't wait to cradle my sweet baby in my arms.

## Chapter 30

I had received news the border patrol was getting quite lax in certain areas. I understood people had traveled out of Germany and crossed the border into Austria on occasion without encountering too many problems. There seemed to be no rhyme or reason as to why the guards sporadically granted or denied permission for people to cross over into Austria. I heard there were times when individuals were able to cross the border without being bothered by the border patrol. I'm sure there was money exchanged under the table which helped convince the guards to let them move along without being hassled.

I missed my parents dearly. I had not seen my mother, father or sister in two-and-a-half years from when I had been forcibly taken from my home. Something about being with child made me yearn even more to be closer to my mother and homeland. I longed for her company, her love, advice, and support. It was a feeling difficult to explain; it wasn't just an intense desire. I needed to go home.

I had given a lot of thought to returning to Austria. I had convinced myself I was ready to take a chance and sneak over the border even if we weren't given proper travel visas. Pregnant or not I was going to go. I feared the German officials would not grant me a visa. Oma Engle thought my idea of going home was crazy, and did not want me to take the chance. I desperately needed to see my mother, father and sister Friede, who never was given a chance to have memories of me. She was only a baby when I was kidnapped. Regardless of the consequences, the risk of crossing the border illegally was worth taking.

I wrote to Hinrich and he agreed with my plan to go home, although he was worried about me being eight months pregnant climbing over the Alps. He said he would try to get a leave so he could make the trip with me. He wanted to help keep the baby and me safe from harm as we crossed the border into Austria. I prayed my baby would be born at home in Bleiberg and my mother would be there to help me with the birth. My desire to see and touch mother grew stronger every day. I was nervous about my delivery and believed everything would be fine if she was there with me during my labor. I knew there may never be another chance to get back home because the war grew fiercer and no one was able to predict what tomorrow held in store.

After chores one morning, I went into town to see if I could get a visa to travel. If not granted, I planned to get back to Austria somehow before my baby was born. I thought traveling through Germany would be easy for me since I married a German citizen. Though crossing the border into Austria would likely be more difficult.

I hoped we could ride the train most of the way through Germany. After that what lay ahead for us was unknown. I was unsure how far we would have to walk on foot once close to the border and how long it would take us to get through the mountains. The trip would be risky and require a great deal of stamina and courage, but my mind was made up. My heart was set on seeing my parents before the baby was born and I did not plan on changing my mind.

I heard from Hinrich about a possible leave and began to solidify my plans to travel back home. He said he would be able to get a two-week leave. I stopped at the German immigration office and applied for a travel visa. I kept my fingers crossed our visas to travel would get approved. If not, I knew I was going home one way or another. Even if Hinrich was unable to go with me, I decided I'd make the trip without him. I planned our route. We would first journey south to Hannover, then Frankfurt, staying south toward Heidelberg and continue straight southward through the rest of Germany.

My goal was to get to Zurich, Switzerland because I believed the border patrol in Switzerland might be easier to get through. After we reached Zurich, we would head to Innsbruck, Austria. If we made it that far my home would almost be in sight.  Innsbruck was only about 180 kilometers (116 mi.) from Bleiberg.  Once over the border we would be home free.  Hinrich and Father would help decide the best route to take.

I diagramed each planned step through the various cities we would travel through.  Seeing the plan on paper created a more concrete vision and a more likely possibility.  If everything went well I would once again see my family, and my baby would be born in Austria with my mother by my side.

Map of Germany below
(http://www.atlapedia.com/online/map_images/political/Germanyetcpol.
jpg)

My eyes fixed on the map, I spotted Klagenfurt and Villach both

cities close to home. I wrote to my mother and father to tell them I was

coming home no matter what. I asked if Father would be able to meet us

on the Austrian side of the border and help us get the rest of the way to

Bleiberg. Once we made it to the Austrian border, Father would be much

better prepared than I to get around the trouble spots and areas that were heavily patrolled.  He knew the area well and would know where to go and which route was more promising for our travels.  Father would be able to gage whether or not we would need to travel by foot or if we would be able to go the rest of the way by wagon.  Bleiberg lies a ways from the border and we wouldn't be out of danger until we were closer to my family's home.  I was determined to put together a fail-proof plan and hoped Hinrich would be able to accompany me.  My father knew how badly I wanted to come home.  I told him I would make the trip whether or not he was able to meet us at the border.  I knew he would do whatever it took to help us get home safely from there.

Planning such a specific route stirred up all kinds of emotions.  I lay awake at night going over and over each detailed step that would hopefully get us there safely.  We had missed so much already being apart for so long.  Mother said in her letters there were many midwives in Bleiberg to assist with the delivery.  If we found we needed more than a midwife, the old doctor in town might be willing to come to the house.  We didn't plan on calling on him unless absolutely necessary.  Having my baby at home where I grew up and slept, with my mother present, gave me great comfort.

The doctors in Germany told me my pregnancy was going well so far and they didn't anticipate any problems during my baby's birth.  I thought about what we would need during our four to five day journey.  Gathering suitable food for the trip was easy.  On the farm we dried, smoked or salted all of our own meat, which stayed fresh and preserved for many weeks without any type of refrigeration.  I needed to bring appropriate clothing as well.  Hiking high into the mountains in March would be cold.  If we had to climb to a high elevation to avoid the patrol, the snow would likely be deep.  No matter, I was ready and nothing was going to stop me from trying to get home.

I received some great news.  Hinrich was on his way home.  His leave had been approved and having him with me was a Godsend.  Along with this news, I found out we were refused a visa to travel across the border into Austria. Trying to avoid the border patrol would certainly create more obstacles. We wouldn't have the proper documents to legally travel once we reached the border. Hinrich and I knew we would be taking a chance of getting caught at the border. He understood how badly I wanted to go home and said he would do whatever he could to help me get there.

## Chapter 31

I secured train tickets for both of us.  On March 2, 1941, we started
out on our journey.  Once aboard the train, both of us sat quietly waiting
for it to pull away from the railway station.  We both wondered if we would
make it to our destination.  In my heart I knew I had made the right
decision to go.  Thinking about all the things that could happen along the
way including getting caught trying to cross the border from Germany into
Switzerland was nerve-racking.  I had heard stories of others who had been
beaten or killed after being caught without their proper paperwork.  During
the war trust was in short supply just like everything else.  Women trying to
make their way across country borders with no papers had far worse things
that could and did happen if they were captured by military authorities.
 The act of Hinrich risking his own safety to be with me made me love him
even more.

The hours of silence in the travel car while we crossed over German
territory gave me ample time to go over the planned route.  I found myself
repeating it over and over in my head.  Under my breath I recapped every
step we would take including all of the towns we would be passing through
as we moved southward.  Father and Hinrich had discussed the planned
route thoroughly when they wrote.

First, we had to travel several hundred miles south to pass through
Germany.  To cross the border into Switzerland and then again into
Austria, we would be hiking by foot up into the mountains to avoid the
border patrol.  If able, Hinrich had friends in Switzerland that would help
transport us.  My father planned to meet us in Innsbruck where we would
travel by horse and wagon the remaining distance to Bleiberg.

Time passed slowly as I watched out the window while we moved
down the tracks.  The countryside whisked by in a blur and seemed almost
artificial.  Within days I hoped to be reunited with my family.  We changed

trains along the way and although the train moved along at a fast pace, the ride seemed endless. Hinrich and I each carried a small suitcase to bring just a few belongings with us. We thought once we were off the train, it would be easier to carry and possibly hide a small suitcase if necessary. I knew the mountain range was steep, heavy with snow and may be dangerous to travel by foot; carrying a light load made sense. We brought a few supplies and extra warm clothing along. Thoughts of my family and homeland kept me on track. My determination was rekindled every time I knew we were getting closer.

As we got closer to the border, I was startled by the loud warning whistle. We were approaching our last stop, the Konstanz railway station. Konstanz was a German city directly adjacent to the Swiss border that was not bombed by the Allied Forces during World War II. The city left all of its lights on at night. They hoped to fool bombers into thinking it was part of Switzerland. Apparently it worked.

When the train came to a halt, we grabbed our bags and hastily stepped onto the ground. We felt compelled to move quickly even though we were still in German territory. Once off the train we needed to act casual like domestic German citizens. Hinrich wouldn't have a problem, of course, because he was a citizen. I, on the other hand, might have problems convincing the guards I was German born especially since I had not yet perfected the various German dialects or the language. If we were stopped or questioned by guards, we decided Hinrich would do all the talking. We planned to proceed on foot after becoming familiar with the landscape and had directions in mind. With no compass or other guiding devices it was vital we accurately determine our position. We had gone over all possible routes and talked about all of our traveling options.

To avoid the patrolled border, we began our ascension of the Alps. Hinrich carried our belongings and we talked little. We wanted to be sure to avoid any border patrol or any others wandering along our route. Hiking up the mountains triggered many memories from my childhood.

118

Thoughts of herding goats with Father and gathering flowers for Mother passed through my mind. We concentrated on our path and after hours of hiking, we hadn't encountered anyone. The higher we climbed the colder the temperatures became and snow flurries soon began to fall.

I put on my winter scarf and gloves. I was grateful we had thick wool socks and high boots for the trip. Hinrich tried his best to keep me comfortable and helped me through the entire journey. Being very concerned about my condition, he made every effort to make the trip up the mountains easier for me. He asked me several times during our journey if I was hungry, tired, or if I needed to take a rest. Once up on the mountain side we felt safe; we were far enough away from the border guards we no longer worried about being caught. We needed to keep walking as long as we could.

We wanted to make it out of the rough, mountainous terrain as soon as possible. The trip was grueling and occasionally we stopped to eat a few morsels of dried meat we had brought along with us. We ate snow to supplement our water supply and carried little to drink. All in all we were able to keep up a relatively, steady pace. Somehow I found the energy to keep going. The thoughts of being home boosted my adrenaline. Picturing my mother and me peacefully sitting in the front room warming ourselves by the pot belly stove gave me the determination to reach my destination.

We had traveled in the mountains for a couple of days before meeting up with Hinrich's friends that took us as far as they could to the Austrian border. We made it over the border safely and had not run into any major problems. We were able to connect with complete strangers who helped us get to Innsbruck. Being back in Austria was an amazing feeling.

Innsbruck lies approximately 200 kilometers (135 miles) from Zurich. Once we made it to Innsbruck, we journeyed toward the coordinates where we planned to meet my father. As we neared the designated meeting place, I saw with blurred vision, the vastness of the landscape, which made it hard to distinguish what waited ahead for us. I focused my eyes on a single object, and as we drew nearer I saw it was the shape of a man sitting in a horse-drawn wagon. The figure I made out was of someone familiar. His silhouette mirrored my memory of my father; it was a perfect profile. The likeness of the man in the distance who waited patiently was my father and that image of him has remained fixed firmly in my memory to this day. The closer we got to the wagon, the more familiar he looked. I couldn't help, but question myself if it was really him.

The deep yearning for my mother intensified even more. We made it through Germany, across the border and over the mountains; I had made it home. When we got close enough to the wagon I recognized with ease the slim stature of a gentle man. Tears of happiness streamed down my face; I was really home and my father stood before me. We had only a short distance to get to Bleiberg where my mother waited with open arms.

I started to run for the wagon. I was so excited I forgot all about being almost nine-months pregnant. I shouted and waved. When I reached my father, he jumped down from the wagon and I hugged him tightly. I never wanted to let him go, afraid if I loosened my grip, he might slip away and disappear.

## Chapter 32

I saw my father's eyes begin to well up with tears. He didn't cry yet I could tell it was difficult for him to hold back his tears. After we had hugged and hugged some more, Hinrich and Father introduced themselves properly. Hinrich helped me up into the wagon. We started the rest of our journey home. My father told me it was time I rested. He could see I was exhausted and totally wore down from the trip. I was tired yet at peace with myself knowing I would soon be home surrounded by the rest of my family. We had missed out on so much since I had been seized and taken to Germany. I wanted to make up for all the time we had lost.

I couldn't find enough words to explain to my father how I felt. I was bursting with joy and wanted to share the events that had taken place in my life since I'd last seen him. Once we started to talk it was as if I had never left home. We talked non-stop as we traveled down the narrow dirt road that would eventually bring us home. My father was always an easy man to talk to, and being together again made it a wonderful journey home. Father and Hinrich chatted along the way and got to know one another. The three of us had been touched by the war in many different ways. The voids left in each of us disappeared in that moment.

We traveled another full day before we arrived at the old house where I had grown up. By the time we arrived I was exhausted. It was a good feeling of fatigue because I was home at last and soon to be surrounded by the people I cared about and loved most! We had traveled for over four and a half days with more than half of that time spent traveling by foot and horse drawn wagon. I had not allowed myself to think much about our travels back to Germany. I knew making the journey with an infant would be much more difficult. I refused to think of it. I was home with my family and we were overjoyed with happiness, nothing else mattered at that moment.

My mother waited at the front door when we arrived just as I had imagined for so long. The minute we saw one another we were overcome by tears of happiness. She was so excited to see me I thought she would faint in my arms. I was truly overjoyed to have my family back and that euphoric moment would last until it was time to say goodbye. I just knew whatever was happening in the world, I would not let it interfere with this utterly perfect moment. I embraced my mother with open arms and truly felt at home. My sister, Friede, at nearly three-years-old stood near my mother and looked at us curiously. An overwhelming sense of peace consumed my body; a feeling I hoped to carry with me when I traveled back to Germany.

Mother wanted me to get settled in right away and waited on me hand and foot. Mother, Father and Hinrich catered to my every whim. I never lifted a finger the entire time I was there. Knowing it wouldn't be long before my visit came to an end, I wanted to enjoy every moment there savoring the breathtaking scenery and the love I felt emanating from those who cared about me. Hinrich had been granted a short leave and needed to return to Germany soon. He didn't have much time to spend with us in Austria.

I was due any day and hoped, as all expectant mothers, I would not go over my due date. I wanted my mother to be present when I delivered my first child, and we had risked our lives to get to her. I, of course, wanted Hinrich present when the baby arrived as well.

I was committed to staying in Austria until the birth of my baby regardless of how long it took. Hinrich and I planned for me to stay several weeks in Austria after the baby was born. We would return to Germany at a later date than Hinrich. He had to return to his base ahead of me. Neither the war nor his commanders waited for our baby to be born. They wanted him back in the air doing their bidding.

As time passed, I began to worry about our return trip back to Germany. Traveling by foot through the mountains and hiking to high elevations with a baby would certainly make the return trip more complicated. We had made several contacts with friends and family members at the beginning of the trip and had asked them for assistance when it came time for me to travel back to Germany. Most of them were willing and had agreed to help in any way they could. Perhaps to provide a place to stay or hide us if it became necessary. Some were willing to help me with transportation and promised to keep my whereabouts secret from the German authorities. Some of our contacts would be scattered throughout the mountain range, others having homesteads where I could rest.

Hinrich, my father, and I talked about the possibility of taking another route back to Germany. We agreed it might be easier traveling through Munchen, then Nurnberg, proceeding to Frankfurt, and then on to Bremen. The new route would make traveling by foot a bit easier so it was definitely something for me to consider. I thought I'd worry about that closer to the time I'd be returning to Germany. I wanted to try and savor the time I had left with my mother and father.

**The picture below is of Hinrich and me when he was home on leave.**

## Chapter 33

We thoroughly enjoyed our time in Austria with my parents. Days had passed since we arrived and it was approaching the time Hinrich would have to head back to Germany. I was worried he would have to leave before the baby was born. There were no other options for Hinrich, the penalty for not returning was too extreme. I hoped he could be here with me.

With only a few days left before Hinrich had to leave me, I worried he'd miss the birth. Luckily a few days before he was to depart, I began experiencing a few stomach pains. I hadn't felt well most of the day. The ill feeling lasted through the evening. That night, I tossed and turned and found it hard to fall asleep. The next morning I woke early from pains shooting down my leg and my back ached terribly. The pains were so intense it frightened me.

I woke Hinrich and then my mother. This being my first baby I wasn't sure if the pain was caused by labor or from some other possible complication. Mother knew exactly what was taking place and how to prepare for the delivery. She sent my father down the road to summon the midwife. A half-hour passed until her arrival and by that time, I anxiously waited for her help. My pains were stronger, closer together, and more intense. The pain was like nothing I had ever experienced before.

Mother told Friede to go outside and keep a close eye on the chimney to watch for the stork that would soon visit our house. Despite the cold snowy weather, Friede went outdoors and faithfully waited for the stork to come. My labor pains had become much worse and I was unable to stand up any longer. I lay in the bed where I had once slept as a child. Fortunately my mother and the midwife were by my side as my pain intensified. I still had enough energy between contractions to laugh at the thought of Friede pacing back and forth in front of the house. The pains became even more intense. I had excruciating pain down along my lower back. It was a good thing Friede was outside because the last 15 minutes of my labor felt unbearable. I screamed after each agonizing contraction began. My screams echoed throughout the house.

The pains came so quickly and close together I had no time to breathe between contractions. The pressure was so great, I worried my insides were being pushed out. My knowledge was very limited when it came to childbirth. Not knowing how long my pains would last was the most frightening aspect of giving birth. They kept telling me it would soon be all over and I would feel fine, but I wasn't sure I believed them. Father and Hinrich waited patiently in the living room while the midwife and my mother tended to me. It was soon time to push and within a half-hour my sweet baby girl was finally born. As I felt the weight of her in my arms and held her close to my chest, I looked down at my precious baby. With one glance I saw her perfect tiny face and the pain all but disappeared. I was amazed that pain so excruciating could dissipate in a few short moments.

My mother and husband were both able to be present for the birth. Hinrich and I decided to name our little girl Ingeborg. Ingeborg was born March 17, 1941. I was 18-years-old and surrounded by the ones I loved. With everything going on in the world at that time, life was good. I was thoroughly happy, and gave thanks to God for being given such a precious gift.

**My baby girl, Ingeborg. Inga means, protection. Ing was the Norse God of peace and fertility. A perfect name for a perfect baby girl.**

When I awoke the next day after Ingeborg's birth, I had to think about Hinrich's return to Germany. My father planned to take him by wagon as far as he could go. Hinrich had to cross the border back into Germany on his own. Traveling alone this time he would likely attract less attention. If he was stopped by the border patrol, his story of travel would seem more believable if he was not accompanied by a foreign woman with a newborn baby.

I knew the trip back to Klenkendorf for me would be more dangerous and difficult. I did not want to worry Hinrich any further so I did not share my fears with him. I was glad for the friends and family along the way that had agreed to help on my return trip.

When Ingeborg was only three-days-old it was time for Hinrich to leave. Both he and I wished our circumstances were different. I gathered up all the hope, courage, and strength I could muster and prayed he would travel back to Germany safely. After Hinrich left, I cried for hours wishing he could have stayed with me longer. I know he wanted to stay, but he had to go. My mother helped console me after he left, yet I longed for him. She did her best to keep Ingeborg and me safe. After Hinrich was headed back to Germany, I decided to stay in Austria another month before I returned to Oma Engle and Opa Brase.

## Chapter 34

Being in Austria with my family that month reassured me there was some normalcy left in the world. I hoped perhaps someday in the future I'd return to Austria when Ingeborg was older. There was no fighting in the area and I felt safer in Bleiberg, at least for now. It was a good feeling not to take cover in bomb shelters or worry about being killed by a landmine that had been buried in a field nearby. I didn't want to stay too long and become a burden on my parents, even though my mother begged me to stay.

I was aware of the dangers back in Germany, however, I felt obligated to return to my husband and my home in Germany with our daughter. I needed to be there for Hinrich when he came home. I did not have to worry about providing basic needs for my family such as food, shelter, and clothing once back on the farm. I had no choice but to return.

While in Austria I worried I'd be discovered by the Nazis, who would take my baby and me away from my homeland once again. I was frightened when I thought of the possible consequences for our defiance of the law. From what I had experienced and read, Nazis held little value for human life, particularly infants.

My father continued to follow world affairs and politics closely. Every evening he listened intensely to multiple radio broadcasts that reported details concerning air raids or threats that drew allied fire in Europe. We had heard through sources that Hamburg, Bremen, and Berlin were being bombed. Hamburg was one of the main targets. We understood the ship yards and oil refineries were being hit and knew civilians were also killed in the raids. Father talked of errors during bombing raids that were at times 50 miles off target, creating dangerous situations for all civilians. Father was fearful of the increased bombing, believing my return to Germany might be more challenging and dangerous.

Security was tighter and getting back across the border to the farm in Klenkendorf could prove tricky since it was in close proximity to all of the cities currently being bombed.

The month I was in Austria sped by and the day soon came for my return to Klenkendorf. Father thought it would be a smart idea to take the second route we had discussed hoping it would reduce the time I would spend traveling on foot, especially now that I had a small baby with me. My mother was having a difficult time accepting I was leaving again. She was especially worried knowing I was traveling with a newborn infant. It was difficult to witness my mother's pain. I hated seeing her this way.

It was the end of April making the weather more agreeable for traveling. The day I was to go, there was no turning off Mother's tears. When I climbed into the wagon with my baby and sat alongside Father, she cried endlessly. I was heartbroken for her and shared her pain. I tried to reassure her everything would work out fine and we would hopefully return within the next year. She looked at me with disbelief and watched me get ready to leave helping me with the baby. She hugged me tightly and kissed both Ingeborg and me goodbye. After a long embrace she said goodbye. Father and I were off, this time headed for Munchen, Germany. I'd be traveling far north back to Bremen after climbing the Alps to get over the mountains. Father had brought his pistol he had found on the dead soldier a few years ago. We hoped the need to use it would not arise.

Since my father knew many people in Austria, it was easy to get us close to the German border with few problems. Many friends, local farmers, and family along the way were willing to help my sweet Inga and me get close and smuggle us across the border. Once in the mountains, we'd be on our own. The challenge was getting on the train in Austria without being stopped by the guards. The border between Austria and Germany lay somewhere in the middle of a long tunnel, which was approximately 50 kilometers (31 miles) long. The trick was to get through the tunnel undetected so I could make it back into Germany unnoticed.

Once in Germany, I could catch a train with the help of relatives and friends then travel north to Bremen.

Father and I traveled by horse and wagon for many hours. I would have to continue on by foot for several hours after he dropped me off with my small suitcase and Ingeborg in my arms. My goal was to reach the rail tunnel to get free passage back into Germany.

When we reached our destination close to the border we had been traveling for over a day. Saying goodbye was agonizing for both of us. During wartime, our uncertain futures made goodbyes all the more difficult. So many had been killed, had their homes destroyed, or were imprisoned in nameless camps when discovered crossing the border illegally. Father told me to stay strong and make sure I wrote as soon as I arrived home. Our friends and family that were to help me along the way would try to get word back to him that I had made it as far as their town or village.

We talked about the possibility of me being caught when I tried to cross into Germany. We had come up with our best believable story to tell the border patrol if for some reason I was stopped and questioned. The plan was to act disoriented and puzzled as to why they were questioning me, tell the border patrol I just had a baby and when I was released from the hospital, I had lost all my travel documents. When Father spoke to me he conveyed feelings of confidence and assured me I would make it back to Germany safely. We had several safety measures included in my travel plan. If stopped while traveling with the individuals risking their lives to help me, I was to act like the daughter of whichever friend or relative who was helping me along the way in hopes the guards would pay less attention to families traveling together.

I was hesitant to get out of the wagon and leave him but I knew it was time to go. I walked slowly down the dirt road and waved goodbye. I looked back at my father. I wanted to remember him just as he was. His willingness to do anything to help me was apparent; his love was unconditional. I wanted that final image of him etched in my memory so it would be there forever just in case I never made it back to Austria to see him again. After we parted, I journeyed for a few days on foot through the mountains and finally reached the rail tunnel.

I became extremely vigilant, paying close attention to everything happening around me. I needed to be fully alert to anything that might compromise our safety. I tuned into the movements of the border patrol because so many surrounded the immediate area and controlled the flow of traffic. They patted down most individuals entering the train. The patrols were well organized. They were stationed in various locations along the railroad tracks and throughout the boarding section. The patrol keenly watched the guarded areas, waited, ready to react to any suspicious movement.

I decided it would be best if I stood back several hundred meters from the entrance of the train where the majority of passengers boarded. I looked for a place to hide in case I needed to get out of sight quickly. I remained in the background surveying the entire vicinity to get a sense of the movement among the patrols and the command posts situated around the railway station.

I watched the patrols every move in hopes I would be able to tell when I could make a break for the train. Very quietly and patiently I waited. I hoped they would leave their assigned posts or the boarding area. Without a proper pass, I was unable to board the train in a normal fashion. I would have to board by hopping up between the railcars where they connect to one another and climb into a railcar as the train was moving. If the train moved slowly enough, I would be able to get up into the boxcar if I jumped up on the couplers and pulled myself up to enter a rear door. If the doors happened to be on the side of the railcar, I would have to use all my strength to get myself pulled up through the doorway. My plan was to grab on to the side of the door opening. I would need to jump up almost three feet in order to be high enough to reach the opening of the door. I would have to first put Ingeborg and my suitcase in the opening, then haul myself in. It would be impossible to pull us both up through the doorway while holding her.

I stood in the background for almost three hours as I watched and waited for the right moment to board. The patrols, however, were relentless and never moved away from the main entryway of the train. I needed to make a decision. I made up my mind. As the train started to move, I made my way towards it. I ran for an area where no guards were stationed. I spotted an open door on one of the railcars and dashed toward the opening. Ingeborg bounced in my arms and my bag flopped up and down hitting the side of my hip while I ran. Ingeborg let out a cry, thankfully it was hardly noticeable. She was swaddled tightly in a blanket with her head covered up by another heavier blanket so her soft cries stayed muffled. The noise of the train also covered her cries. When I reached the empty boxcar I swiftly threw my bag up through the doorway, placed Ingeborg in the opening, and jumped up into the railcar myself. We had done it! The baby and I were safe on the train and were traveling north to Germany. I let out a sigh of relief when the train reached full speed.

It didn't take long for us get through the tunnel and cross the German border. Our friends and relatives helped to make the rest of my journey to Klenkendorf less complicated. The ride through the tunnel went quickly and it wasn't long before the time came to get off the train. I traveled on foot for several hours. A distant cousin living in Germany helped me make the necessary train line connections. Along the way several strangers had offered their help and were kind enough to give us food and a place to rest. The war created perplexing situations and circumstances that were unavoidable for all of us. Trusting perfect strangers was sometimes a necessity even though my father had warned against it. The element of the unknown and the volatility of the future kept everyone on edge; learning to trust others didn't come easy but it came none the less.

I felt the worst of the trip was behind us and was thankful we would soon be back on the farm in Klenkendorf with Oma Engle and Opa Brase. On the farm I would go back to cooking, cleaning, and waiting on the farm hands. I was ready for a more predictable and calm setting where I knew I wasn't risking being thrown in jail or worse. I looked forward to a more monotonous life. The thought of milking the family cow everyday seemed welcoming. The long trip I had just taken with all the secrecy, unpredictability, and dodging of border patrols made the thought of being back home on the farm incredibly comforting.

I sat in the seat with Ingeborg next to me. There was plenty of room in the car because few people traveled during the war. As I watched the landscape pass by the open window, I thought about my desire for Ingeborg to have a place she could call home. Most of all I wanted safety for our family and to forget this war. I wanted her to be able to enjoy a normal childhood, one that did not include seeking safety in bomb shelters during air raids.

I fell asleep gazing out the window of the train until Ingeborg began to stir. After several hours we finally arrived in Bremen. Opa Brase met me with a wagon ready to bring us home. We traveled about 50 kilometers (31 miles) back to Klenkendorf where Oma Engle waited at home to meet her new granddaughter. I was sure she'd be excited to see Ingeborg but not so sure she'd be as happy to see me. Still I couldn't wait to get home. Our trip had been long and arduous.

When we arrived Oma Engle came outside to greet us. She was smiling and immediately wanted to hold the baby. Ingeborg was received with love and kindness in her home. She was genuinely welcomed into Oma Engle's heart and was treated as one of her own. I was happy to see Oma Engle willingly share her love with my daughter. Ingeborg's Aunt Anne, however, was another story. She was jealous of the attention Ingeborg was given by Oma Engle. I hoped Anne's resentful feelings toward Ingeborg would subside.

## Chapter 35

Along with caring for Ingeborg once home, I continued to cook, clean, avoid conflicts as much as possible, and wait on the hired farm hands. Oma Engle and Annie helped care for Ingeborg. Oma Engle treated Inga like a little princess. She was growing like a weed, had gained several pounds since we arrived, and was turning out to be a chubby little baby.

Having a few extra pounds on our babies was important. The extra weight helped them if they fell ill or if food became scarce. Our babies were all breastfed, yet I felt especially lucky to have an extra supplement of milk from the family cow. Milking the family cow was one of my chores on the farm. I milked her twice a day, morning and evening.

When Ingeborg was nearly two-months-old, Hinrich came home and was able to spend a short time with us. He was a proud daddy. Watching Hinrich love and care for our little girl strengthened my love for him. While we had been in Austria, I noticed Hinrich had not seemed quite like himself. During this current leave, Hinrich confessed he once again was feeling ill with similar symptoms he had felt in previous months. It was difficult for an outsider to notice he was feeling sick because he covered up his ailment well. He didn't want others to be burdened by him and his superiors didn't care about his well-being. I was deeply concerned Hinrich wasn't home long enough to see a doctor once more. He was ordered to return soon after his arrival to continue flying missions.

About a month after Hinrich left for duty, I began feeling ill. Every morning I felt like I had the stomach flu. I worried something was wrong with me. Getting up to start my day became more difficult. My nausea subsided as the day passed. I suspected I was pregnant once again. My suspicion was confirmed during a visit to the doctor. I wrote to Hinrich to share the good news. He was excited to hear he would be the father of two. He also wrote of his concerns regarding his time spent away from home.

We both shared the opinion it would be good for Ingeborg to have a sister or a brother to play with.

Hinrich took any and every available leave. He wanted to be part of our lives as much as possible and be close to Ingeborg and me. He knew we needed him. He and I both wished for more time together. We were more fortunate compared to some in the Nazi ranks. Hinrich and his fellow pilots were granted leave more often than other branches of the military. The Nazis needed their pilots to be fresh, rested and ready for any mission they were assigned.

I knew having another baby would make our lives all the more demanding especially without Hinrich there to help us. The war continued to rage, yet we were overjoyed with the thought of having another baby. Every major city in close proximity to Klenkendorf was being hit by aerial strikes. The lack of precision when some air strikes took place put all civilian lives at risk. Every day we lived in fear our loved ones were in harm's way. The instability in the world was becoming increasingly nerve-racking. I found it easy to let my mind wander, to imagine death and destruction or being captured. Terrible thoughts of becoming a widow and being left behind to fend for myself with our two children filled my head.

Even though Oma Engle and I had our differences, I was glad to have the strong family foundation and additional care for Ingeborg. It made Hinrich's absences less difficult. I had already started planning another trip back to Austria for the new baby's birth. I calculated the baby would be born sometime in May of 1942. Hinrich hoped to be able to go back to Austria with me when the time came to deliver. He was uncertain if he would get approval from his superiors for leave.

Large scale attacks in close proximity to Klenkendorf made it more dangerous to travel and much more difficult to get visas. Hamburg and Bremen were under constant fire. The British continued to target industrial sites. The miscalculation of target locations during the bombing raids took out entire neighborhoods. We all worried as civilian casualties mounted.

## Chapter 36

Time flew by that first year of Ingeborg's life.  She was a healthy happy baby and Oma Engle coddled her everyday giving Inga her utmost attention.  Oma Engle had become more accepting of me over the year. She constantly pampered the baby and fussed over her every chance she got.  Having Ingeborg brought Oma Engle and me closer together.  She finally accepted me as one of the family.

My belly grew bigger as my due date neared.  My second baby would soon be born.  Again I applied for a visa in hopes we could travel across the border legally.  I didn't look forward to having to cross the border again with a newborn baby.  Hinrich and I continued to write and make plans to travel to Austria sometime around the beginning of May regardless of the visa situation and restrictions to travel.

Fortunately, Hinrich was granted leave to come home.  It had been a year since I visited Austria, and I longed to be with my mother when my second child was born.  Just as our plans were set, I received notification we were turned down for a visa to travel into Austria.  I wrote to father to let him know the situation and he said he was committed to helping us if we decided to come without legal papers.  He would greet us at the Switzerland/Austrian border and help us with the rest of our journey.  The plan for this trip was to use the original route we took during the first visit, proceeding south through Germany, crossing the border into Zurich, then on into Austria.  We heard reports of less fighting along our planned route.

Hinrich would accompany me and stay a few weeks until he was required to return to duty.  We decided to leave Ingeborg with Oma Engle knowing she'd be safer and our journey would be less complicated.  If I decided to stay longer with my mother, I would have to return to Germany on my own once again.

We embarked on our trip to Austria boarding the train in Bremen. The excitement of seeing my family again overwhelmed me. Hinrich and I took our seats and thankfully no one on the train questioned our travel plans. I believe Hinrich's Luftwaffe uniform helped us avoid any unwanted attention from the authorities. The train was comfortable and we traveled for many hours. We changed trains multiple times before we reached the border between Germany and Switzerland.

We were hopeful we wouldn't have any problems crossing the border this time. As before we had to cross on foot. Many areas of the border were not patrolled as meticulously as they had been during our last trek, which surprised both of us. We would, however, have to hike back up into the Alps to avoid any possible confrontations with the border patrol. It was late spring and travel through the mountains proved less arduous than our journey over a year ago. It wasn't easy by any means. It was difficult to pack enough food for the trip because we needed to travel light and food spoilage limited our supply as well. We picked whatever we could find to eat, though we had to depend primarily on the food we brought because many berries were not yet ripe.

Father was again waiting for us near the Austrian border and helped us with the rest of our journey to Bleiberg. By the time we reached Bleiberg, my body was swollen and fatigued. I was exhausted but ecstatic to be home and able to see my mother once more. Being in the mountains, we were able to enjoy the fresh air. Also to be home with my family was comforting. Even though I was heavily pregnant and tired from our journey, we still took a few short walks through the countryside as we waited for our new baby to arrive.

I loved having Hinrich home with me and spending time together. Our leisurely walks provided Hinrich with plenty of fresh air he so seemed to need. His coughing had grown persistent at times. Our journey by foot was more difficult for Hinrich this time compared to our last visit to Austria though after a good rest he felt a little better.

As we walked, we were able to reminisce and discuss our future together. We discussed our hopes for our children and looked forward to the birth of our second baby. I missed Ingeborg greatly and wished I could have had her with me. I knew Friede would have loved to play with her. Hinrich expressed even more pride knowing he was going to have another child he could boast about.

Mother again catered to my every need while I was home. She waited on me hand and foot. It happened to be a nice, sunny day when my labor began. I knew what to expect this time. I felt more prepared and less frightened. Being more prepared, unfortunately, did not reduce the intensity of my labor pains. My mother and the midwife hovered over my bed. My husband and father in the next room listened and waited to hear the baby's first cries. I lay in my bed trying to put the pain in my body out of my mind and I found it wasn't any easier the second time around.

My labor continued for a few hours and after nearly an hour of hard labor our second daughter arrived on May 15, 1942. I gave birth to a healthy, beautiful, blonde, blue-eyed baby girl. We named her Anneliese. Her name means: favor and grace, God is my oath. It was a wonderful day for the entire family; the birth of another precious little girl made the war seem non-existent. For the moment at least, we were able to forget about the war and focus on this very special little gift we were so fortunate to receive. Her innocence and pure sweetness was such a comfort. She reassured us there was still hope and miracles to be had. Our minds filled with memories of a time when things were happier and content. Satisfaction filled our hearts when she looked up at us. She was pure and untouched by the chaos and madness that was happening around her.

Anneliese's birth became a sacred moment for us all; another loveable child had blessed our family. I focused on Anneliese. I couldn't stop looking at her petite little face while I gently stroked and patted her back as I held her close to me. Everything about her had turned out just right. She was perfect. Her tiny fingers clutched my forefinger and gripped it as if she didn't want to let go.  I thought to myself how lucky we were to be blessed with two lovely daughters.  Anneliese, another miracle, during a time when miracles seemed scarce.  She was perfect and flawless in every way.

My mother and father were delighted to welcome our new baby girl into the family.  They felt fortunate and blessed to have played a role in her birth at their home.  I was worried and concerned when Hinrich and I first met that he and my father might never get along or be friends because of my father's strong convictions against the Third Reich.  It became apparent Father recognized Hinrich as a kind and loving man and respected him as a person.  He understood if it wasn't for the conditions of war, Hinrich would not have chosen to be a part of the Luftwaffe.  I was proud of my father for being able to see past what appeared on the outside and accept Hinrich into his family.

## Chapter 37

Our time with my family went quickly. Shortly after Anneliese's birth, we knew that Hinrich had to return soon to his base. For most of our trip I noticed Hinrich had poor color and felt ill often yet he rarely complained to anyone. At times in the night he would wake up soaked with sweat. My mother did her best to help Hinrich feel better. She made him her Edelweiss tea, but it did not seem to help.

My family and I convinced him to see a local doctor and have further tests run to try to determine why he felt so ill before he returned to Germany. His superiors never felt his condition was pertinent. He was admitted to a medical facility and spent three days completing various tests. We hoped the doctors would be able to find the cause of his illness and help him to regain his health. Hinrich told me that whatever ailed him had started to affect his normal daily functioning. He said his nausea had become more frequent, and the congestion made his breathing more laborious. I had noticed that myself during our trip through the mountains.

Hinrich told me his grueling schedule and flights had become more difficult for him. He never shared any details of the Luftwaffe missions. We both felt troubled by the lack of consideration he was given from his superiors regarding his current health issues. Both of us knew it wouldn't help to complain to his commander about his poor health and his inability to fly. As in the past, the military demands made on him were unrelenting and his superiors unsympathetic. The Luftwaffe wasn't about to discharge him from duty; his grievances about feeling ill were not considered serious enough to warrant him a permanent discharge. His superior's most critical concerns were to keep Hinrich flying so they could win the war. Caring for the welfare of the men who served in the Luftwaffe was not a priority for the Nazis; they didn't care about anyone. Their only concern was to keep the fighter pilots in the air flying regardless of the personal issues or health problems they may have encountered as human beings.

We received the results for Hinrich from the medical facility. The doctors informed us that Hinrich had tuberculosis (TB). The unexpected report was a shock to both of us. I didn't know much about the disease except for having been around my father and the grieving family members of victims he had worked with. I knew people died from it.

They slowly withered away becoming thin, pale, unrecognizable, and eventually unresponsive. Such a far cry from the person they had once been before they contracted the disease. It was hard to rid myself of these intrusive thoughts. In my mind I pictured the adults and children who had died from this cursed disease. I was determined to help Hinrich fight to stay alive. The doctors said they were unsure how fast the disease would progress. They told us tuberculosis at this stage might prove to be incurable, yet they still showed some hope for Hinrich's recovery.

I couldn't bear to hear the news. Thoughts of Hinrich lying ill, wasting away, and dying filled my head. I certainly hadn't given up hope and I wouldn't ever let him see the bleak look of hopelessness on my face. I couldn't help but think about the possibilities, of losing the man I loved and being left alone to raise our girls. I found it hard to believe he had a life threatening disease. He still functioned quite well and had only a few days at a time where his symptoms took their toll and got the best of him. I tried not to think about him becoming more debilitated. I tried my best to stay hopeful.

I was glad to be at Mother's and Father's home, surrounded by my family when we received the bad news about Hinrich. They did everything they could to help us through that emotional time and I was thankful for their love and support. The time I spent with my family after delivering Anneliese and after Hinrich had left went far too quickly. Even though I dearly missed Ingeborg and felt I needed to be at the farm for Hinrich, I also needed my parent's strength and support. I wished so much they could come back to Germany with me.

It seemed to me as though anytime things were going good it didn't last long. Despair lurked constantly around the corner waiting to pounce, to diminish any type of happiness or pleasure that had been given to us. Having our baby was a wonderful event and I looked forward to our life together as a family. Then the news about Hinrich put a halt to those feelings of happiness. Regardless of what happened, I promised myself I would stay positive. I needed to hope for the best for Hinrich and the children. I found no other choice but to support and love him. I refused to give up on him and prayed with all my heart every day for his good health and survival.

Before I left Austria, Mother felt a rollercoaster of emotions. She worried about my trip back to Germany, she worried about my children and now Hinrich's health. In a given moment she expressed sheer delight having a newborn grandbaby in her home and then the next moment she cried her eyes out because she knew we would leave her soon.

She was well aware of all the bombings taking place near Klenkendorf and the deteriorating conditions. She knew that innocent families like ours living in Germany were not out of harm's way. Klenkendorf, Hannover, Bremen, and nearby cities were becoming more dangerous and many civilians were being killed. She heard Father describe how destructive and common the night bombing attacks had become as well as the horror stories about the starvation, torture, and mass killings of the Polish, Russians, Jews, Gypsies and any others the Nazis saw as inferior. The negotiations for peace between Allied and Axis forces did not seem a possibility. I felt it was my place to be with my husband and both of our children; especially now knowing of his illness.

After Hinrich was diagnosed the doctors did not prescribe any type of medication since there was no known cure for TB at that time. Also there had been severe sanctions placed against Germany by the Allied governments so medicines were difficult to get even if they had been available prior to the war. The doctor's recommendation was for Hinrich to rest. Once back in Germany, Hinrich continued to receive orders to fly and participate in military action in the Luftwaffe squad despite informing his superiors of his illness and declining health. His commander showed no sympathy for his condition and most of the officials above him acted as if they did not believe he was ill. This development was incredibly difficult to cope with for the both of us. He did not get the rest the doctors recommended. We both refused to lose hope and believed someday someone in command would take notice of his condition and let him come home.

Before I returned to Germany, Mother tried to talk me into staying with her longer. She felt we would be safer in Austria. She begged me to stay saying she would help me with the baby as much as she could, but I couldn't stay in Austria longer. I needed to return to Ingeborg and be available if and when Hinrich was allowed to come home.

Oma Engle took the news of Hinrich's illness very hard. She had already lost a son to the war and worried endlessly about the wellbeing of Hinrich and Klaus. I tried to reassure everyone as best I could including Hinrich in our letters back and forth. Our little Ingeborg and Anneliese helped to bring joy and distraction to our lives which was much needed at the time. Hinrich wrote about experiencing days where he felt fatigued and other days when he felt he wasn't sick at all. I hoped he wasn't writing the words just to ease my fears.

Hinrich wrote he felt horrible he wasn't able to be home to protect our girls and me. He knew our area was being hit hard. He was much more concerned about our well-being than his own. Over the next year Hinrich lost weight from his illness but managed to make it seem like he was doing okay when he was home on leave.

## Chapter 38

During the summer of 1943, the bombings near Klenkendorf became more frequent and there was even less regard for civilian life. I feared for the girls' safety. They were never allowed too far from the house nor could they venture out in the yard too far from us. Ingeborg and Anneliese had a small sand box at the side of the yard they played in. It was one of the few normal activities they were able to enjoy during their childhood. The risk of being injured or killed during a bombing raid remained present and constantly worried me. I was always watchful of them. I continuously looked out the window, combed the skies, and watched and listened for aircraft overhead that carried bombs our way. I was always ready to dash for safety in case they came close to the house or yard. The sound of droning plane engines signaled us to run for shelter or to any other safe haven that was close by hoping to survive the bombs.

Within a 100 kilometer radius of Klenkendorf fire bombings took place routinely. The devastation the bombings caused was unforgettable. I remember the air raids, the smoke filled skies, and the fear embedded in everyone's eyes when the bombs exploded. When I think back, my thoughts become clear, immediate and present, as if we had been attacked yesterday. Large numbers of incendiaries fell very close to the farm. They burned and obliterated everything around the strike zone. Block after block was destroyed, burned and demolished.

The fire bombs lit up the sky as they exploded. There never seemed a single moment when I could let my guard down. We reacted within a split second and knew where to run for safety when we heard the planes coming. Air raids took place mostly during the nighttime. Lights were shut off quickly to avoid becoming a lit target waiting to be destroyed. The first sound of an airplane headed our way cued us to turn the lights off and if we were close enough to the city during a raid we heard the sirens warning all to take cover.

Everyone acted quickly when the bombers closed in. Sometimes we jumped out of bed in the middle of the night. When awakened by the noise and disoriented, we tried to find our shoes in the dark beside our beds. Many wore their shoes to bed so they didn't have to look for them in the dark just in case we needed to run to escape the fire bombings. Rubble and shattered glass were scattered everywhere so wearing your shoes was a necessity. Always startled by the unexpectedness of the attacks, no one slept easy. Once in bed we slept lightly knowing we needed to wake at a moment's notice to run for our lives.

We became sound experts as we distinguished the noise of an aircraft coming from several miles away. The engines roared loudly and one of the sounds we heard came from a uniform formation of fighter planes that dipped and dove close to the ground firing at anything that moved. The bombers flew low enough at times we were able to identify what country had arrived to bomb us.

There were numerous times we would have to run over the top of broken glass, metal pieces, rubble, hot surfaces, broken rocks, bricks and mortar to flee from the dropping bombs to get to a shelter or to a safer place. It was hard to see through the cloud of dust and dirt from the impact of bombs exploding. The bombs penetrated the ground forcing dirt and dust up into the sky creating a haze that made it hellish for us to see anything. The thick smoke filled the air from burning buildings. The horrifying stench of burning flesh and the screams from those injured and dying was terrifying. Piles of bodies lay in the streets injured or waiting to be buried after a raid was over.

When an air strike began, bombs exploded and within seconds the sky became illuminated. During the darkest night I could see as if it were daytime until the dirt, smoke and fire clouded the air. The array of colors that filled the skies were incredible. The devastation from the destruction of property that followed the brilliant light was unimaginable. These images remain stored in my memory. They hide, waiting to come out in my dreams, always there, coming out at unexpected times, prompted by the smallest reminder. I remember being told when the raids began not to look directly at the light when the bombs exploded because the flash could damage my eyes. I tried to cover Ingeborg's and Anneliese's eyes when bombs exploded instructing them to look away. I have wished over and over I had looked away more often.

The shocking sights were numerous when we emerged from the bomb shelters. The destruction to human life was sickening. I've learned since that incendiaries could actually cremate a human in an instant. At the time I wasn't sure what type of weapons had been unleashed upon us. I was puzzled by the kind of warfare being used that caused a full grown man or woman to shrink to the size of a small child. For the longest time I thought the bombs contained some type of chemical and when released would scorch and shrivel people until they were unrecognizable. I was five feet tall, weighed 110 lbs., yet could have easily picked up a grown man and carried him in my arms after they were exposed to the incendiaries. Later in life after the war was over, I realized it was not chemical agents they used to employ such horrific damage, but the wrath of the infamous incendiary bomb.

Sometimes the charred remains of people were in positions that told of their activity prior to being incinerated. Some were stiff and motionless, situated in a way that told a story. A mother still holding her baby. Others in sitting positions hugging one another for comfort, scorched and unconscious. Some barely alive dragged themselves along unaware of the severity of their own injuries. Many were unable to walk or stand. There were arms and legs not attached to bodies. Many had parts of their bodies charred, scorched and blistered from the heat. Some bodies would lie rotting in the streets for weeks.

Planes flew heavily over Hamburg and Klenkendorf. After the war it was disclosed that Hamburg had over 2,300 tons of bombs dropped on the city including 350,000 incendiary bombs.

(http://www.historylearningsite.co.uk/Hamburg bombing 1943)

No one was safe and the smoke looked like it went 10,000 feet up into the sky. The gusts of wind blew people over. Everything was on fire; people, houses, the trees, and anything that would burn. The girls and I were caught in Hamburg a few times during air raids. Fortunately we made it safely to available bomb shelters. The city would be nearly destroyed with enormous loss of life by the end of the war.

In 1943, many of the German people still believed Germany was going to be victorious in the war. This can be heavily credited to the propaganda promoted by Joseph Goebbels. After Hamburg burned, during the summer of 1943, many of us still prayed for peace. The common people like us who were stuck in this hell hoped Nazi Germany would call for peace and put an end to the war.

Toward the end of 1943, Hinrich wrote to me with news of his illness worsening. I could tell by his words he was scared. No one within the military listened to his grievances. He had dizziness, lingering fevers, and wasn't sleeping well at night. He wrote he felt weak and his ailments were now most definitely affecting his military performance, yet his superiors continued to make him fly. I was more concerned about his health than ever before.

I wanted my husband home with us. I wanted to take care of him and ease his aches. An uneasiness constantly flowed within me. My fears increased that Hinrich's weakened condition would jeopardize his safety. My thoughts were with him constantly. Ugly thoughts filled my head and I couldn't help but think the worst. I feared being abandoned if anything happened to Hinrich. I wondered if his family would continue to let me be part of their family if he died. I was scared of the possibility of having to raise my two small daughters in the midst of the war all alone. Oma Engle and Opa Brase had been supportive this last year, and tried to lessen my fears. I dreaded the thought of losing Hinrich and desperately wanted and needed him by my side.

## Chapter 39

The air raid sirens sounded endlessly. The Allies bombed more heavily to the south of Klenkendorf closer to Hannover but continued to bomb near us towards the German army base. The Brases and I were not only in fear of the bombings but also feared the Nazi military. One day as I watched out the window checking on Ingeborg while she played, I saw several Nazi soldiers harassing the neighbors. The soldiers were yelling. I couldn't turn my eyes away. They forced the family to gather outside by their barn.

The family of eight had been our neighbors for several years. I believe the Grandpa's name was Alfred. He was probably close to 75-years-old and his wife nearly 72. Her sister lived with them, along with the couple's adult daughter, her husband, and their three children. I can't seem to remember all their names. I do remember the baby as a cute, little, six-month-old boy I had helped care for on occasion while his mother worked in the field. He was a happy, smiley baby with locks of curly, blonde hair and big blue eyes. The family was very religious, but I'm unsure what faith they practiced. If memory serves me correctly I believe they were of a Quaker faith.

They were a typical German farm family, but they practiced a religion that had no affiliation with the local Lutheran church prior to Hitler's takeover. During the years Hitler was in power no one attended church services because it wasn't allowed by the Nazi government. The neighbors had expressed disagreement with Hitler's policies, were against the war effort and didn't believe in killing or harming others even in the event of a war. They had shared their religious beliefs with me on several occasions and told me that no matter what the circumstances were, they would never support the war effort nor would they ever harm another human being. The baby boy's father though of draft age had never entered the military service because of his religious beliefs. He stayed at home and worked on the farm with his father-in-law. Their beliefs and convictions were a breath of fresh air as it was good to have people still not afraid to voice their convictions and opinions toward the Nazi Party.

The neighbor's barn stood fairly close to our house. I saw clearly what the soldiers were doing when they entered the neighbor's property. I realized the soldiers had gotten Ingeborg's attention and her curiosity caused her to watch their every move. I thought she would be safe because the SS troops usually left German children alone. Still I wondered why the Nazis had the neighboring family congregated outside by their barn. We hid our children far away and out of sight when we thought someone was coming to harm us. Sometimes we hid the children under a bed, in a closet, or under a mattress to keep them safe. This family apparently had no chance to hide their children from the Nazis.

I thought perhaps the SS were looking for food, a cow to butcher, or wanted to take a pig to roast for the soldiers. The SS came to the local farms and confiscated livestock as food for their units. They helped themselves to any of our livestock without consent. When they took possession of the livestock no one argued with them or confronted them because the end result could be deadly. On one occasion they took our only cow and we could do nothing about it; we just watched them lead her away. The German people were given no leeway nor were any extra exceptions made by the SS to tend to our safety. On occasion the SS provoked an argument with local farmers just to show they were in control. Being German didn't ensure your safety as far as the Nazis were concerned; people feared harassment and persecution constantly.

As I watched out the window looking toward the neighbor's barn while Ingeborg played, I heard the Nazis raising their voices as they yelled at the 30-year old father. They argued about his refusal to take part in the war efforts and in the armed forces. I saw one of the SS soldiers draw his weapon and point it at the baby's father. Another of the soldiers went to the mother and snatched the baby boy, wrapped in a light blue checkered blanket, out of her arms. The soldiers continued to argue with the baby's father. The mother became frantic as the SS soldier held her baby boy hostage and would not give him back. I heard the soldier who held the baby telling the mother if they didn't cooperate they would all be killed. Her husband must go with them. By this time, I had hurried Ingeborg into the house. I worried about her safety and wanted to protect her. She stood at my side, peered out of the doorway and hung on to the hem of my skirt.

We heard the neighbor man tell the soldiers he would not leave his family and go with them. He and the SS men argued back and forth for several minutes. The baby started crying. As his cries became louder, his mother became more hysterical and distraught. I could see the officer losing patience with her. I prayed and asked God to help this mother, her child and family. The baby's mother fell to her knees with her empty arms held up in front of herself and pleaded with the officer to give him back to her. The soldier dismissed her pleas. To my shock and horror the soldier gripping only the baby's blanket, slammed his tiny body against the solid, wooden barn wall. The blanket fluttered to the ground. The cries stopped and the baby lay dead next to the barn, broken and silent. His mother raced toward him but the soldiers intervened and held her back. She screamed and cried. I stopped breathing. How my legs continued to hold me up, I do not know.

The SS efficiently lined the mother and the rest of the family up against the barn. The officers shot all of them at the same time, execution style. The family never had a chance to run or save themselves; they all died in a matter of seconds. Horrified, I watched the entire family as they lay dead or dying. Grandpa Alfred, Grandma, her sister, their daughter, her husband, their small son and daughter and their baby boy with the golden curls, all sprawled on the ground, some motionless while others still twitched and jerked after being left to die. I turned away and became physically ill, the contents of my stomach heaved out of me. Shocked, I could hardly believe what I had just witnessed.

The soldiers casually walked away, indifferent and unconcerned, some stepping over the fallen bodies with an unexplainable ease. They moved toward the livestock they wanted to seize. They eventually moved the dead bodies. I'm not sure where they took them, but they were no longer where they fell. At the time I thought Ingeborg's innocent little face was buried in my skirt while I stood at the window watching. Unfortunately that was not the case. She recounted the story from the perspective of a three-and-a-half-year-old. She has never been able to completely forget that dreadful scene.

I had nightmares for countless months after the incident. No one felt safe anymore, and my fears grew stronger. The feelings of helplessness, chills crawling under my skin, and the essence of being physically and mentally sickened by the sight of the murders was difficult to shake. For many months after the execution, the details played over and over in my head. The snapshot of the family's panic and dying screams are never gone from my memory.

## Chapter 40

It was hard for me to write Hinrich about the events happening at home. He was already worried and I didn't want him to worry more. Knowing his illness was taking a toll on his body, I certainly didn't want to add any more stress. I received a letter from Hinrich sharing news that his superiors finally released him from duty. This only after he collapsed while flying on a mission. He had also reported having difficulty getting in and out of bed.

Hinrich was placed in a German medical facility to evaluate his condition before he was released from his military service. The only treatment offered was the advice to go to Austria high up into the mountains and breathe the clear thin air. They seemed to think that once he got into the mountains, the clean fresh air would help to relieve some of his symptoms and perhaps cure his TB. The medical team who cared for the servicemen in the *Luftstreitkräfte*, a special division of the German Air Armed Forces, recommended a permanent medical leave. Hinrich was granted permission and received passports for all of us to travel with him to Austria. When Oma Engle heard the news she was happy to hear Hinrich was coming home, although she struggled with an overwhelming fear of his sickness.

It was close to the end of summer in 1944 when Hinrich finally arrived home and was back in Klenkendorf with us. He had lost a significant amount of weight, was ghostly pale, and suffered from debilitating bouts of nausea. He had been unable to eat properly for the last three months and was failing. I told him we shouldn't wait a minute longer. We needed to go to Austria as soon as possible so he could be exposed to the mountain air and hopefully be cured. We planned to consult doctors in Austria hoping they knew of a treatment that would help. I kept my faith that Hinrich might still be able to overcome this disease. I planned to do whatever I could for him until he was nursed back to health. We decided to leave Anneliese on the farm with Oma while Ingeborg came along with us. I wanted to give Hinrich the attention he needed.

Being home gave Hinrich added strength to fight his illness. We decided he should be hospitalized in Austria as soon as we arrived. So far no one else in the family had fallen ill. An unsettling fear remained that another member of the family could contract TB. Because no one else had become sick thus far despite exposure, we hoped we were immune to it.

We had a sense of urgency to get Hinrich to Austria. He had been back home for nearly a week when we left the farm to make our way to Bleiberg. This time we traveled the entire distance by train since we had been given visas. Upon our arrival, Hinrich was hospitalized in Klagenfurt about 65 kilometers (40 miles) from Bleiberg. We hoped they had options for treatment. Being in the mountain air as suggested by the German military doctors gave us both a ray of hope.

During Hinrich's week long hospitalization, he underwent an array of tests. The prognosis for TB was not good. His doctors didn't want to come right out and tell Hinrich his time was limited, nor did they want to make any predictions on how long he would live. We were told that very few people had been cured, although a handful had survived.

At times he became violently ill. Hinrich was 32-years-old and certainly not ready to give up on life and die. When he was discharged, the physician suggested we stay with my mother for a few weeks while they further evaluated his condition and considered all possible treatments. The only treatment he was given at that time was cough syrup.

Some days Hinrich was so weak he couldn't get out of bed, yet there were other days he seemed quite well. On the good days we walked in the foothills among the pine trees taking in the beautiful scenery and the fresh mountain air in hopes the air was curing his ailments. We held on to the hope that we would return to Germany and live a normal life together raising our two beautiful daughters. We refused to give up hope. We went on fighting and praying his condition would improve. There was still a small glimmer of hope and our faith kept us going. I didn't want Hinrich to see how worried I truly was about him.

Mother prepared various plants she had gathered into a tea in hopes they would help Hinrich. Both Mother and Father tried to lighten up our predicament by distracting us with talk about the family, upcoming holidays and the weather. They tried to give us hope things would turn out fine.

During our stay in Austria, a neighbor living a few blocks down the road died. Father planned to help with the funeral and the burial. All of our neighbors and their friends were invited by the family to the wake. Oma Agnes, Ingeborg and I went to pay our last respects. The family had arranged to have the wake in the deceased's home, rather than at the church.

Customary for the time she was not embalmed and her funeral was planned quickly. Her body was prepared for viewing and many family members and friends gathered at the deceased's home. They brought a variety of beautiful mountain flowers in her honor and placed them around the departed's body. The bed was large enough to hold the deceased and the growing number of flowers that covered her body. Her face remained uncovered. Friends and relatives strolled by the bed saying their last goodbyes.

The priest summoned all to gather while he delivered a final prayer. The crowd fell silent, setting down their cake and coffee. The priest announced we would gather for a prayer around her bed. We all joined hands and bowed our heads and the priest began an invocation. "Dear God, please take this woman into your kingdom." As he spoke the word 'kingdom,' the deceased sat straight up from the head of her bed. With glazed eyes she stared blankly at the crowd surrounding her. She began to move, wiggling her arms and legs as though they had fallen asleep. She then tried lifting herself from the bed, but to no avail.

Everyone stared in shock. I initially thought her jerking may be an involuntary response because I had seen this happen before. Everyone in the room was totally confused, unsure of what was happening. The priest was astonished, but kept his composure. He immediately tried calming the crowd down hoping to keep some order. The deceased continued to move and jerked about. She was as pale as a ghost and had no color left in her face.

She looked dead, but was indeed moving. When she sat straight up, all the flowers that had covered her body fell to the floor. The crowd gasped in shock when she finally gained the ability to stand. With great haste the crowd backed away from her, thinking she was possessed. She screeched out, "What is happening here? What is everyone doing? What is going on?" Everyone started screaming and yelling in fear. Some panicked, and ran frantically out the door trying to escape as fast as they could. People stumbled and tripped over one another trying to get out the front door.

Ingeborg and I stood in awe watching the crowd with amazement. With an unsteady gait, the woman walked toward one of her family members who appeared in shock. One guest fainted and fell to the floor while others tried feverishly to revive her. Another grabbed a glass of water and threw it in her face in hopes she would come to.

Ingeborg was completely terrified yet reacted more calmly than many of the adults. My first thought was there was a mistake pronouncing her dead. She was most definitely alive and moving about her home. The priest finally regained order of those remaining in the house. After her resurrection she lived on another five long years. What a story it was to be told by all in attendance.

There were several local documented cases where someone's death was officially pronounced by a doctor only to later have it discovered the individual was not dead at all. There were a few incidents Father experienced in his duties when he heard knocking coming from inside a coffin. Once Father was in the process of covering a coffin with dirt when he realized the person inside was still alive. The thought of being buried alive was extremely frightening to me and since hearing of the events from my father, I was fearful it could happen to me.

I thought, however, this incident was quite comical. The shock and excitement in the room when the woman sat up was truly unbelievable. Despite the stress of Hinrich's health, Mother, Father, and I were able to laugh about our strange day. Our laughter was short-lived, as on our way home my thoughts quickly shifted back to Hinrich.

Two weeks following Hinrich's release from the hospital, his condition did not appear to be improving. There were no other planned treatments. Everything became a waiting game. We decided to stay one more week in Austria in hopes we would begin to see a change. After the week passed, it became apparent the mountain air had no healing effect on him. We, however, refused to give up hope.

## Chapter 41

We decided to return to Germany and visit another doctor in Klenkendorf. We hoped he would be able to help Hinrich survive this terrible, progressive disease. The trip back to Klenkendorf proved especially difficult for Hinrich. In just three weeks he had lost over 15 pounds and was nauseous nearly all of the time.

As soon as we arrived in Klenkendorf, Hinrich scheduled an appointment with a new doctor. He hoped to get some relief for his pain. According to the doctor there wasn't much left to do or try. Their supply of medications and treatments were limited or used up. His prognosis was so poor they gave him little hope they could stop the progression of the illness or relieve his pain. His mother and I were both willing to try just about anything at this point. Oma Engle mixed raw eggs with beer and fed it to Hinrich daily in hopes this home remedy might help cure him or at least help relieve some of his pain. She had heard from others this treatment could help cure his TB. Hinrich drank this concoction to please her, however the remedy didn't help him much. He hardly ever complained to any of us but the look on his face and his nightly moans told of his great suffering.

**Our girls during this time, Anneliese on the left and Ingeborg on the right**

When night fell things became quiet, giving Hinrich and I time to talk and more time to think. He whispered how much he loved me and his hope he'd live at least until our girls were grown. Hinrich told me how sorry he was he hadn't been home as often as he would have liked. The war had taken him away from us often and he felt he had missed out on much of our lives. The war had interfered with both of our lives. It had interrupted our hopes, our dreams and our plans we had for ourselves and for our girls. I knew he regretted his long absences and the opportunity to be the father he wanted to be. Hinrich was not willing to give up. He said he planned on growing old and we were destined to be partners, a team that would work side by side just like his own mother and father had for many years. He fought hard for the next several months to survive and stay alive. I was inspired by God, my mother, and children to not give up on him and fought this threat right alongside him.

Hinrich saw his doctors on a semi-regular basis. We were always told Hinrich's TB had progressed to a point where there were no treatments left to try. Seeing we were not ready to give up, the physicians sat us down to express their belief that Hinrich did not have much longer to live. Hearing their words was devastating. I was so tired. I had remained strong for so long for Hinrich and my family I felt as if I couldn't bear this information. I was angered by their words and accused the doctors of not doing everything they could to help save him. The despair I felt destroyed the hope I had once felt for him and for us. I wasn't sure how we would get through this terrible ordeal. Hinrich refused to admit his illness was terminal. I embraced his courage and strength as mine wavered. I hoped he could remain strong in his faith for the both of us as I was unsure of my own.

Concerned that others in the family may become ill with TB, the hospital medical staff tested me and suggested the girls and I move off of the farm. I tested negative, but was warned because of my frequent close contact with Hinrich my chances of becoming infected were elevated. I wasn't ready for any kind of separation from my husband, especially knowing he desperately needed me. Our family divided by war, now together, was being asked to separate once again.

For some reason the doctors did not recommend our girls get tested for tuberculosis during his hospital stay. This decision not to test our girls was relieving and increased my confidence we were somehow safe from the disease. The fact no one else in Hinrich's family or my family had contracted the illness also added to my confidence. At that time I believed Hinrich became so ill because the Nazi officers had not allowed him to rest as the doctor who diagnosed his illness had recommended.

I wanted to keep our girls protected so I followed the doctor's recommendations and moved down the road a short distance from the farm into a duplex. Since the farm was located right at the edge of town Opa Brase was able to find a place for us to stay that was only a few blocks from our home.  I was close enough to still tend to Hinrich every day.  Many times Oma Engle came to the duplex and stayed with her granddaughters while I took care of Hinrich.

I felt I couldn't leave Hinrich stranded and alone to fight the disease on his own even if it meant risking my own safety.  Everyone else in the family, including Oma Engle feared TB and sadly, often avoided Hinrich even though he needed someone to help him.  I loved him and wouldn't leave him especially when he needed me most.  Dying of TB was one of Oma Engle's worst fears, and she was frightened of her own son.

Oma Engle had become very helpful caring for our girls during this time.  She loved Ingeborg and Anneliese dearly and treated them like little princesses.  Our girls loved their grandmother and enjoyed spending endless hours with her.  They had a difficult time understanding why they couldn't go home to the farm.  Hinrich and I had discussed that if both of us died before our daughters were raised, they would live with their grandparents on the farm.  I had no intentions, however, of dying prematurely and wished wholeheartedly Hinrich wouldn't either.

Officials from the local Department of Health came out to the house and checked on us several times per week to track symptoms and to test for the illness from time to time.  Every time the girls and I were tested the results came back negative.  It had been four years since Hinrich's first symptoms had appeared.  For some reason I was being protected perhaps by God, knowing Hinrich needed me.

Seeing my children carry on with their carefree nature was a source of healing during that time.  Some days almost seemed normal and I thanked God for those days.  I loved to watch our girls play together and hear them giggle.  It seemed no matter what happened children somehow sifted through all the rubble and managed to have fun by doing the simplest things.  Just like all children, mine had a tendency to get into mischief.  With our girls being so little, I had to keep my eyes on them at all times to avoid any mishaps.

I tried to keep our faith in God strong during this time and recited prayers from my Grandmother Margarette's prayer book to Hinrich. It was difficult to believe our time together was nearing its final chapter. I found myself weeping alone. I did not want Hinrich or our girls to see me crying. I cried for Hinrich, for myself and our daughters until there were no more tears left to cry. I felt alone, no one could help; destiny had set its course. I was already in mourning and he hadn't died yet. I prayed to God to keep me strong so I would have the strength to help my husband and daughters through this horrible time. I wished dearly that my mother was near.

Hinrich only got worse. Our prospects for any kind of recovery were gone with the inevitability of death clearly apparent. Hinrich saw the despair in my eyes. It was ironic because he tried his best to comfort me, told me things would be okay and not to worry. He was the sick one, yet he consoled me. When I recognized he felt he needed to take care of me, it broke my heart. I didn't want him worried about me, he had enough to think about. It was hard to hold back the tears when we talked about our future. I didn't want him to see me cry. I wanted his last days at home to be peaceful and happy. I had to find the strength to keep moving forward.

Hinrich insisted the time had come to talk about what would happen to our daughters and myself after he died. He called me into the bedroom where he lay and asked me to sit with him. Hinrich talked about his hopes for us and his thoughts on how he'd like the girls and me to move forward with the rest of our lives. He stressed his desire for our happiness. We talked about the war and how we thought it might affect our future. He, still thinking of us, was concerned with so much fighting going on because he wanted to make sure we would be safe after he was gone. He apologized to me for what the war had done to our family and said he wished things had been different. The words we spoke at the edge of his bed were heartbreaking. I was beside myself and could not bear to think about going on without him.

I couldn't plan for what was to come no matter how hard I tried. He had come to terms with his own impending death and was more accepting than I. He insisted we needed to be as prepared as we could for when the time came. No matter how many times we spoke I never felt prepared to let him go.

It was inexplicable one morning when Hinrich stated he felt better. He perked up, appeared to have more energy, and seemed ready to take charge of the time he had left. It was a lovely late fall morning. He decided he wanted to go to town. He felt he was strong enough to run a few errands. It was as though he wanted to put his illness behind him, at least for a day, and go about his business in the same way he had before he became ill. Seeing him in control and having more strength brightened the day for all of us.

Hinrich spoke to his father about having one of the laborers who usually worked on a neighboring farm, but was working for us that day, take him to town. Opa Brase arranged for the laborer to take Hinrich with his horse and wagon. From Hinrich I learned the laborer was a Slavic man who had been taken as a German war prisoner in 1941. He was later ordered to work as a laborer on local German farms that surrounded our area. I learned later this prisoner's name was Djura Stefanovic and he was born in Yugoslavia. I also learned Hinrich and Djura talked with ease and covered many topics during their trip that day.

Upon returning to the farm it was apparent the trip had taken a toll on Hinrich. Having been out and about all day plus riding back and forth on the bumpy road had worn him out. When Hinrich left he was able to walk to the wagon on his own, but when they returned, Djura and his father had to help Hinrich back indoors. All of the optimism sparked in me from seeing him earlier that day feeling well, faded quickly.

## Chapter 42

As time passed Hinrich grew weaker by the minute and became frailer with every day that passed. He sensed death was closing in on him as his condition worsened. He began vomiting blood and became almost entirely bedridden. By November of 1944 Hinrich had become a wraith. He was thin, weak, and tired with barely enough energy to get out of bed.

Hinrich's mother had become terribly paranoid of the disease from having watched Hinrich waste away before her eyes. The thought of catching TB continued to terrify her. She asked me one day to come to the house to care for Hinrich because he was so very ill and she had become too afraid to go into his bedroom. She knew I was not afraid and wanted desperately to help him in any way I could.

His severe symptoms caused him much pain. He coughed and choked on his own bodily fluids. He aspirated his own blood as he tried to catch his breath. He found himself gasping for air. I would pound on his back to help him in attaining much needed oxygen. I carried buckets of vomit and blood from his room to the outdoors. With each bucket I emptied it felt like a bit of Hinrich was slipping further away.

Hinrich had not seen Ingeborg and Anneliese for some time and asked to see our girls that day. I knew he didn't have much longer to live and even though the Department of Health didn't think we should be together, I brought the girls to see him. He was dying and I worried this might be the last chance they would ever have to see their father. Both girls had missed him through this whole ordeal and had very limited time with him the last two months. Ingeborg and Anneliese continued to ask to go see their father. These requests tore my heart out each time they asked. I couldn't help but let Hinrich see his children.

Hinrich asked to see Ingeborg first and I felt so glad I had brought them. I went to get Ingeborg from the other room. I told her how much her father wanted to see her and not to be afraid. I wanted to prepare her for how much his illness had changed his appearance. She smiled at me, then she calmly walked into his bedroom. I think she sensed something was very wrong even though she was only about four-years-old. She had heard us talking about him and his problems many times. She knew he was sick.

Hinrich smiled as she entered his bedroom. He waited patiently for her to come sit beside him. He had grown so weak in the past few days he was only able to visit with her for a short time. Hinrich had some very important things he wanted to discuss with her. He didn't have much time to help her understand how much he loved her and missed her. Hinrich wanted so much to help her grasp that he would no longer be here in a physical sense for her. He knew he was dying and the words he spoke would probably be his final words to her. Hinrich also knew this was the way she would remember him for the rest of her life. I stood in the doorway and watched them hug. It was agonizing to see the sorrow in his eyes. It was all I could do to hold back my overwhelming emotions.

Hinrich's voice was gentle as he spoke softly to Ingeborg. Without hesitation she went up to him as if nothing were wrong and asked him what he wanted. Ingeborg loved her father dearly. If you speak to her today, she remembers how her father liked to put her on the kitchen table and ask her to dance. He bragged about her intelligence, her beauty and how someday she would be a famous movie star. Hinrich reached out and asked her to sit with him on the bed. He held her so gently and told her how very much he loved her. I listened quietly in the corner as he asked her to watch over her mother and her little sister after he was gone.

I could barely stand it. My knees grew weak and I slid down the wall. I broke down and silently cried. He told Ingeborg he would be leaving soon and wouldn't be able to come back. She seemed to understand that very shortly he would no longer be with us and then asked him where he would be going. He did his best as he tried to reassure her

167

she would be alright. He told her she had Oma and Opa Brase and her mommy here and they would take care of her when he was gone. I knew Ingeborg couldn't understand everything that was said, but she sensed something was terribly wrong. She asked her father not to leave her, and asked why he couldn't stay with us. He explained he would always be with her and thinking about her. The family had practiced the Lutheran faith in the past so Hinrich spoke to the girls about God, a heavenly place, and prayer. He went on to say that she, Anneliese, and her mommy would be in his heart forever no matter what happened.

It crushed me that my little girl had to experience this at such a young age. I was angry she would not get a lifetime with her father. Hinrich wanted to talk to Anneliese next. He sent Ingeborg out after giving her one last, long, tender hug. Ingeborg bravely told him she would help take care of me. I turned my head so Ingeborg wouldn't see the tears running down my face.

I carried Anneliese into the room and over to the bed. She was a little over two-years-old and didn't understand anything about her father's illness. Hinrich needed to see her one last time even if she didn't realize what was happening so he could tell her goodbye and he loved her. Anneliese crawled up on his bed and gave him a big hug. He told her goodbye and to be a good girl for her mommy. She climbed off the bed and came running to me. I picked her up and held her in my arms. I was unable to stop crying. She patted me on the back saying "Mommy it will be alright." Hinrich just smiled and laid his head down on his pillow too weak to carry on.

That evening I stayed with him and when we went to bed he actually got a bit of sleep. I stayed awake most of the night to help him. Hinrich did not want nor was he ready to die even though he was coming to terms with succumbing to this illness. Together we made it through one more night. The sun shined in on us through the window the next morning.

## Chapter 43

November 7th of 1944 was a day I will never forget. Hinrich began vomiting pints of blood. His lungs had totally deteriorated. He heaved chunks, at times large enough to stick in his throat and block his airway. I wondered if the chunks were pieces of his lungs. I had to use several towels to sop up the massive amounts of blood that had spilled over the top of the bucket sitting next to his bed. The pail sat in a pool of blood. He was too weak to get out of bed. When he had to throw up, he leaned over the side of his bed and positioned himself over the opening of the bucket so it would catch the clots of blood and pieces of lung his body purged from his insides. When a large chunk passed, it caused him to gag until he turned blue.

Fearing he'd choke to death, I removed obstructive clots numerous times having to reach into his throat to retrieve them. I emptied the bucket when it overflowed as blood clots and lung tissue floated freely to the top. I dumped the buckets of blood in the nearby field where no one traveled. I wanted to make sure no one else would be affected by his tainted blood. It was agonizing and awful seeing Hinrich that way. I desperately wished I could take away some of his pain. I was covered with his blood from head to toe. Every time he coughed he lost what seemed to be quarts of blood. I'd never seen so much blood and didn't know how long he could suffer this way. He was in agonizing pain and there was nothing I could do to help end his unrelenting discomfort and suffering.

Oma Engle remained afraid to enter Hinrich's room, scared she might catch the illness and die. She was afraid the germs would spread throughout the entire house and everyone would be infected. God must have been watching over me. I never contracted the illness despite all the close contact with Hinrich. I was angered by his mother's fear for her own life and the fact she wouldn't step one foot in his room or offer him any help. I would have been overwhelmed with guilt if I had left him to die alone in his room. I sat by his bed, watched, waited, and hoped for a miracle to happen but knew it was too late. I stayed by his side until he drew his very last breath.

Hinrich had given up his fight and accepted his destiny. The life that had once filled his body vanished. He died and was finally at rest. His body lay quiet on the bed; his soul I hoped was on its way to Heaven. He was no longer mine to hold. An empty numbness came over me. There was nothing more I could do so I broke down and cried.

I have no idea how long I sat there with him and held his hand before I could move. He was still warm, still my husband. I picked up his hand and held it to my cheek. I didn't want to let him go. His hands were soft to the touch. I could still feel the warmth from his body. I stood up and put my arms around him cradling his lifeless body. Expression and emotion were absent from his eyes. He was gone and no matter how badly I wanted him to be with me, I knew he his soul had departed.

## Chapter 44

Nothing seemed harder than to leave his body knowing when I returned all that would remain would be the shell of the man I loved. I carried out the last bucket of blood after Hinrich had passed. I had to be the one to do it. I felt I owed him that act of respect. As I poured the life of my beloved husband to the ground, I dropped to my knees in desperation. Knowing I could not be seen in the field, I clutched my blood soaked apron to my chest, turned my head up toward the clear blue sky and allowed screams of anger and anguish to erupt from the innermost core of my being.

When I was capable of returning to the house I walked into the kitchen, broke down and cried again. I didn't have to say a word. Everyone knew exactly what had happened before I shared the news. I wanted to return to Hinrich and I wanted to avoid Oma Engle. I was truly infuriated by her avoidance of her own dying son. I thought I shouldn't feel that way and I knew my anger wouldn't bring Hinrich back. It would take all the strength I had to deal with Hinrich's death. I had nothing to feel guilty about and had done everything I could to help him yet I wished there had been more I could have done.

I returned to sit beside his bed. Opa Brase wasn't as fearful as Oma Engle and joined me. I was glad he was there. Oma Engle did not want to come into Hinrich's room to say her last goodbye. She worried about the infection, feared a similar death and refused.

We sat for an hour after his death. Oma Engle suggested we burn everything in his room to make sure the infection could not spread throughout the house or to the others in the household. I was greatly saddened, yet realized getting rid of Hinrich's bedding made some sense. Oma Engle told me to burn his things which didn't help resolve any feelings of resentment I held toward her. She wanted me to do all the work as well, because she was afraid to walk into his room. I agreed to remove Hinrich's bedding, but told her I wanted to wait until morning to get rid of most of his possessions.

Oma Engle insisted it was necessary to burn them right away and remove all items from his room that might be contagious. I felt totally exhausted, yet somehow found the energy and strength to help go through Hinrich's things. I thought of our two daughters and I wanted to keep them safe. I found it hard to contain my feelings toward Oma Engle. Especially my urge to blurt out how insensitive, selfish and unsympathetic I thought she had been through this ordeal. It was nearly impossible to control my emotions and not lash out at her because of the loss and the pain I felt. Both girls and the rest of the family had been in close contact with Hinrich for several years prior to his death so I was unsure how burning his items now would help the situation.

That night Opa Brase and I moved Hinrich's body into another room. Then I thoroughly cleaned the room where he had died. I took out his clothes, sheets, and finally his mattress. I buried each one of the blood-soaked towels deep underground so animals wouldn't dig them up. I picked up any items that couldn't be completely cleaned and carried them outside to be burned in a nearby field. When I was done, his room stood almost empty. I walked out of the house and lit the heaping mound of his possessions on fire. I stood and watched while they burned to ashes. I gazed into the fire, watching the pile burn, fixated on the flames and embers as each item turned to ashes.

Transfixed on the rolling flames, my memories were sparked of our encounter with the Gypsy fortune teller several years ago. Did she really foretell Hinrich's death? She predicted he would die on November 7th of 1944 and it was exactly the day he died. I wondered to myself as the flames withered down to a glow, how the Gypsy woman could possibly have known the exact day of the end of his suffering and death. Her prophecy was puzzling and frightening.

The entire ordeal had been horrible and heart-wrenching, yet I couldn't help but feel a sense of relief for Hinrich. I knew how much pain he had been in the last few weeks and knew he no longer suffered which gave me a sense of peace. I faced a future without him. The war, cruel and unforgiving, had taken Hinrich away from me. I blamed the Nazis for his death by forcing him to fly when he was so sick. I was angered by the sanctions that had been placed on Germany, leaving Hinrich without proper medications to ease his suffering and maybe cure the TB. I was deep in thought about our past and contemplated how I would get through the next few days.

The day after his death we began to plan the funeral. Making arrangements for the funeral was difficult for me. I was emotionally drained, and was just going through the motions. I felt as if nothing really mattered. His funeral was planned very quickly and took place at home on the farm. The entire family was present and many of them helped during the wake and the funeral. Hinrich was buried in the local Klenkendorf cemetery three days following his death. Both girls asked me over and over when Papa was coming home. I was unsure what to tell them, because they were too little to understand he would never return. After we buried Hinrich I just wanted to get away.

## Chapter 45

Everything felt foreign, and nothing felt quite right. The house where we lived, Opa Brase and Oma Engle, and our daughters, everything was exactly the same yet everything seemed so different. I desperately needed to leave and try to figure out how to proceed with the rest of my life. I was young and healthy and hoped I had a lot of life left to live. I needed to think about what would be best for my girls and how I as a single parent would survive the war. It was hard to think straight and plan ahead, yet I knew that keeping Inga and Anneliese fed, a roof over their heads, and protecting them from any harm were my first priorities.

My first thought was to go back to Austria and stay with Mother and Father for a few months. I hoped Mother could help me get through this awful time in my life and help me move forward. Once I had some clarity that was exactly what I did. I went to see my mother.

I traveled with my girls back to Austria shortly after the funeral and had to experience the same trials and tribulations I had during previous trips home without visas. I crossed the mountains with them, avoided the border patrol and connected with my father once over the border to help us get the rest of the way home. Once home, my mother's strength, love, and support helped reinforce to me the many wonderful people remaining in my life. I was truly grateful for my loved ones. I don't think I would have made it through the whole ordeal without Mother. She kept me grounded when I needed it most. Her thoughtful, gentle way gave me the will to continue and move forward with my life.

I also had two wonderful daughters that would be part of my life forever, no matter what else happened, they would be here with me. I would always be their mother and no one could take that away from me. Somehow I found the strength within myself to move on. Mother helped me rekindle my faith. She gave me hope I could still find happiness. There was much good that lay ahead for both my girls and me.

I stayed with Mother, Father and Friede for a few months while time seemed to drag on, almost at a standstill. I loved being back home with my mother, though her unconditional love couldn't fill the emptiness I felt. Hinrich's undying love for me, heartfelt tenderness and constant kindness had become an integral part of my life. My emotions were conflicted, I was thankful for everything I had, yet I was in agony.

Given their age, my girls seemed to deal fairly well with Hinrich's death. They didn't understand the finality of death. Gratefully, my mother and Oma Engle helped immensely with them. I didn't want Inga and Anneliese to ever forget their father and I planned to do whatever I needed to ensure they knew the man their father was.

At the end of two months I decided it was time to go back to Germany. The girls missed their home and talked often about their grandparents. Hinrich and I had decided the girls and I would be safer living near his family after he passed. Living close to the farm was practical and familiar for the girls. They could visit Opa Brase and Oma Engle given we only lived a few blocks away. Within a few days after making the decision to go home, we left Austria and traveled back to see their grandparents and to make a new home for ourselves.

The trip over the border was never easy and two small children made it all the more difficult. There was always the risk of being stopped by the border patrol and being jailed, harmed or killed for trying to cross illegally. The war, in full force, left few places where we felt safe. Winter was upon us and travel in the mountains proved most dangerous for the girls and me. We had to climb high over the mountains and the snow was deep that time of year. The weather could be quite severe at the higher elevations and there were heavy snow falls on the way back home.

Somehow we were always able to avoid avalanches while in the mountains, yet hiking up the steep mountainsides always proved to be treacherous. Despite the danger, I was happy Mother and Father were able to see Ingeborg and Anneliese during this trip. Luckily again some local farmers along the route and a few friends offered to help us get over the border and on our way back to the farm. Even though the trip to Germany was long and arduous, we made it back safely.

## Chapter 46

Once back at the farm, I helped Oma Engle and Opa Brase on the farm, but we still lived in the house down the road where Ingeborg, Anneliese and I had been quarantined when Hinrich was ill. The Brases paid my rent and made sure we were taken care of. In return I cleaned, cooked, and served food to the farm hands. I tried to keep as busy as possible. I hoped it would keep my mind off Hinrich and the many other problems I faced being on the farm and in Germany without him. I found myself doing whatever I needed to do in order to survive and kept going primarily for my girl's sake.

For several months after Hinrich's death, nothing I did seemed the same as when he had been alive. It took me some time to get over the shock of losing him before my life felt somewhat normal again. I had plenty to do, my girls kept me busy and I helped Oma Engle during the day which kept my mind distracted. It did me good to stay busy leaving me little time to think about my troubles. There wasn't a place for self-pity. It seemed as though almost everyone we knew had lost someone very near and dear to them. Everyone was dealing with their own losses and grief.

Four months passed by quickly and it was soon mid-March of 1945, a day before Ingeborg's birthday. Much had happened during the months after Hinrich died, and I didn't feel like celebrating. However, I didn't want Ingeborg's fourth birthday to go unnoticed the following day. Celebrations didn't happen often during the war. Ingeborg's birthday gave us good reason to enjoy a few hours together.

Oma Engle and I planned to make Ingeborg's birthday cake. I had made cakes for all previous birthdays for the girls and wasn't going to break the tradition now. I knew she liked large, cream-filled tortes, decorated with fried oatmeal, filled with fruit and pudding, heaped full of strawberries and topped with thick, whipped cream to cover the entire cake. I hoped Oma Engle had some dried or canned strawberries or blueberries handy for the cake. It was customary for us to make tall, cream-filled tortes for celebrations. Tortes were one of Germany's traditional desserts we made for various occasions. Ingeborg's birthday was a perfect opportunity to bring some pleasure and joy back into our lives. I hoped maybe together we would create an enjoyable memory and not have her birthday memories solely connected to the war or her father's death. Ingeborg talked a lot about her father and remembered much about him, which warmed my heart. I never wanted her to forget him. It saddened me that Anneliese was so young and probably would have no memories of Hinrich.

I counted my money and thought perhaps I could afford to buy Ingeborg a pair of shoes or a doll. Times were hard and I wasn't receiving any kind of pension or death benefit after Hinrich's death, but I had a little money we had saved. I decided our resources for such things were too limited and there just wasn't enough money to buy her something new. However, all of the women in Oma Engle's household knew how to sew. Anyone of us could have made her a new dress or a homemade doll. She would have been thrilled with either one. She probably wouldn't expect anything other than her cake. If I made her a doll I would use bits and pieces of material we had laying around the house; making her a dress though would be another story. Finding and affording nice material to make a dress was difficult.

Anneliese was almost three-years-old, could talk up a storm and had begun to form her own personality. She had reached the age where she instigated many fights with her sister. I broke up occasional battles over toys between them. Neither of the girls had many toys of their own, but what they had they considered theirs.

Anneliese being the willful child that she was, tried to steal away Ingeborg's things and aggressively claimed Ingeborg's possessions as her own. She had a more domineering personality, became the aggressor if provoked and sometimes resorted to biting if she didn't get what she wanted. I had separated them a few times because of their arguing. Even though Ingeborg was the older one, Anneliese was at times able to get the best of her.

Anneliese was, however, just as sweet as she was determined and most of the time was a charming well-mannered little girl. Anneliese was at the age where she wanted everything she saw. She would put a claim on the item even if it belonged to her sister. It was hard to believe someone as little and cute as she caused so much havoc in our household. Those clear, innocent blue eyes tricked you into believing she was totally angelic and blameless in any given situation. Many times her funny laugh, kindhearted smile, and gentle touch revealed how sweet and loveable she really could be.

We had managed to make Ingeborg a doll and sure enough after she unwrapped it, Anneliese tried to steal it away from her. Nearly three, it was hard for her to understand it wasn't her birthday and it wasn't her doll. Ingeborg being the kind-hearted, big sister she was, willingly offered to share her new doll with Anneliese at least for a short time. The birthday party turned out to be a success and we all enjoyed the tasty cream-filled torte Oma Engle and Anne helped make that day. We all enjoyed the much needed distraction.

## Chapter 47

With so much to do on the farm, there were farm hands that came and went. Sometimes the German military rotated war prisoners working on farms, depending on the farmer's needs. Many times though, if a prisoner was placed on a farm, it was possible they stayed on that same farm to work for many years. Several months after Hinrich died the Slavic war prisoner, Djura Stefanovic, was introduced into my life when he came to work for Oma Engle and Opa Brase. He had taken Hinrich to town near the end of his life. Djura had been transferred from the neighbor's farm to our farm. Opa Brase had heard he was a good worker and requested Djura be placed on our farm, and the German commander granted his request.

I remember after I had served Djura the first few times, he was brave enough to make eye contact with me. He gave me these looks that hinted he wanted to talk. His stares of interest never lasted too long for fear he may get into trouble for flirting or looking at me. I tried not to look at him, but it was hard not to glance back. He was nice looking, seemed harmless, and was very mannerly when I came around to set his place at the table. Opa Brase liked him as a worker. Djura worked long and hard hours, didn't complain, and was willing to do extra tasks without being asked.

After Djura worked for us for several months he became quite talkative with me and it wasn't long before I considered him a friend. He gained my attention by speaking of Hinrich and how they had met before he died. I find it ironic when I think back that Djura was the one who had taken Hinrich to town that day shortly before he died. A Serb war prisoner paired up with a German pilot in the same wagon discussing various aspects of their lives and befriending one another as they rode to town. There was something about Djura that appealed to me and his connection with Hinrich made him all the more intriguing. Djura and I had somehow met through fate and made a connection.

As time went on during some of our talks, Djura opened up to me. He shared many stories about his life. He felt he was luckier than other war prisoners because he had been placed on farms, rather than having to stay locked up in the concentration camps like many of his Slavic friends. Even though I had lived in the midst of the war for the last several years before Djura was captured, I wasn't aware of how badly many of the Serbian prisoners had been treated while they were in the war camps. When Djura was first captured he had been imprisoned in a concentration camp with many others from various ethnic groups. Many different groups had been strategically captured one by one during the war and were forcefully taken to the prison camps in Germany. Millions of them died during war time in the 1940's.

Djura told me there were Russians, Poles, Serbs, Czechs, and various other groups that had been placed in the same camp with him around 1941. He spoke of how he had been released after a few months from the camp to work on farms as a forced laborer instead of being jailed behind barbed wire fences. Djura believed nearly all of the Jews had been exterminated from the Klenkendorf area, had fled in fear, or were in hiding somewhere in the country. Djura spoke of the danger to those in hiding and of his hopes they would not be discovered. I remember Djura had said, "No Jews were left in the camp where I was; they had already been murdered or moved somewhere else." We both struggled with the horrors happening to innocent people around us.

Through the next few months Djura and I continued to talk. I shared my story with him and he spoke of how he came to Germany as well. He told me how he had been taken prisoner when Hitler took over Yugoslavia. His experiences with the Nazis were somewhat similar to mine. He went on to tell me how he was treated while detained in the camps and what it was like being a war prisoner.

Djura said he was drafted twice into the Yugoslavian army. The first time he was 18-years-old. Then he was drafted again after the war broke out. He had been drafted the first time and served nearly 18 months in the Yugoslavian army at which point he returned home to Kormont, Yugoslavia. He had been having some medical problems and was unable to stay in the army at that time because of these. He wasn't able to return to duty until he recovered. He said he had problems with his kidney. The doctors were unable to cure the disease but helped him feel well enough so he was able to function and eventually return to duty.

Djura said when he was drafted a second time he was 23-years-old, re-entering the army in 1940. When Djura reported for duty the second time Hitler had not yet annexed Yugoslavia. It was approximately one year after being drafted that Djura and the Yugoslav army were recalled into action in April of 1941 to fight the Italian invasion of Yugoslavia under Mussolini. Yugoslavia was able to repel the Italians, but Nazi Germany came to Mussolini's rescue. The Axis Powers overthrew Yugoslavia because Hitler was fearful that Yugoslav leaders would side with the Russians.

At first it seemed strange to me for him to have been drafted twice during the same war, but then again nothing that happened during those trying times surprised me. If men were able bodied anything was possible, so being drafted twice during the same war was not that unusual. When Djura was drafted into the Yugoslavian army both Muslims and Christians were housed in the same area and used the same mess halls. He told me that mixing the two faiths in the same mess hall sometimes had its challenges.

Djura spoke of a time when a practical joke had gone sour and how several men could have been killed. One of the Serb men in his group was almost killed by a Muslim soldier over a dip of the communal soup they served for supper. It was against the Muslim religion to consume any kind of pork. The Serb soldier had snuck some pieces of ham into the big pot of soup while it cooked for the platoon. Both Muslims and Serbs would be fed from this same big pot of soup and unbeknownst to them would end up eating the ham hidden in the stew.

The Muslim cook somehow found out the man had placed pork in the soup and had become so furious with the practical joker he grabbed his meat cleaver and began chasing after him. Both men were running through the mess hall, the cook chasing the Serb crazed with anger for disrespecting his religious beliefs. His sharp metal meat cleaver raised high above his head was ready to strike and hack off the Serb's arms or legs. Djura said he pursued the cook, calmed him down and eventually managed to get the cleaver away from him. If he wouldn't have been able to stop him, the cook would have certainly hacked the Serbian joker to death. Even with the occasional issue it sounded like for the most part things operated fairly smoothly and both ethnic groups continued to ban together to battle Hitler during the conflict to annex Yugoslavia.

Djura told me the story of the downfall of Yugoslavia from his own recollection. He said German troops entered Yugoslavian territory in the spring of 1941. He was unable to recollect the exact date it happened but remembered vividly the early spring morning when his entire platoon was taken as war prisoners by the Nazis. At almost 24-years-old, he was in charge of 15-20 men. As the leader, he directed several other men who did the blacksmithing work for his platoon. Djura said he performed various tasks in the company, which included supervising others and doing blacksmithing jobs himself. He remembered putting up camp in a small town close to Sabac, Yugoslavia where their group was captured. His recollections of the event were clear and he remembered the event as if it had taken place yesterday. Djura told the story of one quiet spring evening when all hell broke loose.

## Chapter 48

Djura and the rest of the platoon had just settled down for the night. Most of them had already fallen asleep, other than the night guard who patrolled the immediate area around them. Djura said the evening started out like any other night. He had drifted off to sleep in the back of a horse drawn wagon where he stored all of his blacksmithing tools.

Unaware of what was going to happen that evening, he went to sleep with ease. He felt quite secure because the night watchman was wide awake and faithfully patrolled the area for possible intruders.

It seemed as though he had just fallen asleep when suddenly, without any warning, a commotion in the camp broke out and he was awakened. He felt someone nudge him on the shoulder with the barrel of a gun. He was ordered to get up. Once fully awake it took him a moment to get his bearings. He opened his eyes, looked up and there overhead stood two German soldiers ready to seize both him and the wagon. He soon realized German soldiers had entered his camp and had them surrounded.

The soldiers who woke him continued to prod at him with their guns. He explained how the Germans had covertly snuck into his camp during the night and surrounded the Slavic platoon, taking them all by surprise. He realized there was a man out of uniform who assisted the Germans and spoke the Serbian language fluently, which was Djura's native language. He was totally confused why one of his own people would be a traitor and help the Germans.

Djura later found out the sympathizer was a civilian from town, who had been born a German citizen and lived in Serbia for many years. He was a Nazi collaborator who translated for them and assisted in the capture of many Yugoslav troops during that time. Everyone in the camp understood everything they were being ordered to do after they had been taken prisoner. Djura remembered he had his gun laying beside him somewhere in the wagon when he had fallen asleep. It must have fallen or rolled off in the wagon somewhere between his tools because he couldn't put his hands on it fast enough when he was awakened by the enemy. The two soldiers standing over him with their guns pointed at his head dashed any thoughts he may have had of searching for his gun.

His group had been surrounded very quickly when the Germans quietly crept into the camp. The Germans were heavily armed with high powered weapons and tanks. Djura's platoon was armed with simple weapons, including hunting rifles and knives. His group moved across the countryside on foot and by horse drawn wagons. The Yugoslavian group was no match for the Germans, they had been outnumbered and lacked the weaponry to fight a fair battle. They were all taken prisoner in a matter of minutes.

While the attack was taking place Djura, already captured, looked over the side of the wagon where he could see his platoon leader, a Yugoslavian sergeant. The sergeant pulled out his sidearm to fire on the Germans during the uproar. The sergeant had his gun pointed, ready to fire figuring to kill as many Germans as he could before they were taken. Djura's commander yelled at his group to get up and fight, "We can take these Nazis. There are only a few of them!"

The Nazis saw the commander raising his gun, saw he was ready to shoot, and gunned him down. The Nazis riddled him with bullets and within seconds he was dead. It all happened very fast, no one doubted they would be next if they attempted to resist. Any further resistance from his group would have been an immediate death sentence. They all would have been shot to death without any hesitation. Forced to cooperate at gunpoint, they had no choice but to surrender.

After being captured, Djura and the other Yugoslav soldiers were marched on foot for a short distance until they reached a small building where they were detained. His entire group later moved to another town, to a building where the Nazis were holding other prisoners that had been captured before his group. Djura recalled they were held in the smaller building for several hours. All the prisoners were ordered to put their hands behind their heads and marched to the large building nearby. Then they marched them on foot approximately three to four miles to the city of Sabac just across the river Sava.

**This is a map showing the city of Sabac (west of Belgrade) where Djura was taken after being captured by the Nazis.**

(http://www.embassyworld.com/maps/MapsOfYugoslavia.html)

It didn't take long for the group to get to the building where the Nazis were already holding other prisoners that had been captured. When they arrived at the larger prison site they realized they were guarded more heavily. The building where they were held was similar to a large warehouse. The Nazis outnumbered prisoners ten to one. The guards were stationed around the perimeter of the building and guarded both the inside and outside of the warehouse. They had captured many other groups beforehand and put Djura's unit in with the rest of the captives to hold them all together in the same building.

The Nazis threatened to shoot anyone that tried to resist. Djura remembered several fights that broke out between the prisoners and the guards. Some of the conflicts got out of hand and there were several serious scuffles within the confines of the prison. If a prisoner became too disorderly or unmanageable he was shot and dragged off. When Djura first entered the building, constant gunfire rang out, bullets were heard overhead hitting the ceiling mostly to get the prisoners to settle down. The threat of being shot was a scare tactic that worked and most of the prisoners were afraid to cause too much of a disruption.

Once the prisoners were all settled in and things calmed down, Djura's unit was given a small morsel of food. He heard lots of yelling and occasional screams. The crowded conditions and all the commotion made it impossible to keep track of everyone inside. Djura said so many prisoners were packed into one area, that one of them could have been easily shot and killed by the guards and he wouldn't have known the difference.

The sound of gunfire in the holding camp was never good. When the guards shot, beat or injured a prisoner, word spread quickly among the rest of them. The killings and beatings helped maintain control among the prisoners. Djura said, "Those damn Nazis, the sons-of-bitches, they don't care about anyone and now look what they've done to our country and our people." He hated Hitler's rhetoric, his ideals and the cruelty of the Nazis he witnessed toward the Serbian people. He had absolutely no tolerance for Hitler's politics or the Nazi Party. He was imprisoned along with thousands of his countrymen; all with no idea where they would be taken.

## Chapter 49

After a few days of detention in the warehouse, the Nazis loaded all of the prisoners into boxcars, and brought them to Germany by train. Their final destination and drop point was Bremervorde. Once in Bremervorde they were transferred to a smaller town close to Klenkendorf. Djura was eventually imprisoned in a concentration camp close to Klenkendorf near the town of Sandbostel. Djura said when they got off the train in Bremervorde, all of those who had been captured walked nearly ten miles to Sandbostel. They were held in the prison camp along with many other war prisoners. Some, not as lucky as he, were held there for many years after he was released to work on the farms. Bremervorde was a larger city approximately seven miles from Klenkendorf which was located very close to the Brase farm.

Many ethnic groups were housed together in the concentration camp. Djura was kept in the locked and guarded concentration camp for about two months. After that he was taken to Gnarrenburg to work on a farm harvesting potatoes for local farmers. Then he worked on another farm located close to the Brase farm where I lived with Hinrich and our girls. Eventually he came to work for Opa and Oma Brase and was housed close to the farm along with the other prisoners.

A small group of Polish prisoners were part of the forced labor pool on the Brase farm and worked on the farm nearly every day. Oma Engle had done most of the cooking for the workers and made sure all of the prisoners working for us were fed a few small meals each day. Opa Brase and Oma Engle had few problems with the forced laborers. If any of the prisoners caused too many problems, they were sent back to the concentration camp where they were treated with cruelty and lost all rights as a human being. The workers were well aware of this so most avoided any sort of trouble.

Djura recalled the prison camp near Sandbostel and described it as large buildings with tall fences around them. The fences had barbed wire along the top to prevent prisoners from escaping. He told of the many guards stationed around the building, and said it was very difficult to break out without being seen and shot down. Djura told me the prisoners were not fed well. Most were as thin as rails with their primary nutrition coming from bread and water. He described the bread as black and hard as a rock. Swallowing the stale tasting bread proved challenging with water a necessity to accomplish the task. Those that complained about the food had their ration withheld. On a rare occasion the guards gave the prisoners a snip of jelly or a pat of butter to put on the bread.

Some mornings Djura, along with other prisoners were taken to Bremervorde by train to work. At the end of their work day that stretched well into the evening, they were forced to walk back to the Sandbostel camp 10 miles from Bremervorde. Guards marched alongside the fatigued prisoners to ensure their return. Prisoners selected to work on local farms were more fortunate. Eventually Djura and a group of 20-30 men were taken out of the prison camp every day. They were assigned to a work group that labored on local farms with many of them assigned to the same farm each day. The laborers picked vegetables and completed any of the other necessary farm chores.

Djura was imprisoned in many different locations during the war. After working in Gnarrenburg he was moved to Fahrendahl. Then within a month was moved from Fahrendahl to a smaller camp with fewer guards where he found a bit more freedom.

Once he was moved from Fahrendahl he found stability in his work placements. Eventually some of the prisoners, including Djura, were moved closer to the farms they had been assigned to. They were housed in a separate building near the farmsteads where they worked. The Nazis wanted increased productivity so they eliminated the walk time to and from the camp.

When Djura moved closer to the farm where he worked, his entire work group was guarded by one or two soldiers. They were identified as men that were less likely to attempt escape. If Djura had caused problems while he was inside the concentration camp, he would never have been hand-picked as one of the men who went to work on the farms. Each day the guards walked them back and forth to the work site, watched over them while they were in the fields, and then escorted them back to their barracks when the day's work was complete. Djura felt lucky there were only a few guards that watched over his group and they were fortunate to be able to sleep in a building that wasn't surrounded by barbed wire fences.

Hitler's policies inferred that by utilizing prisoners to help local farmers, improvement would be seen in the farming industry and the local economy. He also drummed up support by using this labor method to fulfill the need to feed the existing prison population, increasing local food supplies, and contributing to the overall war effort. The draft took many German men from their home and work and slave labor was Hitler's solution to address the problems it created.

**Picture of Djura Stefanovic a German war prisoner working on a German farm that was in close proximity to the Brase's farm.**

While working on the neighboring farm, Djura heard that Opa Brase was a good man to work for from other prisoners who had worked for the Brases. Djura told me while he worked for Opa Brase's neighbor, he learned of Hinrich, his illness, and the Brase family. He had hoped he would be transferred to the Brase farm. After the day he had been asked to take Hinrich to town, he wasn't sure if their paths would ever cross again. Six months later he was given the opportunity to work for Opa Brase.

## Chapter 50

Opa Brase tried to treat most of the prisoners fairly yet at the same time they were being taken advantage of by being forced to work long grueling hours. They labored from daylight till dark. War prisoners were not to be considered friends or allies. Most German families would never consider socializing with them. Most prisoners who worked on the farms were not treated in a brutal manner. However, they clearly received the message they were nothing more than forced laborers.

The prisoners had few complaints about working for Opa Brase; most thought he was a nice man and they felt fortunate to be out of the camps. Even if they had a grievance though, it wouldn't have done them any good. The farm owners had the upper hand and were always in control. If they didn't like the way a prisoner performed, a complaint was made to the guard in charge and that prisoner was sent back to the concentration camp where life was miserable.

All the prisoners were considered Auslanders and therefore not to be trusted. I recalled being treated the same way when I first was taken to Germany, but not to the same extreme. The Slavs were despised by Hitler. Djura's tanned darker skin, and black hair made him even more foreign looking. Slavic individuals were definitely among the people stereotyped by the Nazi propaganda that promoted the Germans as being the supreme race. His ethnicity was considered inferior. He was looked upon as less intelligent, and treated with less compassion and respect than I was met with, when I first came to Germany. Most domestic Germans I had encountered didn't like foreigners and they particularly didn't like the Slavs, Jews, or Poles.

Djura's Yugoslavian heritage was not appreciated by the locals and the propaganda fed to the Germans led many of them to believe they were indeed the supreme race and as such superior to everyone. Hitler had nothing good to say about anyone who was not a true German. His hatred and prejudices spread throughout Germany and brainwashed nearly all of the citizens. Overall, if you were not of German descent, you were treated like someone less capable, and less intelligent. Most foreigners, including me, would never be totally accepted into German society. Djura would always be considered inferior, and worse yet, he was a war prisoner, which further lowered his status in the ethnic hierarchy.

If I had not married Hinrich, I know for certain I would have never been accepted into the Brase family. Having Hinrich's children was a significant factor in my being allowed to stay with the Brases. Djura, however, had not been as lucky as I. He had a more difficult time gaining their trust and proving himself and would always be considered a foreigner and a prisoner of war.

Djura was slowly able to start breaking down my wall of fear, apprehension, and grief by sharing his own story with me. It was nice having someone I could talk to again even if our encounters were brief. With Hinrich gone I felt so alone. I did not feel I could talk or confide in any of Hinrich's relatives as our relationships remained strained. It was nice to have a friend even if our association with one another would have been frowned upon by everyone around me.

Ingeborg and Anneliese also greatly helped me deal with my grief over losing Hinrich. It was reassuring and heart-wrenching at the same time as I saw the resemblance of their father in the girls' faces. Each had inherited their father's blue eyes and blond hair. Their childish antics brought a smile to my face, making my life bearable. My work provided another distraction from my grief.

The chores I did in the house were not hard for me. It was nice for me to have my girls around when I was working. Ingeborg and Anneliese were allowed to play and run freely through the house, dashing about as they played. They sometimes ran by the prisoner's table and stopped to try to talk with them. Their Aunt Anne, Oma Engle, or I, would give out a yell when we saw them getting too close to the prisoner's table because we didn't want the girls to have any contact with them. I had seen and heard how some men behaved during the war toward women of all ages. I highly distrusted them.

I never felt comfortable when I was around a group of men because I suspected their intentions were probably not good. It might be unsafe for me and for other women around them. I knew they could have ulterior motives and possibly behave even worse in groups. Although I felt great empathy for their situations, I also felt the prisoners might feel as if they had no reason to carry on living. The potential for this mindset made me wary of the possible actions of these men at any given moment. The war shook my faith in mankind. With Hinrich gone, I couldn't help but feel the girls and I were more vulnerable.

Djura, however, seemed different than the others. I felt I could trust him. He gained the children's attention when they ran by. He smiled or acted silly whenever they stopped and talked to him. He was able to entertain both Anneliese and Ingeborg, and they grew to like him. They told me they thought he was a nice man. They wouldn't listen to me when I yelled at them to not run around the workers table while they were playing. They trusted Djura and weren't afraid of him though they hadn't known him long. Both girls liked the playful attention he gave them when he joked around. I didn't know him well, yet he appeared to be a friendly man. He was funny, kind, and I also grew to believe my girls were safe around him.

Ingeborg was old enough to know they were not supposed to be talking to any of the prisoners. I tried to shoo both she and Anneliese off when they played too close by. I didn't trust everyone that worked on the farm, but they were drawn to Djura. I was especially afraid for my girls if they were too friendly with any of the prisoners because the men were right in our home. They could have easily caused us harm if they became angry enough since there were only two guards watching over them.

When the farmhands came inside to eat, they all sat at a big wooden table Opa Brase had made from rough-cut lumber. The table was heavy, bulky and hard to clean because of the rough wood grain. We had wooden chairs around the table and each prisoner had his own place to sit. The table was long enough to seat 12 to 15 men, and they all gathered at the same time to eat. I had my hands full carrying bowls of potatoes, vegetables and whatever else we rationed up for them that day.

While I served, some of the men tried to talk to me; others just gave me a look or a stare. Most of them were respectful and mannerly and very aware that if they misbehaved, they would be sent back to the concentration camp where life was a nightmare. I tried not to engage them since I didn't want to contribute to a situation that might cause their return to the ghastly camp.

## Chapter 51

I remember seeing many of those poor souls when I rode my bike by the different camps on my way to town for supplies. Their bodies were so thin they looked like walking skeletons. I could count every bone that poked out of their skin, their heads disproportionate to their bodies with their belly's bloated from the lack of nutrition they needed. When the guards made them march down the streets to get back to the camp, I watched them. I could pick out every vein that showed on their heads and saw the purple blood vessels in their arms and legs. Their skin was thinned and almost transparent. Their bodies so frail many of them could barely stand, yet the Nazis marched them across town weakened and battered.

The prisoners looked ill, feeble, and bruised. Sometimes all their hair fell out from disease, starvation, or simply because their heads had been shaved. I saw when they came close to the fence, they were black and blue from the beatings they had endured, some limping and barely able to walk, naked at times as they held an arm or leg that had been twisted or broken. They were a horrific sight and I felt more helpless every time I passed.

In some camps young and old were held together. Some were small children. The poor souls were imprisoned because they happened to be born into the wrong family or ethnic group. I saw men, women and children begging and crying out for food, sobbing in misery, while they clung to the fence, which stood over ten feet tall. They hoped I or someone would throw them a morsel of food.

The doomed spirits hoped for an ounce of compassion from anyone who cared and prayed for anything that might help them survive one more day. They were filthy and starved. Some too weak to walk, others just lay in the dirt where they had fallen because they didn't have the energy or the strength to get back up.

Despite knowing I could get shot or killed if I was caught giving them food, I did it anyway. I felt it was the only way I could help. I couldn't stand to see them suffer and often wished I had done more for them. So many people, helpless and powerless. I knew many died from malnutrition or from the severe beatings they received. I went to town multiple times a week. Each time I packed the basket of my bike full with sandwiches and snuck prisoners food whenever I could.

I tossed food to the Polish, Russians, and Serbs when they were marched down the street toward the Sandbostel camp. I waited until the guards were far enough away so they did not see them pick up food that fell in the road. When the guards weren't looking I threw pieces of sandwiches to the prisoners in the street by their feet or through the fences where they stood.

I remember many guards watching the perimeter of the fence waiting to pounce on anyone that looked like they were doing something suspicious. Sometimes with sheer cruelty they bashed someone on the side of the head with the butts of their guns just to show they were in control. When I threw food over to the prisoners, they ran toward me, grabbing the food and eating it as fast as they could when the guards weren't looking. Some tried to hide it under their garments if they had any place left to conceal a morsel of food. Some were naked and had nowhere to keep the small ration from being seen. The captives knew they would be beaten or worse if they were seen picking up food from an outsider.

The prisoners they marched down the street were expected to stay standing while they marched and not stop for any reason. If one of them fell because they were too weak to stand, they were run over. No one could stop the march or they would be trampled or shot. Their bodies lay where they fell as an example to the other prisoners and the civilians. The Nazis wanted everyone to know the fate of anyone who broke their cruel directives.

It amazed me how many different languages were spoken by the prisoners in the concentration camps. Many of those languages I didn't speak, much less understand. None of them needed to tell me out loud they were hungry or sick. I'm not sure how many nationalities there were that were being held captive, but I could recognize at least five different languages being spoken by the prisoners.

## Chapter 52

Unlike the prisoners in the camp, the POWs that worked for Opa
Brase and Oma Engle were fed on a regular basis and had plenty of food to
eat like potatoes, vegetables, and bread.  Most of the time they were not
served meat because it was scarce during the war.  There was barely
enough meat to feed the family much less give good meat to forced
laborers.

During the war food was in short supply and it was necessary to
ration.  Starvation was a very real threat and everyone feared the available
provisions could easily be depleted.  I was fortunate to be living on or near
the Brase farm during most of the war.  The productivity of the farm left us
better off than most.  When we butchered a cow or a pig every piece was
used; nothing went to waste.

We butchered our own meat, salted the pork, and hung a steer or
pig carcass for days while the meat cured.  The heads of the animals, their
internal organs, brains, tongues, and the blood drained from their bodies
would be used to make various sausages and other dishes.  Sometimes we
made pickled pig's feet.  I remember stirring blood in a bucket for hours
that had drained from an animal so it would thicken and eventually turn
into blood sausage.  The heart, kidneys, and liver were cooked and served
as a main meat dish for some of our meals.

The men in the family and the hired hands seemed to favor the
internal organs more so than the women in the house.  From the animal
heads, we made head cheese.  Some actually found it to be quite tasty.  A
large pot was placed over a fire outdoors.  It was filled with fat strips cut
from the pig's skin to make lard.  We fried up leftover strips, called lard
crisps, and ate them with breakfast or as a snack.  The large pot cooked for
hours at high temperatures allowing the fat to melt away from the pig skin.
Eventually the fat turned into a liquid.  When it cooled but had not yet

hardened, we filled the crocks and other containers with the liquid. In time it set into a solid. In those times of struggle, we were grateful to have lard as part of our diet.

Nearly everyone was thin during the war and there never seemed to be enough food to keep a person's stomach full. Eating fat was a customary way to ensure good health. To survive any number of illnesses one could be subjected to, it was vital to include fat in our diets to maintain an adequate weight. A thin weakened body struggled to fight the ailments of the time.

Indulgences, like chocolate or any kind of candy or sweets in our diet were rare. Our meals were plain and basic and second helpings were unheard of. Your food was portioned, placed on your plate, and when it was gone you were done. During an occasional celebration, however, we would try to gather up more meats and desserts like baked tortes or cookies. It was considered a very special treat to have such items during war times. Mostly we ate speck (bacon), potatoes, and soups.

then four and we wondered how long this could continue. We were all packed in the small space, dirty, wet, uncomfortable, and cold. It was too dangerous to run back to the house for anything. The bombs, bullets, and grenades did not stop coming.

Huddled in the shelter I thought about Djura. He risked his own life to help my family. I was so grateful he had come into our lives. His concern for us, my children in particular, caused a stir of emotions. I let my mind wonder. Could an Austrian woman, widow of a German soldier, and a Serbian war prisoner come together and form a relationship? Would it even be allowed? So many questions and reservations ran through my head. I felt an intense desire to be close to and learn more about this man.

The fighting continued throughout the day and we hoped nightfall would bring an end to the battle. We were all very tired and hungry. I tried to make space in the shelter for the girls to rest. They were both exhausted and scared. With each loud boom and intense light from the explosions, their fear never subsided. They kept close to me all night long; both of them too afraid to move away.

That night drew to a close while the fighting escalated. We huddled in the muddy hole listening to the endless gunfire as bullets whizzed over our heads. No one slept that night. The girls dozed off for moments at a time only to be awakened by loud bangs from gunfire and booms from explosions. The next day came and went. We were stuck in the shelter with nowhere to escape. I felt sorry for Oma Engle having to endure this at her age. She sat in the mud and rain, wet and shaking as she prayed we wouldn't be killed.

We had been in the hand-dug, dirt shelter one full day and night. My stomach hurt and I was experiencing cramping. It became evident why I was feeling this way when I noticed a stickiness between my thighs. I discreetly looked, which was hard to do with all of us crammed together, and saw blood trickling down my inner thighs from my period. Even with our lives in very real danger, I was so embarrassed. I had no idea how long we would be stuck in the shelter. I had no supplies to clean the blood from myself or stop it from flowing. I tore a piece of material from the hem of my skirt, used it to clean myself and to help contain the blood. Survival for us all was my first concern, despite the shame and embarrassment I felt.

We endured a second day of terror burrowed in the hole without food or drink. While we sat on the drenched soil, staying warm was impossible. The girls, frightened out of their wits, screamed in terror when sudden explosions burst overhead and lit up the skies above us. Oma Engle, Djura and I tried to calm them with little success. We held them close and reassured them we would be alright. I held Anneliese in my arms most of the time so she wouldn't be as frightened. The fighting continued through the night and we were resigned to another sleepless night.

At daybreak the next morning the air was silent. The battle between the two opposing armies came to an end at last. The bullets had stopped flying and the explosions dwindled to a halt. Despite the quiet, we waited a few more hours to make certain the area was safe before we ventured outside the shelter walls. We scooped up the children in our arms and ran back to the house as fast as our legs would carry us. Things appeared safe at the time, yet everything happened by chance. The unpredictability of the situation made it impossible to know for sure if we were indeed safe or if another grenade, bullet or bomb might come our way.

## Chapter 55

My respect for Djura deepened after that day. He had shown me such compassion during the two days and nights burrowed together, it felt natural to relax my guard with him. He had gone out of his way to come to the aid of my family and myself and had kept us safe. He had put his own life on the line for not only me but also for Opa Brase and Oma Engle. From that day forward Opa Brase began to see Djura in a different light as well. He had watched Djura racing in from the field to warn us all of the incoming fire and danger. This heroic act of courage helped Opa Brase develop a newfound respect for Djura.

After days of not having bombs dropped, the girls and I ventured off to Sandbostel to buy some needed supplies. I rode my bike to town. Anneliese sat in the front basket while Ingeborg rode on the back. We hadn't been riding down the road long when I heard plane engines rumbling. We were near the bridge that lay close to the farm. Without haste I peddled to the bridge. We got there just in time for me to throw my girls in the river under the bridge where I joined them until the bombing stopped and we were able to come out from hiding. We came out from under the bridge dripping wet. They had bombed the area heavily. Standing on the river bank we saw trees that had been uprooted and buildings that were totally destroyed. We were lucky to have survived another bombing.

I worried about my children and the impact on them having witnessed the atrocities of war and the effects it would have on them at that time and for the rest of their lives. How I, as their mother, had found it terribly difficult, to shield their small bodies from harm and innocent eyes from witnessing such savagery. Anneliese was almost three-years-old and Ingeborg had just turned four in March. They learned at a very young age the real threat of war and the need to protect oneself from harm.

One memory held to this day was Ingeborg witnessing a neighbor being blown to pieces when his horse and buggy rolled over a landmine. She stood in the yard watching his horse and buggy hit the mine. She saw him, the buggy and the horse explode blasting them into pieces. The driver's and the animal's remains lay scattered and broken in a nearby field. The man was killed instantly. My poor little daughter had witnessed the entire event. Fragments of his charred body lay on the ground. He never had a chance. How could these children ever forget such horrific sights? The sadness of the reality was they never would.

Many landmines had been placed close to the farm and no one knew exactly where they all were buried. I was never sure which path was safe, every step a life or death decision. Every trip to town for needed goods or supplies could have been our last.

Some of the German soldiers in the area knew where many of the mines were, although most times they weren't around to warn us where the mines had been buried. Many local citizens died as collateral damage. An unfortunate but normal consequence of war. We found our best hope was to walk the exact route we knew was safe from previous travels. This worked most of the time, although sometimes the Nazis buried landmines in new locations.

## Chapter 56

Even with all the dangers the girls managed to experience some fun, playing with their dolls inside the house and on rare occasions outdoors. Although they had few toys, both Anneliese and Ingeborg each had their own doll. Ingeborg had a little baby buggy she put her doll in and strolled around the house.

It was war time and buying toys was not a concern for any parent. We had much bigger things to worry about so one doll for each daughter seemed enough and was all we could manage to afford. My girls used their imaginations to make up games to play or used household items pretending they were toys. They spent a great deal of time playing house, talking, singing, and dancing with each other.

They drew pictures for hours and made up stories. Anneliese enjoyed annoying her sister and stole away her sister's drawings and sometimes ripped them in half. Most of time fights began when Anneliese antagonized her older sister. I tried to distract Anneliese with something else and at times that worked. There were other times she wasn't about to listen and pestered Ingeborg all the more. Anneliese didn't pay me much mind when I asked her to stop. If she had her mind set on something she was determined to get it done. She also had an innocence about her and her overabundance of sweetness more than made up for her defiance. It was impossible not to love this little girl. I thought of her willful personality as a positive characteristic.

**Below is a picture of Anneliese when she was four-years-old.**

Anneliese was a charming little girl. She captivated nearly everyone with her pleasant personality and her persuasive blue eyes. She wasn't the favorite in the family, however, since Oma Engle catered to Ingeborg and spoiled her more. Perhaps it was because she was the first born grandchild that Ingeborg seemed to effortlessly capture Oma Engle's heart. I could tell Oma Engle truly loved her and gave her lots of special attention. Oma Engle always sneaked Ingeborg special treats if there were any baked goods to be had, and many times the other children didn't get the same treat as she. Aunt Anne sensed the favored treatment, and believed her children should be treated the same as Inga. Oma Engle's coddling caused some obvious tension between Ingeborg and her Aunt Anne. Over the years their relationship seemed to improve and the envy dissipated some, yet I don't believe Anne ever fully let go of her resentment toward Ingeborg.

We did have our good moments. My girls and I had many enjoyable times together while we lived with Oma Engle and once we moved to our own home. We began creating our own personal traditions. We also started several daily and nightly rituals we practiced for years. When the girls got ready for bed they laughed and giggled and never wanted to go to sleep. I told them a story or sang them a song right before they went to bed. I thought this helped quiet them down and because they enjoyed listening so much. We said our prayers together, faithfully, every night. After we talked to God we relaxed and slowly drifted off to sleep. My girls always tried to get me to tell them one more story or sing one more song right before they finally fell asleep. It was impossible to say no to them. I kept them entertained by singing one more bedtime song. They generally would be satisfied after I sang and finally drifted off to sleep.

**One of the prayers we recited every night before we went to sleep went like this:**

**Mein Hartz ist Klein**
**Mein Hartz mach rein**
**Darf neimad drin wonnen**
**Als Jesus alien**

**Translation: My heart is small, my heart is pure, and no one may come into my heart but Jesus alone.**

To this day Ingeborg says this prayer every night before she goes to sleep. Every one of my children was given a hand-stitched pillow in adulthood with these same words to remind them of the bedtime prayers we said together when they were just little girls.

**Another simple prayer that we said together at bedtime every night:**

**Lieber Gott**
**Mach mich fhrom**
**Das Ich in den Himel Kom**

**Translation: Dear God make me holy so I can go to Heaven.**

When they finally drifted off to sleep, I gazed upon their faces as they slept so peacefully. Their unconditional love was precious, a priceless gift no one could ever take away from me. Caring for my girls made it possible for me to overlook the uncertainties of war, let go of all the heartache, and feel an overwhelming contentment so heavy it overshadowed all of the bad things that were happening in my life. I could only think of the love I felt for my children and hope for our futures.

## Chapter 57

Djura was given more freedom every day. He was able to come and go with little explanation as to where he was and what he had been doing. Opa Brase also trusted Djura more. He didn't mind if I had an occasional conversation with Djura or if I sat and visited with him for a short time after supper in the dining area. Djura visited me after he was done working. He and I had many heartfelt talks before it was time to turn in for bed. He was becoming a close friend. I was able to confide in him telling many things about myself and my past. He began to confide more in me as well.

I continued to develop strong feelings for Djura and it seemed he was doing the same. During one of our evening conversations, Djura shared the feelings he was having for me. With some hesitation, I told him I felt the same way. Djura didn't have the freedom nor was it acceptable for him to court me openly. Everything we did together had to be kept a secret from the rest of the Brase family. I couldn't act as though he were my equal or openly share my thoughts and feelings about him. Things would have been much easier for us if he had come from a German family. It was hard for me to believe Opa Brase and Oma Engle would ever accept Djura in any role other than a forced labor farmhand.

As the months passed we became much closer. I began caring for him in ways I didn't think were possible after losing Hinrich. He proved to me he was a trustworthy and honorable man, which drew me closer to him. He was becoming a trusted friend of the family as well. Djura was considered more acceptable in Opa Brase's eyes as being someone they would associate with and have into their home. Yet their prejudices were apparent and I didn't think they would ever learn to overcome them.

Djura wasn't as well educated as Hinrich and wasn't able to express his feelings for me in the same heartfelt way, yet I was attracted to him. He wasn't a sweet talker like Hinrich nor did he have the ability to always say just the right thing to make me feel special. He instead showed me he cared about me through his actions of endearment and thoughtfulness. One of the most attractive qualities Djura possessed was his sense of humor. He had a way of making me laugh even amidst the violence, destruction and death around us.

I was beginning to fall in love with this man and wanted to know more about his family and his upbringing. Djura told me he had grown up in a small village in Serbia called Kormont near the town Sabac. His family was very poor and lived on a few acres of land. His father, Luka, was a mean, callous man. He drank too much and without provocation beat Djura's mother or his children if he felt the urge to lash out and hurt someone.

Djura, like most boys in Serbia, had to quit school after the sixth grade. He then went to trade school to make money to help support himself and his family. He grew up in a poor village and at age 16 finished trade school and became a blacksmith. He didn't make much money being a blacksmith, and didn't have much left over after paying for his clothing. He said he usually made enough money to buy his own clothes and if necessary he would borrow money from his sisters if he needed anything else. His sisters worked on neighboring farms to bring income into the home.

He was the oldest child in his family and the only son. The entire family worked, except for Luka, helping to contribute to the family's welfare whenever possible. The family worked on their own few acres raising some crops and a few farm animals. His sisters went as far as the third grade in school because girls were not expected to get an education. Most girls never went to school. They stayed home doing what was considered traditional women's work, hoping to marry someday and find a man that was able to provide and take care of them.

His father, Luka, was a manipulative and cruel man once alcohol entered his system. He severely beat the children and Djura's mother, Leposava, without reason or remorse. Djura's father was bigger and stronger than Djura, which made things more dangerous and complicated when Luka got intoxicated and came home drunk.

Although Luka was a mean drunk, Djura told about the few times when he saw him sober. When Luka was sober he was a hard worker and was one of the best people and fathers in the world. Once intoxicated, however, the person closest to him was in the most danger. He was a fighter and Plum Brandy (Slivovitz) was Luka's choice of liquor. Slivovitz was a popular 100 proof brandy in Yugoslavia. Luka, his friends, and many other men in the village got together often to drink. Luka drank nearly every day. Some days he drank Slivovitz until he couldn't stand.

Djura went on to say that everyone in the household walked on eggshells when Luka was around. When he was drunk they all hoped nothing would set him off and throw him into a rage. Djura remembered at age four he witnessed his father beating his mother severely. He recalled trying to help his mother by yelling at his father to stop and jumped on his back. He hit Luka many times thumping him on the back trying to get him off of his mother so he would leave her alone.

Djura fortunately, did not get his work ethic from his father. Luka didn't work much on the farm or anywhere else for that matter. He was lazy and tried to escape work or any type of responsibility whenever possible. The rest of the family banded together and tried to help each other to make up for their father's lack of financial and emotional support.

Djura had a very traumatic childhood especially with such an abusive father, however, he came out of his childhood with hope and determination to not repeat his father's mistakes. He wanted children of his own someday and, with a crooked smile, said he hoped they wouldn't get into as much mischief and trouble as he did when he was a boy. Having few possessions, Djura used his imagination when he was younger to create adventures as he roamed the countryside. Djura told me many humorous stories about his family and his own childhood. One story I believe is worth repeating and Djura tells the story like this:

*Well the Gendarme, you know, is a soldier who is employed doing police duties. It was around 1930, I'm not sure how old I was back then, what the hell, I think I was about 13-years-old or so. It was a nice day and I normally would find things to do outside like exploring the countryside close by our farm. Sometimes I walked for miles searching for something to do, not purposely looking to get into mischief, although sometimes my pranks managed to get me into some kind of a mess.*

*Most days when I set out I was looking to find ways to burn off energy and satisfy my own curiosity. Part of the thrill and excitement in my explorations was when I would discover newfound devices, gadgets, or trails when scouting the neighborhood. I could always find something to do and would never get bored just hanging out in the woods or the countryside. I could stay busy all day long just walking on a nice day and sometimes joining up with friends or neighbors. Our group of boys found trouble and created a bit of chaos in the neighborhood from time to time. In the midst of trouble we'd take off running to avoid getting caught or having our identity discovered.*

*This particular day, I was by myself and decided to head down toward the river. I started walking on the path that led to the hill where we had a community garden. There were a lot of gardens that had been planted on the hill that year. Everything was growing nicely with tall tomato plants, onions, and other vegetables popping out of the ground. Most of the adults who kept gardens were out every day. They worked hard in their gardens hoping to have a substantial crop to harvest at the end of every summer.*

*Several trees surrounded the gardens so it was a nice quiet place to just sit and relax, soak up the sun, and be lazy. No one was working in their gardens as I wandered by so I didn't have to worry that someone was going to make me pull weeds. The neighbor's land joined our property and they didn't care if we roamed about their place as long as we didn't make any trouble. I decided to investigate what I might find in the small river near the gardens hoping to find something of value.*

*I was barefoot most of the summer, so I rolled up my pants and stepped into the stream. I had only been wading for a short time when I stepped on an object that felt hard and pointy. I couldn't resist bending over to pick it up to investigate what the thing was. It was metallic, round, grayish black, and weighed close to a pound. It had red spots all over it and looked as though it had rusted from laying in the water too long. It was small enough I could easily hold it in my hand and it had a metal clip at the top of the egg shaped ball.*

*Examining it closer a wave of excitement passed through me realizing I was holding a grenade. I assumed it must have been left from battles during WWI. Grenades and other explosives targeted a large area during the war and occasionally I heard stories of explosives from WWI being found by other villagers in our area. For a moment I thought about the potential danger, but that was soon replaced with a desire to see if it still worked.*

*A plan began to formulate in my head. I thought the hill where the family gardens were would be the perfect place to test it. The plan was to burrow a hole in the earth, place the grenade in the hole, and start a fire under it to see if would explode. I never gave much thought to the grenade possibly blowing up while I was handling it, although I had convinced myself it would likely be a dud. It must have lay in the river under water for at least ten to 15 years. How could it still work?*

*I dug a good sized hole in the ground on the side of the hill. I remembered soldiers in our village telling stories of having to handle grenades in the war and the need to jump into bunkers for safety when they blew up to protect themselves from the explosion. Considering this, I dug a hole then built a circle of dirt around it, placing the grenade at the*

217

*bottom with just enough room to start a fire around and under it. Next, I packed dirt firmly around it and using matches, I started a fire. After the fire was lit I pulled the pin and ran for cover. For some reason I thought if the grenade blew up it would blow straight up from the ground and all the force would shoot everything upwards toward the sky. I ran away from the lit fire, lay down on the ground on the other side of the hill, and patiently waited for something exciting to happen.*

*Everything was quiet. Nothing happened for a few moments and I was disappointed there were no fireworks. I was about to get up to see what had happened when I heard a big boom from the grenade exploding. The explosion raised all kinds of hell, blowing up plants and the trees that were nearby. It blew a tree right out of the ground roots and all. The gardens were in pitiful shape, dead plants lay 20-yards from the hill and were scattered and shredded all over. I ran back home as fast as I could.*

*The neighbors must have called the Gendarme. The Gendarme came looking for me at my house and questioned me. Someone must have spotted me out and about that day and shared this information with the police. Upon arriving home, I only told my uncle who lived with us about the explosion. The Gendarme questioned my entire family, however were unable to prove I was involved. My uncle staying quiet saved me from some possible jail time.*

## Chapter 58

Djura had no pictures of his father to show me, but described him as a tall stocky man with lighter brownish hair and brown eyes. Djura said he didn't resemble his father much, and he looked more like his mother. He possessed one old picture of his mother, Leposava and his sisters. There were actually seven girls in the Stefanovic family, although only five sisters are listed below. Known names of his sisters were Tamanija, Angelina, Janatija, Krsmanija, and Peladija.

**Three of Djura's sisters and his mother are pictured below with Leposava in the middle.**

I understand Djura's mother suffered the most when Luka drank. Leposava was a small woman who tried her best to protect herself against Luka when he became abusive. Since she was much smaller in stature than he, it was impossible for her to fend off the severe beatings when Luka lashed out at her and the children.

When Djura was big enough to protect his mother, his sisters and himself, he made sure his father could no longer hurt them. There were many occasions when Djura intervened on his mother's behalf. Often the arguments between them turned physical with someone usually getting hurt. A couple of Luka's brothers lived with them and would physically restrain Luka to protect Djura's mother from his vicious temper.

The sound of commotion triggered an alarm for Luka's brother to rush to Leposava's aid and attempt to stop the beatings. Luka was usually too drunk to listen, his temper flared, and he turned his rage onto his own brother or anyone else that dared to interfere. Several confrontations between the brothers, and sometimes a brother-in-law also ended up in an altercation with Luka if it continued to escalate. Vitomir, his brother-in-law or Vojslav, his brother, usually stopped Luka by physically overpowering and restraining him. Many times the brothers had to knock Luka to the floor or wrestle him to the ground to settle him.

During one of the many beatings, Djura came into the house as Luka was screaming and beating his mother. When Djura told him to stop, Luka, angered by the interference searched in the house for a knife to stab Djura. As Luka searched for a knife, Djura called him a coward for beating his mother and dared him to a knife fight. Djura carried his own knife and boldly challenged his father to take it from him if he wanted a knife so bad. Djura told Luka, "Let's see how strong you are against a man rather than a defenseless woman, and we'll see who settles this fight."

Djura said when he offered Luka his knife it surprised and frightened his father causing him to back down once he was challenged. Luka was drunk and he realized his son was no longer a little boy. He could no longer take him down or get the best of him. Djura declared he had no doubt his father would have stabbed him given the chance that day. Djura explained, "That's just the way he was when he drank, he became cruel and violent."

Djura recalls another violent outrage when he was 17-years-old. His father had come home once again intoxicated and began beating his wife. He slapped and punched her turning her face black and blue. Djura, hearing his mother's screams for help ran toward her. By the time Djura arrived on the scene, Luka was sitting on top of his mother punching her in the face. Djura picked up a small wooden three-legged stool that sat in the living room, swung it as hard as he could hitting his father in the back of the head, knocking him out cold.

Leposava was a passive woman. She felt trapped in her situation, afraid and unable to leave. She had eight children, lived in poverty, and was an uneducated farm girl. Her children were all at home and she was afraid to leave them alone with Luka. Divorce was not an option for women in the village of Kormont during that era, even if they were beaten and mistreated. The patriarchal society left men in charge of providing financially for the family and it was common for the man of the house to have the final say in any important family matters. Women were expected to honor their husband's wishes without question. There was no such thing as a democracy between a husband and wife. Most of the time the wife did as she was told. Fortunately not all men in the village behaved like Luka. They treated the women in their life with kindness and respect.

Luka was known as a deserter and had gone AWOL many times while he was in the service. He was drafted during WWI and WWII by the Yugoslavian army, but soon after being drafted, he escaped from duty returning home for refuge. Djura remembered him being at home while being AWOL. Luka was still dressed in his uniform as he tried to hide from the army police to avoid being forced to return to duty. Luka was afraid of being killed. Both Luka and Djura were drafted by the Yugoslavian army during WWII. Luka was 42-years-old at the time. Luka again deserted while Djura moved up in ranks until he was captured by the Germans. King Peter II was the new leader of Yugoslavia at the time of the Nazi invasion. He along with other government officials fled the country.

Following Germany's annexation of Yugoslavia, two Serbian anti-Nazi guerilla groups developed. As the two groups got organized, Djura was held captive in a German war prison. Throughout the time of the Nazi occupation of Yugoslavia, the Nazis as well as their Croat, Bosnian Muslim, and Kosovo Albanian collaborators met stiff resistance from the Serbian people organized in two anti-fascist movements. The first to fight the Nazis in Serbia were the Royalists led by Serbian Royal Officer Draža Mihajlović. This group was known as Chetniks. The second resistance movement was led by Croat Communist Josip Broz Tito. These fighters were known as Partisans.

Both Tito and Mihajlović were not only focused on forcing the Nazis out of their country, but each had their own political agendas. General Mihajlović was loyal to King Peter II and the Kingdom. He dreamed of the day when King Peter II returned from exile and the country would return to its former government. Tito, on the other hand wanted to take advantage of the turmoil caused by the war and take control of the country himself. His goal was to change the political system and to prevent the King's return.

(http://www.srpska-mreza.com/History/after-ww2/Chetnik-betrayal.html)

While open to be joined by anyone who wanted to fight, both guerilla groups were overwhelmingly Serbian. The common Serbs would join one of the two forces almost at random. Luka joined the Mihajlović group. The Nazis occupying Yugoslavia fought to kill any person affiliated with either group.

The Nazis suspected Luka was an enemy collaborator. They approached him one day while he and his brother-in-law Vitomir walked up the hill together near the family gardens. Vitomir lived in a different town during this time, and unfortunately happened to be visiting Luka that day. The Nazis questioned Luka about his affiliation with the guerillas. Luka pleaded he was a civilian and fully supported the Nazi Regime. As the soldiers questioned Luka, a Nazi tank rumbled loudly as it approached the men while they talked.

Hearing the approaching tank, Luka and his brother panicked and started to run. The tank revved its engine and chased both men down as they ran up the hill. The tank caught up to them easily. The tank rolled over both men crushing them underneath its tracks. Their bodies too damaged from the devastating force, they were never recovered for burial. Luka met an untimely and gruesome death at the age of 43.

## Chapter 59

It was imperative that Djura and I keep our relationship a secret. Oma Engle and Opa Brase liked Djura as a farm hand, although he was still considered an *unter menschen* (sub human) by most other Germans. I was at a point where I no longer cared what others thought and found it a Godsend to have someone to talk to who cared about me. Someone whom I trusted and had begun to care for deeply.

Another young lady, who came from the East, also lived with the Brases. I had gotten to know her quite well. She had been kidnapped from her home in the 30's when Hitler began his reign of terror in Europe. Tina was her name and she had been forced to work on the local farms after her own abduction. Tina was a pretty 25-year-old woman and did what she was told to do in order to survive after her abduction. Eventually she ended up being placed on the Brase farm where we worked together to feed and serve the war prisoners.

Working alongside Tina, I noticed she had her eye on Djura. She flirted with him at every opportunity. I also noticed the way she moved in close to talk to him and lingered while serving him. I'm sure she was drawn to his good looks. I found myself becoming jealous when Djura returned her friendliness. I hoped he wasn't confiding in her as he had been with me. I believed Djura felt the same towards me as I did for him, but was uncertain if he desired a long-term future with me.

With the war and our current situations it was hard for either of us to look too far into the future. I had two young girls to raise. Djura remained a war prisoner. He had never been married or had children. He seemed responsible enough, treated my girls kindly, and cared about them. To be honest, I felt uncertain about the future and was unsure how this man fit into my life. I didn't look forward to hearing about how a relationship like ours would never work from Oma Engle and the rest of the family.

In the spring of 1945 there was much talk about the war ending. We were hopeful, but unsure what our futures held even if the war did end. I continued to work on the farm with Oma Engle every day. I got lonely staying in our small home all by myself at times. I stayed at Oma Engle's often with the girls as they wanted to stay overnight with their grandmother. I didn't want to be alone at night.

One night while at Oma Engle's I had put the girls to sleep. They were tired from playing all day long and went to bed easily. Before I went to bed myself I checked all the doors and windows to make sure no one could get in the house. I often left my bedroom window cracked open just a bit. I needed some fresh air and liked to feel the cool breeze flutter against my skin. Most nights I fell asleep as I listened to the wind blow, the cow moo in the pasture, or to the soft clucks of the chickens as they settled down to sleep. I never left the window wide open because I was too afraid someone might crawl through with the intentions to harm us.

Listening to the rustling noises from the animals outdoors usually put me to sleep. While I lay in my bed I heard tapping against my window. The noise startled me and I jumped hastily out of bed terrified someone was trying to get into my room. I recognized the man standing outside. Djura stood there laughing, obviously amused by my fright.

That evening Djura had snuck out of his barracks when he was supposed to be sleeping and came over to the house to see me. I told him to hush as he continued to laugh; afraid he would wake the others in the house. Anneliese was sleeping in bed with me, while Ingeborg slept with her grandmother. Anneliese hadn't heard a thing and didn't move a muscle. It would have taken a lot to wake her up that night. She had played hard that day and had fallen fast asleep.

I dreaded the thought of Oma Engle and Opa Brase waking. Djura said he made sure the guard was sound asleep before leaving the barracks.

Djura didn't seem stressed at all that he might be caught outside the camp. Apparently the guard drank a lot of whiskey that night. Djura said the guard drank often and if he drank enough, there was no waking him. He assured me there was no need to worry.

He intended to come in through the window and I pleaded with him to not take the risk. He climbed in anyway. I was afraid we would be caught for sure. We sat on the floor whispering for at least an hour. My ears were on high alert and I quieted Djura multiple times, certain I heard someone approaching. With each warning he giggled and reassured me no one was coming. We talked about the war possibly coming to an end in the near future and what that might mean for us. Djura told me he most definitely wanted me in his future. I continued to worry about being caught so I shooshed him back out the window. He gave me a sweet kiss on the cheek and we said our goodbyes. He returned to camp, but not before we made plans to meet this way again.

Every night when I was staying at Oma Engle's house we planned to meet if possible. After our first rendezvous he came and visited me often. I was soon brave enough to climb outside my window to join him. His nightly visits became more regular and sneaking about seemed to make our relationship all the more exciting and intriguing. Djura sometimes lied to the guard and said he needed to work late at the farm. We met up somewhere close by after my girls fell asleep and spent an hour or more together. I never stayed out too long for fear my girls might wake and call for me.

## Chapter 60

Djura and I wanted more time together so we came up with creative ways to meet. At times we picked a designated place on the farm when we were both supposed to be doing chores. We tried to arrange our errands into town or into the countryside at the same time so we could meet somewhere away from the farm. One of these meetings occurred on a beautiful spring day. I offered to go to town to pick up some items Oma Engle needed. When I was ready to leave Oma asked me why I wasn't riding my bike. I told her I wanted to take a nice long walk and because I wouldn't have much to carry back from the store, walking would be fine.

Djura and I left separately from the farm and found each other at a designated location close by. Once together, we walked toward town. We had decided to take a new route in hopes no one would see us. We took a path that ran parallel along a stretch of woods close by the farm. The wooded area contained thick shrubbery made for good coverage in case we needed to duck quickly and hide. The sun was shining that day and we both looked forward to getting away from the drudgery of our farm chores. I left with few questions from Oma Engle about my plans. She suspected nothing and trusted I was going to walk to town for the few supplies and out the door I went.

We headed toward Klenkendorf which fortunately remained largely intact. Many cities in Germany had suffered heavy destruction or were completely devastated during the past five years. With all of the destruction, a simple stroll to town was something to look forward to for both of us. Quiet, heartfelt moments together offered welcomed normalcy in our lives. I had grown to love Djura and felt safer when I was with him. We needed to be conscious of our surroundings as we walked since there were thugs who preyed upon the unsuspecting. They robbed and also harmed those who were unable to defend themselves.

We had walked for a few miles when Djura heard odd sounds coming from behind us. The sounds intensified and seemed to get closer as we continued to walk down the road. Looking behind us we were able to make out the outline of horse drawn wagons. We heard wheels clicking as the wagons rolled over the road and men's voices were audible as the wagons neared. Djura and I both knew we did not want to be seen together by SS soldiers.

We rushed to take cover before being seen. We hid behind some thick bushes along the side of the road. Both of us heard the wagons getting closer and closer. As they approached, we saw it was a German convoy coming down the road. Many soldiers walked alongside the convoy while others sat on benches that were constructed on top of the wagons. The horses and soldiers labored toward us. As the soldiers drew near I began to shake. Their voices became distinguishable when they got close enough that we could hear and understand them.

I was so frightened I tried to talk to Djura about what we should do and if we should run. Djura understood the trouble we were in and knew we needed to be silent. He whispered in a soft voice, told me to be quiet and to sit perfectly still. He was worried if we were caught by this band of SS soldiers' we would be instantly killed. He told me to hush and when I didn't, he held his left hand over my mouth gently, and quietly motioned for me to be quiet by putting his index finger of his right hand in front of his mouth.

We watched them travel toward the hillside and we could hear the soldiers as they talked about dumping the cargo they carried as they pointed towards the hillside just ahead of us. We sat quietly and peered through a small opening in the bushes where we were hiding. Luckily none of the soldiers spotted us as the wagons rolled by.

The caravan moved to the south and headed up the hill. The wooden wagons were large and appeared to be about 12 feet long and seven to eight feet wide. Without back gates, we were able to see what the SS soldiers were transporting as the wagons rolled by in front of us. It was difficult for my mind to comprehend what I saw with my eyes. My senses initially were not willing to accept the reality in front of me. I felt Djura's grip tighten around my mouth as he wrapped his other arm around me. I felt his strong frame shudder then stiffen against my back. I knew then he also recognized the contents of the wagons.

It was horrific to witness. Toward the back, I could see the wagons had been filled to the tops with the bodies of men, women and children. Some were clothed, while others were stark naked. They were as thin as skeletons and piled high, one on top of the other, like a load of lumber all stacked into a messy pile. I knew I had to stay quiet, but I found it so very hard not to scream out. I probably would have if Djura hadn't kept my mouth covered.

The mountain of bodies rose high, rounded in a clump, and heaped up above the side boards. Many looked like they could easily have fallen off the wagon to the ground. I was surprised none of them did as high as they were piled. Seeing the many tortured and starved corpses, I imagined the misery they must have experienced and it repulsed me. They lay every which way in the wagons, some faced up others faced down, thrown in like garbage.

Djura didn't trust I would keep quiet. He thought I might still let out a scream so he kept my mouth covered with his hand and whispered to me to keep quiet. He told me once more we were in mortal danger and would both be shot and killed if discovered. I was terrified and shook in horror. Both Djura and I knew it was forbidden to witness these Nazi activities and we knew, beyond a shadow of doubt, if we were seen we'd be dead. We had to remain behind the bushes until they were out of sight.

Some of the bodies that were lain in the wagons no longer looked human. I had to turn my head and stop looking. I covered my eyes with my hands because I couldn't stand it anymore. There were at least four or five wagons full. The odor from the dead was indescribable and lingered along the roadside.

The hill wasn't far from where we hid and when they reached the top, the wagons all came to a stop. We watched as the soldiers, one by one, climbed up the hill with their wagons. Djura and I continued to watch while the drivers pulled their loaded wagons up to what looked like a giant crater that had been dug into the ground. Each one took their turn backing up their wagons to the edge of the pit, then emptied their load of dead bodies into the gigantic hole. The gravesite was unlike anything I had ever seen. One by one, hundreds of bodies tumbled into the pit, thrown with less thought or respect than the soldiers would have given a bag of trash. We sat for the longest hours of our lives watching them dump the dead, unable to move. The soldiers were unaware of their audience.

Djura held very still, whispered and pointed at his ear as he motioned for me to listen. He heard a voice crying. It was someone crying for help. The voice came from one of the wagons that had been backed up close to the pit. Djura heard moaning and then a scream for help. The words at first sounded muffled, then became much clearer.

I then recognized it as a man's voice yelling for help. He pleaded for his life. He shouted out words in his given language saying, "Hey brate, Ja sam jos ziv! Ja sam jos ziv!" ("Hey brother, I am still alive! I am still alive!") He was a Serbian prisoner who had been thrown in the back of the wagon at the concentration camp. He had been buried under many of the other dead in the wagon, a mountain of corpses lay heavily on top of him. He was trying to dig himself out from under them all, raising his arms for someone to help him.

Then others that were still alive and trapped started yelling for help. Those calling out were speaking Russian, trying to communicate they were still alive. The trapped men were helpless, unable to free themselves. They were too weak to work themselves out from under the mass of the dead. We saw the men were still alive as they waved their arms, begging for someone to help them. I couldn't stand hearing their cries. I was sickened by the brutality I witnessed.

The first man continued to yell for help at the SS soldiers, he yelled over and over, "Brother, I am still alive! I am still alive!" The SS soldiers didn't care, and paid him no mind. One of the soldiers yelled back to the Serbian man saying "Ne Brate, doktor kase da si mrtav!" (No brother, the doctor says that you are dead!) He laughed, turned and walked away leaving the man to be dumped into the mass grave.

The soldiers dumped the entire wagon of bodies, including the men who yelled for help, into the pit. I wished I could have stopped listening as I heard the words yelled out over and over "I'm alive! I'm alive!" The Nazis didn't bother to listen or help them. It was an agonizing sight no one should ever have to endure. Their screams became muffled; the wagon where they had lain was empty. None of the victims were strong enough to climb out of the massive hole. After all the bodies were in the hole they were doused with gasoline, set on fire and burned. The screams of those not yet dead were unbearable. After the flames and screams died down, the soldiers buried what was left not caring if any remained alive.

We weren't sure, but thought all those people who had been transported to the gravesite had come from the concentration camps nearby. I was never sure how many of the victims in those wagons were still living and breathing. We could only tell by the ones we heard that still had the strength to scream out for help.

I cried for all those who had suffered and died that day. No one in the back of those wagons could have possibly survived. I prayed to God while all this happened it would stop. It happened anyway. I did not understand how God would let something like this happen to so many innocent people.

After the Nazis dumped all the bodies, they drove off like nothing had happened; as if it had been a routine daily occurrence. The soldiers were immune to the horror, no remorse or compassion was displayed. No one tried to intervene or change the course of their actions. They appeared exempt from any kind of emotion. Djura and I had borne witness to true evil.

I continued to pray for an end to the war and such savagery. My only solace was knowing the concentration camp victims who had died and were thrown into that mass grave were no longer suffering or in pain. Their suffering was over. I knew if heaven existed those poor souls had to be there. What we witnessed broke my heart, haunted my waking and sleeping moments.

Following such a sight, I began to recognize how I had changed. War strips away humanity, it breaks your faith, unfairly steals away your ability to grieve and creates a numbness in part of your soul that for me was everlasting. To this day I still have nightmares, haunted by the voices of those who were still alive. I try hard not to think about those things, but the memories intrude my consciousness, never truly gone.

After the Nazis left, Djura and I looked at each other in dismay, unable to speak. We left and did not look back. It was too awful. I had to try and make my mind forget what I had just seen. It was necessary to forget for my own sanity. I needed to get back home. I needed to be with my girls and be reminded there was still good in this world.

## Chapter 61

The world learned Nazi soldiers in Italy surrendered to the Allies on May 8th of 1945. World War II in Europe had ended. The Americans and the British became heavily involved in patrolling the area where I lived.

The Red Cross planes flew over the prison camps and dropped care packages full of supplies for the prisoners that had survived. The acts of kindness from the Red Cross gave everyone renewed hope the war had really come to an end. We looked toward a better future for all of us. It was wonderful to know someone was there to help us and they cared about what had been happening in Germany over the last five years.

The Americans and British were stationed in many places in Germany helping those imprisoned in the camps. Djura and I were now able to walk freely about without worry we'd be in serious trouble. We learned of a plan in place to release all prisoners from the camps and from their work details on the farms. It didn't seem like there were enough American or British troops stationed in Klenkendorf and the surrounding area to take care of all the needs of the people who had been abused so terribly during the war.

The number of Allied soldiers were sparse other than the groups of American and British soldiers that had been stationed in the prison camps close to the farm. The Americans and British took over the prison camps. Some combat on the ground continued with Nazi stragglers unwilling to give up the fight as they battled to their deaths. There was gunfire and grenades being thrown and various other light artillery being used to fend off adversaries.

Along with the end of the war nearly all of the prisoners of war (POWs) had been released from the concentration camps in Germany. These lost souls roamed the streets, the countryside, and the cities. Most of the former captives were forlorn, having lost their dignity and self-respect. Many had lost their entire families, friends, and anyone that had meant anything to them. The war had taken a huge toll on millions. The POWs newfound freedom had brought them out into a country that was unfamiliar, unfriendly, and a place where they were considered outsiders and unwanted.

At least nine or ten different ethnic groups who had been held in the camps throughout the war had been released. Some were enraged and full of resentment toward the German people. I did not begrudge any of them for the way they felt. They were treated like criminals and subhuman filth. I was appalled and horrified by what I had witnessed through the years. The pain, torture, forced labor, cruelty, and countless murders that took place by the Nazis came back to haunt those who perpetrated such evil.

Innocent bystanders also suffered the consequences of the Nazi's massive crimes. Unconfined and free, some former POWs were uncontrolled, able to commit their own atrocities, and take their revenge out on those who lived close by. They had been damaged by their hunger, torture, and had no money. They needed to fend for themselves, looking for food, work, or just a place to rest. Others were more than ready to steal to get what they wanted or needed; some willing to kill.

So many POWs looked for revenge and wanted the Germans to suffer in the same ways they had for so many years. They were ready to get even and wanted justice. Many of those who were incarcerated had survived being beaten, starved, tortured, and used for unethical and gruesome experimentation. Their bodies cut, bones broken, limbs severed, or parts surgically removed. Many had been forced to undergo and tolerate unbearable pain for extended periods of time. I feared all of us who lived in Germany were in danger. Even though I had never supported Hitler's regime, and despised him for what he had done to me and millions more, this did not set me or anyone who associated with the Germans, apart from the Nazis by those who sought revenge.

Some released prisoners plundered households. They raped and abused the women, including the very young and the very old. They burned belongings, destroyed property, and took what they wanted from the locals. It was as if the world had gone mad and these men had lost their minds. They were no longer able to comprehend there were good people left in the world. Some of the freed had also found guns to use. Other POWs carried spear like weapons and sabers to search for objects that had been buried in the ground, which they stole to trade for food and other material goods they wanted or needed.

When they broke into homes they didn't care if their victims were rich or poor, young or old, all they found or saw was for the taking. They did not hesitate to harm others. Many on the loose had threatened, intimidated, and terrorized the locals. They pocketed whatever they could carry, using the livestock they stole for food or to carry what they had robbed from the surviving citizens.

The joy and relief we felt with the war's end was short-lived. Post war by all rights, should have been a time to heal and recover, however, in Germany I had a different experience. It was a time that proved to be just as treacherous and dangerous as the war. Some did not know or care that people like us had also suffered, had never condoned Hitler's ways, and never wanted anyone to suffer, or be treated inhumanly. There were no considerations if you lived with or associated with a German family. You were despised.

Djura was free himself with the ending of the war. With this freedom he was able to leave the farm and connect with other Serbs in Germany. He continued to stay and work for Opa Brase. There were no other jobs available in the area. He lived on the camp grounds staying in the old prisoner's barracks even though he had been released. This way he was able to stay close and we could continue to be together. Also as an ex-prisoner of war Djura really had no other choice for living arrangements at the time. The girls and I remained in the duplex just a few blocks from the farm but would stay with Oma Engle often. Djura and I decided for our safety to continue to keep our relationship a secret. It had not been easy to keep others from learning how fond I'd grown of Djura and about the love we now shared. Our relationship became increasingly difficult to hide. Though, I believe Oma Engle and Opa Brase had their suspicions.

The borders were being patrolled by the Americans and the British. Travel was not permitted anywhere outside of Germany. I wondered how we would ever get back to Austria to see my mother and father. I had hoped when the war ended, I would be able to move freely back and forth to Austria. It looked as if it would be a long time before we could legally travel into Austria. Visas and passports were not available to civilians for any reason. The passenger trains and many of the railways had been destroyed during the bombings, making travel anywhere in or out of the country more difficult.

The country remained war weary. It would take decades to repair all the damage done in the last five years. I had written to my mother and told her I planned to visit her sometime in the next year. I hoped by that time I could get a legitimate visa to travel to Austria. Djura said he would travel with me if I wanted and if he was permitted to leave work.

I was glad I had Djura helping me during those times. I was often frightened due to the circumstances that surrounded us. There were many Russian POWs that had been released and they seemed to be the most needy and vengeful. The American and the British soldiers patrolled the area as best they could, but there wasn't enough of them to keep order in the cities and countryside.

I was afraid to let my girls go outdoors alone because there were just too many dangerous men that came close to the farm. I was suspicious of any strangers or uniformed men. So many soldiers had been killed and their uniforms were stolen. It was impossible to trust anyone. Life was unsettled and there were many things we were unable to control. We stuck close to the farm and only made trips to town when absolutely necessary.

My friend Elke who worked on a neighboring farm came to me one day to share a horrific story. As she told me what had happened to her, my heart ached for her while at the same time I felt a sense of rage burning within me. Nearly 30 Russian soldiers that had been released from the camp broke into her home, took her captive, and forced her outside. They carried Elke out into the field cursing and mocking her for befriending a German. They beat her with their fists and sabers. Each of the men took their turn raping her. She pleaded for them to stop. She sobbed telling me she couldn't stop them no matter how hard she tried. Her body was bloody, beaten, ravaged and left for dead.

Bloodied and battered she lay in the field until someone was able to come save her after the soldiers left. She was ashamed such a thing had happened to her. She insisted she fought as hard as she could to fend them off. I tried to reassure her there was nothing she could have done. I hugged her trying to comfort my poor friend. Her misery and self-loathing after the incident was nothing I wanted for my girls, myself or any female to experience.

The Russians didn't care if you were 15 or 80-years-old. Their wrath was the most violent of all the POW's. If we saw Russians coming, we ran and hid. Years later, despite wanting children of her own, Elke was never able to have children. She blamed the Russian POWs for the damage they inflicted on her body.

## Chapter 62

It was a scorching hot day in August of 1945. Djura had gone to work in the fields. Oma Engle, Opa Brase, my girls, and I were at home doing our usual chores as we tried to get through another day. Tina and Mata were not home on this day and I don't recall their whereabouts. Mata was Opa Brases's mentally challenged sister and Tina was the young lady from the East who was a war prisoner and worked for the Brases.

It was close to mid-afternoon when I heard some commotion outside the house. Men talked and some yelled. I could hear them shouting at Opa Brase, and I saw them nudging him along. They pushed and shoved him, hitting him with their weapons. I wasn't able to tell exactly what was going on, but I knew right away it wasn't good. As I looked out the window I noticed there were perhaps 50, possibly up to 100 men outside our home. Some lay on the lawn all sprawled out, others limped as they walked toward the house. Some just stood, many were injured. They ordered Opa Brase to come to the house.

When I heard the men yelling, I instantly ran for my girls and rushed them into the bedroom. Oma Engle was in the house with me and went to the bedroom as well to help keep the girls calm and quiet. I told Ingeborg and Anneliese it was important to be very still because bad men were coming toward the house. Ingeborg was old enough to peek out the window when they first came and saw the angry and injured soldiers laying in the front yard. Anneliese was crying as I tried to quiet her, putting my hand gently over her mouth. Ingeborg was four-and-a-half-years-old at the time, yet she realized she needed to be perfectly still while they hid in the bedroom. I told them to be very quiet and not to make a peep.

We hid the girls under the bed. Both girls were afraid and Anneliese, still so little, wanted to come out from under the bed to be with me. I handed Anneliese her doll and motioned to Ingeborg to keep

Anneliese quiet. She did what she was told. I needed to leave them before any of the men came in the house and I prayed neither one of my girls would come out from hiding until the men were gone. As I walked out of the room I told the girls not to come out for any reason and when the men were gone, and it was safe, I would come back to the bedroom to get them.

The girls stayed shut away in the bedroom quiet and did not make a sound. Eventually Oma Engle came out to the kitchen where I was standing to help me. We stayed in the kitchen because we hoped to keep the intruders away from the bedroom if they entered the house. We prayed the men wouldn't search our home. Many of the men that lay on the ground were injured and we could tell they were Russian from the language they spoke. We looked out the window at Opa Brase. Oma Engle and I saw the men wanted Opa Brase to help them. A few of the men were coming toward the house. My heart began to pound in my chest. We were in grave danger.

I needed to protect us. My mind raced to think of a way to get us out of the situation unharmed. I quickly ran into the bedroom where Oma Engle slept and looked for some of her old clothes to wear. I found an old tattered dress, a ragged old scarf and some wore-out, muddy old boots. I changed my clothes as fast as I could. I messed and tangled my hair, then shoved it over the top of my face. I quickly snuck out the back door into the barn where I smeared dirt and cow manure all over myself. I tried to look as old and undesirable as I could in hopes the men would leave me alone.

One of the soldiers out in the yard was all banged up and needed his wounds dressed. I heard one of them that spoke German tell Opa Brase to go get some bandages out of the house. Opa Brase flatly refused to help and told them he would not tend to any of the man's injuries. I heard the Russian soldier get angry and threaten Opa Brase. He ordered him to bandage the injured man's wounds. He refused so they beat him.

The men outside had served in the Russian army prior to being captured and many of them were carrying sabers. They also held long sticks with sharp homemade swords tied to the end so they could poke and prod the ground. They walked as they searched and covered every inch of the ground in the yard and the nearby field. They stabbed and poked the earth, searching for trinkets, goods, and anything they thought we had buried to hide from them. The vandals learned locals buried much of their property to keep it safe and began looking for objects we or other farmers had hidden or buried in the ground.

We had buried many of our valuables outdoors in the fields, after hearing about the robberies. We hoped to save some of our more valued possessions after we heard of their pillaging and had buried them to keep them protected. We buried jewelry, keepsakes, clothing, food, and whatever else we felt we needed to hide and keep safe. This group of Russians who invaded our front yard weren't about to leave until they had found something they thought was worth stealing. The soldier's pierced the ground with their sabers and looked for any freshly dug ground, raised or mounded dirt.

Opa Brase happened to be the only man close to the house that day. He was getting up in years and, though he was still fit, he wasn't nearly strong enough to fend off so many volatile trespassers. They had already beaten him up for not cooperating earlier and threatened to harm us all if he didn't do what he was told. Opa Brase had been forced by the soldiers to bandage up their wounded. He tried his best to distract them to keep them away from the house, Oma Engle, the girls, and me. It was only a matter of time before they forced their way inside, and searched for more things to rob, steal, or destroy.

I was more frightened than Oma Engle and worried about what they would do to us when they came inside. I went back to the bedroom one more time and told the girls to be very quiet and not make any noise because the bad men outside were walking toward the house. The girls stayed hidden safely under the bed where I hoped they wouldn't be found. Ingeborg and Anneliese were terrified, their little bodies frozen from fright. At such a young age Ingeborg had already witnessed what could happen to her if she didn't lie quiet under the bed.

Ingeborg had seen the family of six slaughtered and the neighbor blown to pieces after hitting a land mine. How much more could this little girl stand? My girls had learned very early in life if they wanted to survive they needed to do what they were told. Many times we had to hide both Anneliese and Ingeborg under mattresses, in a closet, or under a bed. Those who pillaged our homes and villages were evil. Danger surrounded us. We hadn't had an incident yet where intruders had harmed the children and did our best to keep them hidden. I didn't trust any of strangers even if they were just asking for food.

I returned to the kitchen as ten of the POWs entered the house. Once inside they began making demands. My thoughts did not leave my girls. Opa Brase was unable to come into the house. They kept him busy forcing him to bandage and dress the group's wounds while several of the others forced their way in. They sat down at the kitchen table, and in a condescending way made themselves right at home. They checked out the kitchen to see if there was anything of value they wanted to steal.

Oma Engle and I stood in the kitchen. Oma talked to them just like she would anyone else. She asked them what they wanted and why they had broken into her house. Then she scolded them for beating up her husband. I was amazed at how confident she seemed and did not appear to show any fear. Then she asked them if they were hungry. She hoped if she fed them, they would eat and then leave our home.

Two of the men demanded whiskey or any other kind of alcohol we might have in the house. We didn't keep much hard liquor around, although there were some beverages with alcohol we kept under the sink. Oma Engle motioned to me, to get the drinks and serve the men. They demanded she cook them food. Oma started to cook. Then she told them they had to get out of her house after they had eaten. There wasn't much food in the house and I was afraid they would get angry because we didn't

241

have enough good food for all of them. Times were very hard so we barely had enough food for ourselves. Even though we had our own cow, she sometimes dried up. Times were so desperate I found myself sneaking milk from the neighbor's cow once in a while so our girls had milk to drink.

Oma Engle never showed her fear and spoke like she was in charge of the situation as she placed food in front of them, which kept them happy for a while. They laughed and joked until their first bottle of liquor was empty. If the men got drunk, it wasn't going to help our situation. The anger festering inside them made me even more fearful. They ordered us around like we were their slaves. I wished there would have been more of our own men in the house to help us that day. My girls stayed hidden in the bedroom.

None of the intruders had paid much attention to me so my disguise seemed to be working. Several hours passed before the men drank up all the alcohol. The others stayed out in the yard. Some had been lying out there for hours, too injured to move. Others were strong enough to continue using their sabers to look for buried valuables. The men in the house appeared to be leading the group. The others took orders from them and continued to search through the dirt. Eventually they found some of our keepsakes I had buried for safe keeping. They took heartfelt mementoes like a necklace and a bracelet Hinrich had given me. My heart ached at the sight.

Djura had buried all of my jewelry in a little box made out of small bricks and hid it under a pile of cow manure hoping it would not be found. When I looked outside I saw they had found many of my things, and were putting them in their pockets. Our larger possessions were placed in a pile or into the Brase's wagon they intended to steal. It was hard to keep track of everything they had found.

Oma Engle was doing a good job keeping the men busy in the kitchen. Neither of us could understand everything they were saying. When Opa Brase finished bandaging the wounded they tied him to a tree.

He was unable to move or get loose to try and help us. The men still hadn't bothered to go into the bedroom where my girls were hiding and the girls had managed to stay quiet. The men were too busy drinking and eating.

Oma Engle had been able to go in and out of the bedroom a couple of times to check on the girls. She made up stories about getting some things that she needed for cooking their dinner. When back in the room she heard the girls whispering to each other and thought it would be best to separate them.

While Oma Engle cooked in the kitchen one of the men called me over and said, "Come over here closer girl, and let me look at you." He looked me over from head to toe and then said, "I don't believe you're an old woman. I don't think you're old at all." I tried disguising my voice, telling him "I am nearly 60-years-old." I don't think he believed me; but the manure smell and dirt on my clothes and face helped me keep him at a distance. He looked at me, shook his head, and kept on drinking, pouring one drink after the other.

The man made me stick out my hands while he was talking to me at the table. I was wearing a ring Hinrich had given me. I didn't hide it with the other jewelry because it was too tight on my finger to remove. The soldier demanded I take it off so he could look at it closer. I tried to tell him it was too tight and I couldn't get it off my finger. He threatened if I didn't take it off, he would cut it off with his saber. He forced me to place my hand on the table with my palm down flat. He slowly raised his saber high above his shoulders lowering it to rest on my fingers. While the saber lay on my hand he threatened to cut off four of my fingers if I didn't give up the ring. I tried to show him I wasn't lying and the ring was impossible to remove. I yanked the ring on my finger praying it would come off, but it was too tight. He suspected I was playing games and again threatened to get it one way or the other.

I begged the man to let me go to the sink where I tried to use the soap and water to slip the ring off my finger. I desperately yanked, over and over as my finger reddened and began to swell. I'm not sure how it happened, but thankfully the ring finally slipped over my knuckle. Off it came and rolled across the floor. He picked it up and put it in his pocket then came closer and we stood face to face.

I was so worried about what he would do next, I panicked. He had frightened me so badly blood started gushing from my nose and I couldn't get it to stop. It bled for several minutes all down my face and the front of my clothes. The intense bleeding scared the Russian soldier bad enough that he backed off immediately, afraid and unsure of what was wrong with me. I believe he thought I was diseased and became too afraid to get close to me. The bleeding eventually stopped. I no longer had to worry about the men attacking me because they treated me like a leper after my massive nose bleed.

The men kept drinking becoming more intoxicated. The longer they remained in the house, the more concerned I became. Oma Engle tried to get the men to leave without upsetting them. She waited on them hand and foot, filled their glasses with drinks, gave them food when they demanded it, and told them afterwards they needed to leave because we had nothing left to give them. A couple of them whispered back and forth to each other making rude jokes and remarks about us. We couldn't understand everything they said, but it was obvious they were mocking us.

In the meantime Djura had come in from the fields when he saw from a distance what was happening. As soon as he saw all the men searching for goods in the ground he knew something was terribly wrong and we were in a situation where we needed help. Thank goodness he could speak a little Russian and was able to talk to them and understand what they were saying. Djura made his way to the house as he spoke to several of the soldiers outside getting closer to the front door. He had been a war prisoner like them and they seemed to listen to what he had to say.

He came in and right away started talking to the men, asking them what they were doing.

When Djura saw me he pointed and told them he believed I was sick and had some nasty illness that was contagious. He wanted to keep them talking and tried to distract them away from Oma Engle and me. He figured out their plans and found out they had been talking about brutalizing and raping both Oma Engle and me. The men talked about raping us in the house and asked Djura if he wanted to join in.

Djura wanted to get us all out of the house. He continued to visit with the men in Russian and poured them more alcohol as he tried to get them drunk enough so they would pass out. He kept the men occupied. Oma Engle motioned to me to try to get out through the back door with the girls. I went near Oma Engle and she whispered her plan to distract the men while the girls and I went out the back door. Djura, devising his own plan, told the men he needed me to come in the other room with him to get more whiskey. The men just laughed certain Djura was taking me into the bedroom for other reasons. They joked and sneered.

They were drunk enough to be fooled into believing Djura was their friend. The men talked and laughed paying no attention to us when Djura and I moved toward the other room. Oma Engle started carrying on loudly as Djura slipped Anneliese and me out the back door. We ran for a nearby bridge near the farm by the town Fahrendahl. Fahrendahl was less than two miles from the house. Ingeborg was in a different room at the time so she was left behind because earlier Oma Engle had hidden her under the mattress in her room thinking the men may look under the bed. It would have been too difficult to get her out the back door without being noticed. I was so worried for her, but Djura assured me he would go back to get Ingeborg next and bring her safely to me.

Djura accompanied us close to the bridge and then headed back quickly to the house to get Ingeborg and try to help Oma and Opa. Djura told me to stay hidden under the bridge until he came back. He hoped the men would leave the farm soon and everything would be alright. I feared for Djura and hoped he could keep Ingeborg, Opa Brase, and Oma Engle safe. I sat under the bridge holding Anneliese and agonized over having to leave Ingeborg behind as I waited for Djura to come back.

Opa Brase at 68-years-old, had been beaten and battered by the soldiers. By the time Djura returned to the house to try to help them, Oma Engle who was in her sixties had been taken outside and repeatedly raped. They had ripped and tore the clothes off her body and beat her. Oma Engle did not want to share the shameful details, she only said several men took turns forcing themselves on her. One after the other took their turn and treated her like she was a piece of worthless garbage. She wasn't sure she would live through the hellish nightmare. She thought they would kill her once they were finished with her. Their excruciating exploitations had degraded and humiliated her. Without an ounce of shame or remorse they left her lying out in the open. Opa Brase sickened and helpless, was forced to hear his wife's agonizing screams.

Ingeborg remained unnoticed under Oma's mattress. Oma Engle sacrificed herself for us all that day as she led the heartless degenerates in another direction out to the field where they attacked her. Her courage and willingness to mislead them had saved the rest of us. Oma Engle eventually recovered from her physical injuries after her brutal attack, although the mental anguish lingered for the rest of her life.

After assaulting Oma, the Russians gathered up their stolen items in the Brase's wagon. They stole our cow, a horse, and all of our belongings they had dug up. Everything they found was either taken or destroyed. The items they did not want were piled up and lit on fire. They burned the items out of spite before they finally left the farm. Anneliese and I stayed under the bridge until Djura was certain they left for good. We all realized our situation could have been much worse. We were all alive and together as a family. All we could do was hope that better times were coming.

I thanked both Oma Engle and Djura for having a hand in saving my girls and me that day. After Oma's harrowing ordeal was over and the soldiers had gone, she gave Ingeborg a hug, held her close and told her she was lucky she was only a child. I shuddered to think what they would have done to the rest of us if they would have found us.

Post-war crimes escalated as former prisoners of war continued to take their fury out on civilians. Oma Engle amazed me when she blatantly refused to help some of the former prisoners when they came knocking at our door. Despite what she had endured, she appeared unafraid and was too stubborn of a woman to willingly give up any of our food or possessions.

Not all former prisoners of war who came to our home were looking to steal from us or harm us in anyway. Some were just looking for relief from their hunger and hoped we could help in some way. Oma Engle felt no empathy for these men. She treated them the same as she would those who sought to treat us unkindly and turned them away. I quickly and quietly packed a few food items I thought we could spare and went out to meet them with what I had before they left our property. I knew what I had to offer wasn't much, yet I couldn't turn my back on those in need and let them leave without trying to help in some way.

Six months passed since the war was considered officially over. Once more we were exposed to several Russian war prisoners that had come on to our property to threaten and antagonize our family. I looked out into the yard and saw 15 to 20 of them headed our way. This time Djura was not in fields and again helped rescue us from them. Opa Brase and Oma Engle were also home at the time.

After our last terrifying experience with the Russians, we had made a plan that would hopefully save us in case our home was invaded again. We planned to get all of the women out of the house first, and had hiding places ready to use. If we saw any sign of intruders and didn't have time to get out of the house we thought of a few places where we could find safety.

Oma Engle had suffered the most during the last horrible encounter. So this time we wanted to make sure Oma, the children, Tina, and Mata were safe from imminent harm.

This time was as frightening as the last when we saw the drifters' inch closer to the house. Djura quickly hurried Oma, Ingeborg, and Anneliese out of the house and he was followed by Tina and Mata the moment we saw the men coming. Our plan to get Oma and the rest of them to the bridge worked. The path that led to the bridge ran in a direction where the ex-war prisoners couldn't see. Once at the bridge Djura told Oma Engle to stay quiet and hidden. I waited anxiously at the house for Djura to return.

Djura needed some time to get back from the bridge, but I knew he would hurry to rescue the rest of us. If we had all left at the same time, the Russians might have noticed the large group leaving together. We thought if we snuck out in small groups, we would be less noticeable.

Opa Brase went out to meet some of the prisoners in the field before they had a chance to get to the house. He was able to keep them away and calm until Djura returned. Unfortunately the Russians forced their way inside before Djura could get me safely out. Once again, acting as if they owned the place, the men ordered Opa about, shouting at him to get them some food and supplies.

The men searched for jewelry or anything else they could get their hands on to steal. Djura made it back and spoke to them in Russian. He asked them what they wanted with us and tried to distract them from harming anyone in the house. This group of ex-prisoners didn't seem as interested in mocking and hurting anyone nor did they look for whiskey or other liquors kept in the house. They came to steal what we had and thankfully weren't as threatening as the last group that invaded our home.

One of the Russian soldiers came straight over to me and stared me up and down. His eyes focused on the side of my head. I was unsure why he looked at me that way. I had put hairpins in that morning to keep the hair out of my face. The soldier stared right at them. Djura tried to divert his attention elsewhere, but the soldier continued to eye the hairpins. He demanded I take the hairpins out of my hair and hand them over. If I didn't do what I was told he would hurt me.

My hairpins were the color of gold, but they weren't made of real gold nor did they have any value. They were cheap costume jewelry, overlaid with gold coloring containing a few small fake diamonds at the ends of each one of the curves. I believe he must have thought they were made of real gold and set with real diamonds. He wouldn't listen to me about the hairpins being worthless and his only concern was to get the pins out of my hair. I refused to take them out, but he reached up and yanked them right out of my hair. He stuck them in his pocket and walked away.

The men ended up taking some of our food and stripped my watch right off of my wrist. One of them grabbed a koogal (a glass paper weight) off the shelf that hung on the living room wall. Examining the paper weight, the man became enraged and with all his might sent the glass ball hurdling across the room. The man yelled Hitler was a murderer and he should have never been born, then cheered his death. The koogal had a likeness of Hitler imbedded within the circumference of the glass. The man was livid, angered by the picture and said he didn't understand how anyone could have such a thing sitting in their home in open view. He considered the koogal a disgrace toward all mankind.

Hitler's picture was a reminder to him of the abuse, pain, suffering and starvation he had endured during the last five years. No one could blame the man for wanting to destroy the image of Hitler or smashing it against the wall. A family friend had given Oma Engle the koogal quite some time ago and she put it on a shelf along with the rest of the knick knacks she had collected through the years. I despised Hitler for the myriad of heinous crimes he had committed. Regardless, the men would have never believed me because I resided in a German household. When the glass ball hit the wall it shattered into a million pieces much the same

249

as the millions of lives that Hitler's evil had touched. I was glad it was destroyed.

The soldiers carried sabers just like the others had before. When they were finished searching the house they went outside searching for possessions hidden in the yard or the fields. They seemed to find nearly all of what we had buried. When they were done, they took it all along with them as they left quietly. No one had been harmed that day. Following their departure, Djura went back to the bridge to get the women and my girls.

## Chapter 63

In late fall of 1945 Djura and I discussed our desire to live together. We definitely wanted to have more privacy and not sneak around as if we were teenagers. We continued to be secretive about our meetings. Finding a place of our own had its challenges. The most obvious was openly declaring we were in a relationship. Another barrier was being able to afford a home. Djura continued working on the farm for a wage that would not support a home so he planned to find a second job elsewhere.

We worried about Opa Brase and Oma Engle's reaction to the news of our relationship as well as Djura's plan to look for secondary employment elsewhere. It was a possibility they might make him leave his job with them immediately once they learned about us. Djura was young and strong. I was confident someone, somewhere would be willing to hire him. I also began going to town nearly every day to get supplies and to look for jobs for myself. It would be more difficult for me to find employment as a woman having two young children. I would need to rely on Oma Engle to help care for my girls.

The duplex we lived in had a tiny kitchenette, a living room, one bedroom, and a store room. I hoped for something larger and wanted a home that wasn't associated with Oma Engle and Opa Brase where Djura could come and go as he pleased. It was likely Oma Engle would not be happy with me for wanting to live further from the farm.

I decided it was time to be honest and tell Opa Brase and Oma Engle how close Djura and I had become and about our plans to live together and marry someday. No matter how they felt about us and reacted to the news, we planned to marry. I would rather they heard the news about our relationship from me rather than from someone else.

Oma Engle and Opa Brase both liked Djura as a farmhand, but considering him as a member of the family would be a very different matter. Oma's pride and Hinrich's memory made accepting Djura into the family next to impossible. She would have a difficult time accepting anyone else in a father role to her grandchildren other than Hinrich. Djura's foreigner status did not help the situation either, however, I felt it was a good possibility I would never meet a man that could live up to her expectations.

I stayed busy, did my work, and when the right time came, I pulled Oma Engle aside and told her about Djura and me. I told her as gently as possible. I revealed we had been seeing each other for quite some time and reminded her of all the good things Djura had done for our family. I told her of our intent to find our own place and eventually marry.

Upon hearing the news of our plan to marry, she fired back in a rage. Furious at the notion I would even consider such a thing, she called him an *Auslander*, a common laborer, and worse yet he was an ex-war prisoner. She said because of his Serbian descent, the family would be disgraced. Sternly she told me she wanted nothing to do with Djura, would never accept him as part of the family, plus he was unfit to be a father to her grandchildren. She said, "Karla if you two get married, I will not come to your wedding, be a part of it in any way, or ever accept the marriage between you two! He will always be a foreigner in my eyes and will never be accepted into this family!"

We left the conversation at that, knowing her feelings about Djura remained unchanged. I wouldn't even try, at least for now, to change her mind about him. I thought maybe someday with the passage of time she could feel differently about him. Her feelings and prejudices were deeply rooted. Her memories of Hinrich became a barrier making her acceptance of Djura an impossibility.

It didn't take long for Djura and me to give up on the idea of finding a larger place to live. It became apparent we were not going to be able to afford a larger home. I decided to ask Oma Engle and Opa Brase if Djura and I could stay in the duplex and, of course, we would pay the rent.

Although they didn't like the idea of us living together, they consented.  Knowing we had considered moving to Gnarrenburg, which was about 11 kilometers (7 miles) from Klenkendorf, Oma Engle was pleased her granddaughters would remain only a few blocks from the farm.

Having our own home and paying the rent ourselves gave us a sense of freedom and hope.  I began a new chapter in my life.  I thought about our renewed dreams and wanted to create new traditions and memories with Djura.  Hinrich would always remain in my heart, but I now felt a sense of peace moving forward.

I was unable to find any other suitable employment so I remained working on the farm.  Ingeborg and Anneliese continued to see their grandmother almost every day and stayed overnight with her often.  Djura continued to work for Opa Brase and had applied to work for the British.  They hadn't become angry enough to fire him, probably because they were afraid I would leave with him.  He found other part-time jobs working for several farmers doing chores and handy work.  I was hopeful the economy would improve so we could enjoy expanded opportunities.  Perhaps by then Djura could find a steady job in town that paid more money rather than doing farm work and several other odd jobs.  We both wanted to save for our wedding and our future.

Soon enough a better opportunity came Djura's way.  After the British had reviewed his qualifications he was asked to join the British Civil Service.  His ability to speak several languages made him a desirable candidate for the position.  His compassion for others, honesty, and past experience of being a war prisoner were also attributes the British found desirable.  Djura stayed with me often though he had to stay on base preforming his duties for the British Civil Service most of the time.  We no longer had to be secretive about our relationship.  Djura continued to bond with Ingeborg and Anneliese and was slowly becoming a father figure to them.

Both girls liked him a great deal. He tried hard to make them laugh and feel comfortable when they were with him. He gave Anneliese rides on the back of his bike and played outdoors with Ingeborg often. He liked playing with them when he had the chance and seemed to enjoy becoming a part of our family. Djura also talked about wanting many children of his own someday.

## Chapter 64

A state of chaos was evident in all parts of Germany. Former POWs continued to roam the streets, not permitted to return to their home countries nor welcomed by the locals. Many were unable to find work. The fighting had stopped and bombs no longer dropped out of the sky, but the current environment sustained the violence in Germany. Getting back on our feet and putting our lives back together after the war was very difficult. I remained vigilant of potential dangers to my family and myself. Thoughts of dying frequently crossed my mind, especially during POW raids. Some Germans who had once been soldiers still wanted to fight and kill their enemies adding to the chaos.

I wanted to visit my mother and father and also hoped for them to meet Djura someday. I decided to make a trip to Austria on my own and bring the girls with me. I wanted to have a chance to talk to Mother and Father about how close Djura and I had become before having him show up on their doorstep. I hoped they would understand the important role he played in our survival since I'd known him. I also hoped through both my letters and my trip back home they would learn what kind of man Djura was and accept our plan to marry.

I wanted to lessen the shock and prepare them for the news I may be marrying another foreigner. I wanted my parents to like him and hoped they'd learn to love him as much as I did. I thought once they finally had the opportunity to meet him they would see for themselves that Djura was a good, decent, and kind man. When I told them about all the good things he had done for us and how he had stepped in and saved our lives, they would understand how much he cared for my daughters and me. They would surely realize he was a good, honest, and trustworthy man.

Mother and Father had liked Hinrich very much after getting to know him. Djura was much different than Hinrich and they would have to respect and trust my judgment when it came to his character and intentions. Djura's and Hinrich's personalities were totally different, their looks opposite. Djura with his dark skin, black hair, and brown eyes and Hinrich with his clear blue eyes, blonde hair and fair skin; the contrast between the two men was enormous.

Neither one of them wanted or agreed with Hitler's propaganda, politics, and murderous insanity. Their morals and values were much the same even though they had contrasting backgrounds. Despite their differences, they had many things in common. Both men placed a high importance on religion, family, work, and values. Once a friend, they stayed loyal, stood by their word, and respected those who were kind and compassionate, were full of humility and always helped those in need.

I knew my parents would express concern for us as I brought someone new into our lives. The fact we were living together without being married was not a concern. The concern would rest solely on the type of man Djura was and his ability to provide for us. With matters of survival on the top of everyone's priorities, marriage was a minor issue of concern. Too many things were happening in Europe; the economy was unstable, the cities and lands of many countries had been destroyed, and millions of people's lives were in shambles.

Like the former POWs, I was also not allowed to travel across the borders. Once more I would have to sneak into Austria to see my mother and father. It was November of 1945, and the weather was getting cold when I planned our trip home.

Djura would accompany us to the train. Once we were close to the border, the girls and I would be on our own. We would, however, have friends and my father helping us at certain points along the way. I yearned to see my parents and sister, Frieda, again. It had been a long time since they had seen Ingeborg and Anneliese. They had written of their hopes to see them before they were any older. The distance that lay between us was troubling and I wished we lived closer to my parents. I wanted my daughters to know their other grandparents better, to experience the love, kindness and compassion I was shown when I was growing up.

The weather had been mild for November and we hadn't experienced any harsh winter weather yet. I thought my girls and I should be fine traveling up the mountain side even though the climb up could be cold. Ingeborg and Anneliese were as excited as I was about going to see their grandparents. They talked non-stop about our trip. The girls hoped for plenty of snow to go sledding down the steep hill that ran alongside their Oma Agnes and Opa Valentin's house.

I dressed us very warmly and brought extra wool clothes plus mittens and socks for the trip along with plenty of food to last us through the trip. British and American soldiers were patrolling the borders during this trip. Regardless I remained determined to see my mother again and I wanted Ingeborg and Anneliese to come with me.

## Chapter 65

Traveling by train would be more challenging this trip. Many of the railways were no longer in service after being bombed or damaged beyond repair. No passenger trains operated and the only way for us get to Austria was on the coal cars. It would make for uncomfortable travel sitting on the heaps of coal all the way to the border.

We said our goodbyes to Opa and Oma Brase and made our way to the train station. Djura felt it was important we travel light because we had to be able to climb up onto the top of the coal filled railcars. We also had to find a safe and suitable place to sit for the girls during the long ride to the border of Austria. We would be on the train for over a day and I hoped the wind would not be blowing too hard. When we arrived at the train station, Djura warned me to use caution and to travel safe. He embraced both the girls and me as we readied to leave. He helped boost us up over the sides of the cars filled with coal. The coal was piled high and shifted under our weight making it hard to keep our balance. Once on top, I made an effort to level out the coal to make the ride more comfortable.

As the train picked up speed, the chilly breeze made the ride feel bitter cold and all the more unpleasant. Trying to hang on while the train sped up proved difficult where the railroad track was bumpy. I kept the girls close to protect them from rolling off the top of the coal if they happened to lose their balance. The girls grabbed onto the chunks of coal when the train began to rock and sway. This left their hands and faces smudged and blackened from the soot lining the cars.

Our layers of clothes helped protect us against frostbite on our journey. Both girls had wool head scarves doubled over their heads and wore long wool socks reaching up to their thighs. The coal filled cars were transported to many locations in Germany to be unloaded at various stops, and then on to other parts of Europe. There was the possibility we would have to switch trains in the middle of the trip if our car was due to be unloaded. I hoped to avoid this because climbing into the car to the top of the coal would be more difficult without Djura's help.

It didn't surprise me when we came upon other people hitching a ride along the way. Some trying to get home to their families like us, while others were trying to reach the next city. It seemed as though every time I traveled back home I ran into someone either on the train or on foot who was willing to help me in some way. I had met many caring individuals during those journeys. All of us who traveled by train had to face the same kind of obstacles including the fear of being arrested.

The wind blew harder and I could see the girls were shivering from the cold. I removed a few of the wool scarfs I had wrapped around my neck and placed them snuggly on Ingeborg's and Anneliese's heads tucking them deep down into their collars. I hoped the wool would help keep their little bodies warm.

It took over a day for us to get to the edges of Germany. The train slowed as it neared a station close to the Austrian border, eventually coming to a complete stop. I climbed down first and helped each of my girls off the coal car. I looked around acclimating myself to the surroundings. We began walking and soon heard voices in the distance. I couldn't tell who was coming and didn't want to take any chances until I knew for sure who it was. I worried it might be the border patrol.

Heading in the opposite direction of the voices we came to a building, and I hurried the girls inside. Off to the right was a big double door. Through the door were several bathroom stalls. I led Ingeborg into one stall telling her to be very quiet. She looked alarmed so I told her bad men might be looking for us and we must hide and not make a single sound. Holding onto Anneliese, we slipped into an adjacent stall.

The voices grew louder and it became evident they were British guards patrolling the area. Their footsteps drew closer. The guards entered the building and opened the double door. They yelled out loud, "Is anyone in here?" They then ordered, "Come out!" They repeated themselves several times yelling if anyone was in the bathroom to come out and show themselves. They paused for a moment, waited to see if anyone answered them. We stood quietly waiting and remained still while they checked each one of the stalls. One at a time, they threw the doors open. I looked down toward the ground and saw Ingeborg had moved toward the door of her stall and her feet were likely visible.

I began to panic trying to think of a way to get us out of this situation. Anneliese never uttered a sound. The guards passed by the two stalls we were hiding in though the tips of Ingeborg's toes were in full view. They circled back toward the double doors and once again did not force either of our stall doors open. The guards' voices began to fade off in the distance and when it became apparent they were not coming back, I hurried to Ingeborg reassuring her all was OK. I was certain the border guards knew we were hiding there and chose to let us be; perhaps it was an act of kindness. I was unsure what the current border guards did if people were caught attempting to cross the border illegally.

Following our close call we continued on to the next leg of our journey, climbing by foot up the Alps. We progressively reached higher elevations and the snow on the ground accumulated. Eventually both girls and I found ourselves tromping through over four feet of snow. I longed for a pair of snowshoes, an accessory to be grateful for in deep mountainous snow. We weren't equipped with such items this trip, wearing only our hiking boots.

I had to carry Anneliese most of the way up the mountain side. She was too young to keep up with Ingeborg and me. Ingeborg, one year older than Anneliese, rarely complained. She walked alongside me and kept up most of the time. She did great for her age and seemed to understand I had to carry Anneliese most of the way. The air chilled as we gained altitude. We climbed steadily up the mountain though it took us hours to get to the other side.

Once over the mountain and into Austria, friends awaited our arrival to help us the rest of the way home. We met up with my father along the way. I was overjoyed to see him after such a long separation. He went on and on about how much his granddaughters had grown and told them Oma Agnes and Friede couldn't wait to see them.

Once back home in Bleiberg, Friede, Ingeborg and Anneliese were soon inseparable and settled in comfortably. As always, Mother catered to us. I planned to stay for two to three weeks this visit. It was a relaxing visit for both my girls and me.

Shortly after our arrival, I sat my parents down and told them of my relationship with Djura. They expressed their concern for their granddaughters and me. They hoped he treated us well. I shared the ways Djura helped to protect us over the past several months. Although they were distressed about what we had endured, they were grateful Djura had been there to help. I was relieved with their acceptance and looked forward to the day they would meet Djura.

Our visit went by too quickly and soon we were saying our goodbyes and heading back to Germany. We traveled the same route back. The return trip had no surprises and we made it back to Klenkendorf without any unwanted attention.

## Chapter 66

The winter months went by quickly and spring began to show its presence. Djura and I planned a trip to the shoemaker in town to pick up his boots. We decided to make a full day out of our venture by bringing the girls and having a picnic. The warming spring air and sunshine gave me a sense of hope and excitement.

I joyfully packed some food while considering where we might stop to picnic. I decided we would stop near the small Fahrendahl Bridge that crossed a little river. Learning of our plan, the girls jumped with excitement and asked Djura to bring his *schifferlavier* (accordion). Ingeborg and Anneliese loved to hear him play and sang along. They begged him to play for hours on end. I was unsure where the word *schifferlavier* came from, but that's the word Djura used to describe his accordion.

On our family outing to the shoemaker we decided we would pick up Djura's boots first then have our picnic on our way home. The girls whimpered some when Djura decided not to bring his *schifferlavier*. We concluded we had too much to carry already. Anneliese's mood quickly brightened when Djura asked her to ride on the back of his brand new, shiny red bike. Ingeborg rode on the back of my bicycle. We didn't have a car so we rode our bikes pretty much everywhere when we ran errands, went to work, and when visiting neighbors and friends. Sometimes we went on family bike rides just for the fun of it.

**Below are a few pictures of Djura and his schifferlavier, (accordion), having a good time and making music for us on several occasions.**

Djura was anxious to get his knee-high boots repaired. He wore them often and the soles had become tattered and damaged from the wear and tear of everyday use. Djura had taken them to the shoemaker days before and dropped them off to be repaired. The shoemaker said he was able to fix them for a small price. He had done a nice job mending shoes for us before so we had no doubt his boots would be like new.

We crossed the small Fahrendahl Bridge over the little river. We decided to stop for a break before continuing our journey to town. It was a picturesque sight, hard for anyone to pass by and resist this restful place. The quaint brick arch at the front of the bridge beckoned those who passed over to sit, take a minute to relax and take in the enjoyable scenic view of two, plush, green meadows in full bloom that lay on both sides. The small arched bridge complimented the countryside nicely. The small iron parts were uniquely incorporated with the brick and blended in with the greenery around it. Its distinctive characteristics were so appealing, it was impossible for anyone to resist sitting down and dangling their feet over the edge. Underneath we watched the gentle current roll by our feet, the rushing water brushed up against the grassy banks. It was easy for me to lean back and stretch out, relax and enjoy the scenery on the soft homemade quilt I brought with me. The small river that ran under the iron bridge was close to five feet deep in places. In certain areas it was possible to see the sandy bottom and the pebbles glistening in the clear pools of water.

After stopping for a short rest it didn't take us long to get to town. Soon after picking up Djura's boots along with the rest of the supplies we headed home. The shoemaker had done a fine job fixing his boots. They were shined, polished, and looked brand new. We took the same road as we headed home. We wanted to go back to the bridge where we planned to stop and eat.

We neared the bridge, ready to relax for a bit and eat our lunch when we were approached by two men who were once German soldiers. They were an uncommon sight once the war was over. Both men were dressed in full uniform with emblems of swastikas still sewn on their chests. Though the war was over, these two stragglers who had been discharged after the war, continued to wander the countryside searching for somewhere to call home. They were once respected, now homeless and penniless, and lucky not to have been killed by the released Russian war prisoners, the British, or the Americans.

Their past military service wasn't of any use to them now. They were despised outcasts with nothing to show for the years they followed and supported a mad man. We assumed right away they were a threat. When we got close enough to recognize who they were, we were already formulating a plan of escape. It didn't take us long to realize these men were dangerous and desperate. Their intentions were to rob us. I also feared they might hurt us as well. It was only a matter of minutes before the men tried to bully and intimidate us. Ingeborg and Anneliese stood right beside me, fearful and hanging on to the hem of my skirt.

The two men started giving Djura a hard time about the boots he was carrying and made rude remarks about his bike. One of the men stepped in front of him while the other stood at his back. The soldier facing Djura continued to harass him, accusing him of stealing his boots and his bike. In a condescending manner he pointed out Djura's foreigner status and the impossibility of him ever being able to afford such items. The other man behind Djura joined in the badgering and called him a worthless thief. The men continued to yell while Djura argued back. Suddenly the man standing behind Djura pulled out a knife, and held it tightly to his throat.

I thought it was a possibility I might be left to fend for myself. I looked around toward the open fields trying to figure out where my girls and I should run. I worried Djura wouldn't be able to defend himself against both men. The soldiers had nothing but the clothes on their backs. They were desperate with nothing to lose.

In a flash, Djura reacted, taking them by surprise. In a matter of seconds, he disarmed the man with the knife and began bashing the thugs. Djura nearly always carried his own knife and brass knuckles for protection. He had slipped the brass knuckles on his fists when the two soldiers initially approached us. He connected his first jab on the soldier carrying the knife with such force the man flew backwards landing on his backside. He whirled around as the other soldier came at him rapidly and landed blow after blow to the soldier's face.

As the soldier staggered, Djura gripped his uniform, lifted him off the ground, and hurled him over the side of the bridge. He walked over to the other soldier, now standing unsteadily as blood dripped down his face, and tossed him over as well. The soldier hollered out in fear until his body splashed into the river. It all happened so quickly we were headed home in a matter of minutes. Djura told me he was never afraid and as soon as he saw them approaching he assumed there would be a fight.

No one had been hurt except for two former soldiers who needed to learn a lesson about picking on people who didn't look capable of defending themselves. Our bikes and boots remained in our possession. We continued on home without any further problems with quite a story to tell. At the time I was scared to death, but now I can look back and laugh about it. The image I remember of those two men disoriented, bleeding, and soaking wet climbing out of the water under the bridge still makes me snicker a bit.

By May of 1946 fewer ex-war prisoners roamed the countryside. Germany remained in a period of instability, but locals began to feel safer and less threatened by thieves and raiders. The German people were more hopeful now than ever before and were given the opportunity to rebuild, forget, and be forgiven. Hitler's reign of terror was over, and his death cheered by an entire planet.

We had been given a chance to look toward a brighter future, and in time rebuild all we had lost. Djura and I seriously talked about marriage, but felt the timing was not right. The entire country needed rebuilding and our lives were in shambles in many ways. The aftermath of war made things all the more difficult for everyone in Germany and so many other countries as well.

During the summer of 1946, Ingeborg and Anneliese were able to enjoy the outdoors more as the violence continued to dwindle. Both girls constantly asked to play outside. We had a tree swing in the yard and Djura spent a lot of time pushing the girls on the swing. Watching him interact with the girls was heartwarming and added to my confidence he would make a good father. He enjoyed their company as much as they enjoyed his.

Anneliese begged Djura constantly for a ride on the back of his bike. She jumped about until he gathered her up in his arms and put her on the back of his bike. She'd wave to me when they passed by and it was obvious with her laughs and giggles she loved his company. She and

Ingeborg grew fonder of Djura every day. I genuinely wanted the girls to have someone to call Papa and we planned to make that happen someday.

## Chapter 67

Cold weather would surely be coming and we needed to cut more wood to burn during those cold winter months. I helped Djura cut and load wood during the fall. We tried to fill the wood room while it was still nice outdoors so we wouldn't run out of wood in the middle of the winter.

When winter arrived that year, I was fairly certain I was pregnant. I had missed a few periods and was feeling a bit queasy each morning when I awoke. Both Djura and I were pleased with the prospect of a baby on the way.

Djura and I had not married yet. The war made us carefully consider any specific wedding plans and having a baby without being married was not uncommon for couples after the war. Survival took priority over marriage. A pregnancy did not necessarily lead a couple to marriage. Common law marriages were widely accepted by the people but not legally recognized by the courts. If you lived with someone and had children together, by most you were considered legally married and should be committed to that person for life.

The economy was poor, most people were needy and had to concentrate on simply surviving. It was hard to make ends meet and provide for your family's most basic needs. Djura and I, although fully committed to one another, planned to marry at a later date. We felt there would be a better time and place to marry down the road.

I finally went to the doctor and he confirmed my pregnancy. We expected I would be having my third baby sometime in late May or early June. Djura looked forward to becoming a father even though he had already begun to fill the role of Papa with Anneliese and Ingeborg. I didn't have a preference whether the baby was a boy or a girl, as long as he or she was healthy.

Even though I was pregnant Oma Engle insisted on being confrontational and started quarrels with me about Djura nearly every day. She belittled him in front of me and in spite of my pregnancy with his child, she was unable to accept our relationship. She told me she planned to have nothing to do with his baby and would only care for Ingeborg and Anneliese. I hoped she wouldn't hold on to such harsh judgments of our unborn child once he or she was born.

Oma Engle's acceptance of Djura and the baby was important to me. I tried to avoid any arguments with her and had no interest in denying her time with Ingeborg and Anneliese. As time passed she seemed to soften somewhat. She eventually no longer talked as if she totally despised Djura. On occasion she spoke in a civil tone without intentionally being rude for no reason.

My pregnancy was going well and I had few problems the first seven months. Oma Engle mentioned to me one day that I should deliver the baby at her house and she along with a midwife would help with the birth. I was touched and appreciated her offer, however, I wanted to have my baby in my own home. I asked her if she would be willing to come help with the delivery at my house. I was surprised and relieved she agreed. I hoped it meant she'd be more accepting moving forward. Ingeborg and Anneliese were thoroughly excited to have a new baby sister or brother on the way and couldn't wait until the baby was born.

Staying busy working with Oma Engle on the farm made my pregnancy go fast. Winter storms had come and gone. Spring had arrived. The baby was active, pounding and kicking inside me. All of my check-ups thus far had gone well.

## Chapter 68

On the evening of April 23rd, I began to feel a bit under the weather. I tossed and turned all night long. Then very early in the morning before the sun rose, I felt a stabbing pain in my side. Going through labor twice before, I knew my contractions had begun.

I became concerned since I was only seven months along. My pains intensified. I knew I would give birth to my third child soon. I was at home by myself with the girls. Djura was stationed in Breddorf on duty with the British Civil Service, several miles from home. It would be impossible for me to get word to him so he could be home in time for the baby to be born. I was heartbroken he wouldn't be there for the birth of his first child. While on duty for the British Civil Service he would at times be gone all week long spending nights in the barracks.

I woke Ingeborg and told her she needed to go get Oma Engle quickly because the baby was coming. I walked around the house with each contraction, hoping Oma Engle and the midwife would hurry. I peeked in on Anneliese who was still sleeping. Before long, Ingeborg returned with Oma Engle and the midwife. I was relieved they had made it in time and I knew it wouldn't be long before I needed their help.

Oma Engle and the midwife patiently counted the minutes between each pain as we tried to figure out how long it would be before the new baby arrived. Ingeborg paced back and forth across the floor wondering what she could do to help. She recently turned six-years-old and had made it clear she hoped for a baby brother because she already had her little sister. In the meantime, Anneliese woke up. She wanted to come in my room and watch for the baby to come. She was nearly five-years-old and didn't understand why Oma Engle wouldn't let her come in the room.

To keep them both busy, Oma Engle gathered coloring supplies for Anneliese and told Ingeborg to go outside to watch the roof for the stork to arrive with the baby. The story she was told was that the stork would be delivering the baby to our chimney or it might come through a bedroom window. When Oma Engle told her to go outside, she was puzzled and had a million questions about the stork. Oma Engle somehow convinced Ingeborg to go outside and she'd explain later how the stork brought the baby.

As hours passed my contractions continued and I wondered if they would ever end. The pain was much worse than my first two deliveries. I worried something was terribly wrong and I ached for my mother. The midwife and Oma Engle discussed what could be causing the delay. My pains became intolerable and I'd scream for help with each hard contraction. When it finally came time to push, I pushed with all my might. I pushed with such a fury, my face turned bright red and I feared the blood vessels in my face and neck would burst. This stubborn little baby who wanted to come early, now resisted the grand entrance into the world.

The midwife examined me and discovered the baby was turned the wrong way in a breech position. The midwife's concerned look and my mother-in-law's fretting about the complications caused me to worry for both my baby and myself. Both of them coached me when it was time to push and I continued to press down as hard as I could to absolutely no avail. The midwife tried to instruct me on what to do to make things easier, but nothing I did seemed to advance the baby further down the birth canal. This was the most difficult and painful birth I'd ever experienced. I questioned whether I was strong enough to survive through the entire labor and birth.

After what seemed like hours of hard labor I continued to struggle to deliver my baby. The baby was folded in half and was trying to come out bottom first. The fold made the labor agonizing, the baby was twice the thickness it should have been coming through the birth canal and was bent

271

at the waist with its feet and toes facing its forehead. My labor involved a pain that words can never describe.

My body finally let the baby move down the birth canal, although my flesh would be torn open and still unable to accommodate the breech birth. The pains were so great, I thought I was going to pass out. As customary at the time, I had the baby naturally with no anesthetic or pain medication. By some miracle the midwife and Oma Engle guided the baby out of my body. As soon as the baby was born my intense pain subsided. I went from having excruciating pain to almost none at all.

The tiny creature they placed beside me was squished and dented, but moved none the less. Djura and I had been blessed with a tiny, new baby girl. Djura wasn't able to be there with me, yet I knew he wished he could have been. Both of us had decided we wanted to name her after one of his sisters. We called her "Krsmanija," (pronounced Kris-maun-ya) and nicknamed her Krs for short.

Born premature, Krs weighed only 4-lbs. Her color wasn't healthy and she felt as cold as ice. She was quiet, barely made a sound, which worried all of us. Since I didn't hear her cry, I was terrified she had died or there was something terribly wrong with her. It wasn't until Oma Engle told me she was breathing I knew Krs was alright. I felt completely exhausted and drifted off to near unconsciousness. It was some time before I was actually able to hold my baby and understand all that had taken place. We were all thankful and counted our blessings the baby was healthy and I had survived such a difficult and dangerous labor.

After Krsmanija was born, Oma Engle and the midwife whisked her off, cleaned her and wrapped her in a small, soft, green and yellow blanket. Because she had come early, her tiny body chilled easily, which caused her body temperature to drop quickly. Her skin was more purple than normal and she had a yellowish tint to her skin and eyes. Her purple coloring concerned everyone so the midwife placed her swaddled body in a cardboard shoe box, then laid her by the heated cook stove.

The heat from the burning wood warmed her cold, tiny bones and after she lay by the fire for a few hours, she began to gain some color. Her face turned a healthy shade of pink, and her cheeks showed a hint of roses. Her breathing became less choppy, steadier, and less labored. She started to squirm a bit and wasn't so quiet and still. She was able to gather up enough strength after several hours that her faint cries could be heard and were so very welcomed.

## Chapter 69

In just a few weeks Krs improved by leaps and bounds, gained weight steadily and appeared to be just fine. It took me much longer to recuperate after her birth compared to the other girls. I was grateful for Oma Engle's help afterwards. I was very sore, weak and unable to properly care for any of us. She was nice enough to help me and I appreciated her kindness. Oma Engle had helped me from the beginning of the delivery to the end, yet I sensed some resentment toward Krsmanija. She wasn't Hinrich's baby and her lineage was not of German descent.

As time passed and Krs grew older, Oma Engle made her resentment obvious. She avoided holding Krs. She instead focused her energies tending to Anneliese and Ingeborg when we visited. She helped me in many other ways, although, I saw clearly she wasn't ready to accept Krs as her grandchild.

After several months passed Oma Engle warmed up to the idea of having another grandchild to acknowledge and slowly began to welcome Krs to the family. She gave Ingeborg and Anneliese more attention and her extra kindness toward them was intentional. The girls were genetically a part of her lineage and were pieces of her legacy. They were little blonde, blue-eyed German children with fair complexions just like their father. Krs, on the other hand, was dark complected, had black hair, and was of Austrian and Yugoslav descent.

With the passage of time, Oma Engle eventually offered to care for Krs when she watched the other children and in time learned to love Krs in her own way. Ingeborg always remained Oma Engle's favorite. She made this obvious to everyone around her.

We were only able to save a few pictures of Krsmanija when she was young. There were so many personal things of ours that had been lost or destroyed during the 1940's. Pictures of my family were my most valuable keepsakes I owned. I wished there was some way I could have saved more pictures of the children.

**The pictures below were taken in Klenkendorf and are of Krs when she was about ten months old. Krsmanija is on right in the first picture. Krs and her father are in the second picture.**

**A photo of Krsmanija and me when she was two-years-old.**

For the next six months after Krsmanija's birth, Djura and I continued on with our lives. I lived in our small duplex across town near Oma Engle in Klenkendorf. Djura was stationed at the British base in Breddorf much of the time, but was allowed to come stay with us when he was off duty. He no longer worked on the farm except to help Opa Brase with an occasional chore.

Breddorf was relatively close to Klenkendorf and we were apart some of the time, but Djura was able to come home and visit us often. Our girls and I made several visits to see him on the base, but for the most part he came back to our home to visit.

**Below is a map of where Djura was located in Breddorf, the base wasn't too far from Klenkendorf. Klenkendorf is not shown on this map although is very near Breddorf.**

(http://www.weather-forecast.com/locations/Breddorf)

We had gone through many changes and so much had happened to my family the last few years. Djura and I had given much thought to what we wanted out of the rest of our lives. Krs was now six-months-old. The warm colors of fall surrounded us, creating a peaceful countryside. It had been almost two-and-a-half-years since the war had officially ended.

Caring for our new baby was a very precious time in our lives. When I looked down upon this innocent child, I closely questioned the future for my girls. I witnessed an overwhelming sadness among the people, lack of opportunity, and hope for many. Much of the world had developed a hatred for the German people.

Deep in thought, I began to wonder about what lay ahead for us and this small child. Her appearance made her foreign descent obvious, and I wondered what opportunities she might have in her life as she grew toward adulthood. Having a new baby brought us both a great deal of joy along with a sense of increased responsibility to get them out of this war torn country. I tended to my girls and our baby since Djura was often gone working for the British. He stayed busy as he tried his best to provide for our family. Somehow we managed our affairs and were able to provide our very basic needs. We were in the midst of an entire country in need of rebuilding as everyone tried to survive the economic crisis.

This little bundle of joy who had recently joined our family gave us both much to think about. We started to talk about setting a date to marry. We had plenty of time to plan and there didn't seem any need to rush into anything. We thought if we married within the next year the situation in Germany may improve and perhaps there would be more stability in the economy. Neither of us wanted a large wedding and planned to have only our close family and friends in attendance. We hoped perhaps by our wedding date, travel over the borders would be permitted so my mother and father would be able to come to our wedding. Considering all that had taken place in the past eight years we wondered what role destiny would play in the next eight years of our lives.

Djura worked long hours for the British Civil Service yet didn't make much money. I had been poor most of my life so being a full-time housewife and living a very simple life was fine with me. We were content regardless and simply wished for good health and happiness.

## Chapter 70

Djura complained occasionally about pain in his back. He thought possibly his work was to blame. He also wondered if the pain was associated with problems he had with his kidneys when he was a younger man. He had problems when he was 18-years-old and was diagnosed with an ailment that would likely cause him more problems as time passed. I grew concerned immediately. Losing one husband had been hard enough for me and I certainly didn't want to lose anyone else I loved. I found myself praying to God nightly to keep my family healthy and safe from harm. No matter how much I prayed, Djura's pain began to affect his quality of life and his work.

He realized he had no choice but to visit a doctor. After seeing the doctor and receiving a thorough examination, we found out one of Djura's kidneys was functioning poorly thus impacting his entire body. If something wasn't done soon, he would suffer from kidney failure and die. The doctor was uncertain as to how much damage had already been done and emphasized the likelihood that one of his kidneys needed to be removed.

Djura's kidney surgery had been scheduled during the winter of 1947 in a nearby hospital. The plan was to remove his right kidney and perform any other procedures that proved necessary while they had him opened up and on the surgical table. This was a very serious surgery and the doctors had already informed us of the possible complications and spoke about his future prognosis. We were told if all went well during the operation, Djura would be able to live a normal life with only one kidney.

It seemed as though there was always something to worry about. We were never totally free from misfortune and uncertainty. We made it over one hurdle, and waited in suspense for another to occur. I felt as though the good times in our lives never lasted long and something insidious always waited in the shadows to entrap us. My only wish in life was that everyone stayed healthy and alive.

Contrary to my worry, Djura's outlook on the surgery remained very positive. He showed very little fear or worry, at least in my presence. If he was concerned about the outcome he never talked about it. He said it was simple, he would have the surgery, get things fixed, recuperate, and everything would be fine. I wished I could worry less and be as positive as he.

The day of the surgery, baby Krsmanija and I waited in the hospital family room. I remember holding Krs in my arms as I paced back and forth in the hallway completely consumed with worry. The surgery was lengthy and nerve racking. My mind raced as I wondered why things were taking so long. I imagined the worst until the surgery was over. Oma Engle had offered to watch Ingeborg and Anneliese, so I took Krs with me since she was left out of the offer. Krs, however, helped distract me somewhat during the surgery.

I was glad Inga and Anneliese didn't have to come with me that day. Ingeborg had already missed so much school. The children attended school sporadically the last six years mostly due to the bombing, rebuilding, and chaos that had taken place during and after the war. There were some makeshift schools built similar to a small one-room country schoolhouse. During the war and in post war times, the children in Klenkendorf didn't attend school on a daily basis.

After nearly seven hours of surgery the lead surgeon finally came to the waiting room to update me on Djura's condition. The doctor explained the surgery had gone as well as possible. They had removed his right kidney during surgery and his prognosis was good. I was so relieved to hear the doctor's positive outlook. Djura was going to be fine. My prayers had been answered, and I was thankful we could move forward, plan our wedding and our future together. Djura's recuperation after surgery was lengthy, but in time he made a full recovery. It took him several months to recover, but he lived and worked like anyone else despite having only one kidney.

## Chapter 71

We began planning for our wedding. The wedding was to take place in June with hopes we would have some spring and summer flowers in bloom. Krs would be 14-months-old in June and we planned on having her in the wedding. She started walking early when she was only nine-months-old, and we figured by June she would be pretty steady on her feet. By the wedding Ingeborg would have turned seven-years-old and Anneliese six. All of our girls would be old enough to play some role in our wedding. I pictured all three girls in colorful matching dresses. I didn't worry because all the relatives would be there and were willing to help care for them during the celebration. Having our daughters present on our special day would make our wedding day all the more treasured, but would take some extra planning.

With Djura's small salary we tried to save some money to buy everything we needed for the celebration. I was unsure if Oma Engle and Opa Brase would help with any of the planning or the celebration. The partying would likely go on for days. The wedding party itself would be small. We planned to include Hinrich's family, Djura, myself, our girls, and a few close friends. Djura wanted some of his Yugoslav friends to stand up for him during the wedding. Some of these men had also been war prisoners along with him.

As was customary for this time, half of the townspeople and neighbors would show up as well. Most of the guests would not show up empty handed, but would bring food and drinks to share. We had to make sure we had enough food for the main course, breads, desserts, and side dishes. I hoped Oma Engle, and Anne, Hinrich's sister-in-law, would help me with the cooking and cleaning if they decided to come.

Both Oma Engle and Anne were excellent bakers. They made the best cream filled tortes, cakes and desserts. They had done an excellent job of baking for Hinrich's and my wedding. I believed we were making progress when Oma Engle agreed to help me make the girl's layered dresses. I hoped for Oma Engle's and Opa Brase's blessing even if they didn't help much with the wedding festivities. Oma Engle seemed to have softened up a bit criticizing Djura less for being a foreigner. Perhaps after all this time she finally realized he had not been brought to Germany because he was a criminal, but because he was considered an enemy of the Nazis.

Talk of our summer wedding persisted during the winter months. The girls grew like weeds. They enjoyed playing in the snow with Djura. They engaged in a number of snowball fights and building snowmen. The renewed post-war safety allowed the girls to run the few blocks back and forth from our home to Oma Engle's several times a week.

The number of renegade soldiers and former POWs that roamed our area continued to dwindle in number. Many landmines remained buried in the ground close to the farm and had never been dug up. Those discovered were marked to allow for safe travels. We had to be very watchful and careful about where we stepped as some of the live mines remained undiscovered and unmarked.

Jobs remained scarce in the area and finding a good job, if you looked like a foreigner, proved more difficult. With fewer POWs left to roam the countryside, I began to feel a greater sense of safety for all of us. Yet there were still some stragglers, thieves, and homeless folk who continued to roam about looking for their next meal. Many living here were beginning to feel a renewed hope and a sense that peaceful times would once again come to Germany.

Watching our girls play together outdoors laughing and singing brought normalcy back into my life. Seeing them play on their bikes and enjoying the outdoors like other children in the world gave me some peace of mind. They had regained a small piece of their childhood, which made our future in Germany less dismal.

Predictability helped me feel more secure. Even though we had very little in regard to material wealth or goods, we all felt blessed to have our health and each other. We knew there were many who had not been as fortunate and this made us thankful for every day we were given. I looked forward to Djura's and my wedding day and cherished every moment I spent with my children. What more could I have hoped for at that point in my life?

## Chapter 72

I loved my girls, each with their own distinct personality. Anneliese was loving, independent, and at times mischievous. She was such a fun little girl. She could be quite stubborn, although her abundance of sweetness overshadowed all that was naughty about her. She was an easy child to love, full of life. Her affectionate and energetic nature was overpowering, and those innocent, deep-blue eyes made your heart melt. She had a way with me that at times caused me to let her get away with behaviors unlike what I expected of the other children.

I remember seeing Anneliese with her pretty blue eyes fixated on the cupboard where I hid cookies and baked treats in the kitchen. Sweet baked goods and chocolates were scarce in our household since there was no money to buy such things very often. Anneliese thought she was being tricky as she tiptoed by me thinking she was going unnoticed. She shimmied up the cupboard as quietly as a five-year-old could manage, grabbed a few cookies, placed one in her mouth, another in her pocket and slipped out of the kitchen. She later came back with cookie crumbs and bits of chocolate smeared on her face. She thought she had fooled me. On her way to play outside with Ingeborg she leaned in to give me a hug and a peck on the cheek. I asked her if she was sneaking cookies and she had a quick reply of "No, I was doing nothing." She then asked if she could take some cookies outside to share with her sister.

I let her go back to the cupboard acting as if I didn't know she had already snuck several cookies earlier and told her to make sure she shared her treats with Ingeborg. As she climbed down from the cupboard she turned and said she wanted to eat all of the cookies herself. She needed much coaxing before she decided she would have to share some with her sister. I watched them from the window and saw Anneliese kept four for herself and gave one cookie to her sister. This wasn't unusual behavior for her. Sharing seemed to be a hard concept for Anneliese to grasp. She also constantly competed with Ingeborg.

Ingeborg, on the other hand, was much quieter, mild tempered, reserved, and always willing to share everything she had with others. She used to worry about those who might be left out or not get their fair share of things. She would give up her own food, toys, or treats to other children if she thought they were being left out. She often played the mother role with her little sister. Ingeborg would pat her sister gently if Anneliese cried or was upset about something. She was 15 months older than Anneliese yet seemed much older. Her ability to care for her little sisters was amazing. She tried to take care of me when I felt bad. For such a little girl, Ingeborg, showed a remarkable degree of compassion toward others.

Krsmanija's little personality was just starting to emerge. She toddled after her two older sisters and delighted in their antics. Ingeborg and Anneliese got her to laugh as no one else could. Both sisters enjoyed being silly and bringing a smile to their baby sister's face.

I knew Anneliese and Ingeborg were both getting old enough that they would have great fun taking part in our June wedding as long as I kept Anneliese's strong will and feistiness under control. I couldn't wait for the day. This was such a happy time in our lives.

Winter was ending. Our wedding day grew closer. I could not wait for June and the warm summer months to arrive. I was in a state of euphoria and was so excited for our wedding. I was hopeful the warm summer weather would cure all the winter illnesses that seemed to be affecting the girls. They all had been sickly off and on during the cold months.

The girls seemed to have cold and flu symptoms and constant congestion that never ended. First it was one, then the other, or all three at the same time came down with something. Home remedies worked the best and I was thankful I had learned many from my mother. The teas and other remedies proved to be beneficial.

Ingeborg had developed whooping cough (pertussis) shortly before spring. The disease was widespread and afflicted many of the other children throughout the city. She coughed so hard that every breath she took pained her. Sometimes she spit up blood from her relentless coughing spells, unable to catch her breath and gagging at times. Ingeborg's bout with whooping cough was much worse than the other children's. She constantly wheezed and coughed uncontrollably. It scared her when her cough took her breath away. I tried to calm her and get her to breathe slowly without feeling panicked, but there wasn't a lot we could do for her. The doctor said the best we could do for her was to keep her comfortable and give her soup to eat. It took months before her cough totally faded and she was finally cured of her illness.

It had been a rough winter for our girls, but somehow Krs was able to escape full blown whooping cough. Anneliese never had whooping cough, although she was having some health problems of her own. The doctor wanted to run several medical tests. Djura and I found ourselves in and out of the doctor's office often with her.

## Chapter 73

On one visit Ingeborg and Krs had come along with Anneliese and me. It was a long day and all three girls soon became restless as we waited for Anneliese's turn to see the doctor. All of them constantly asked over and over how long it would take before it was Anneliese's turn. The doctor's office was full of many sick children that day.

Anneliese went back to see the doctor and he completed his exam. The doctor ran multiple tests to determine what exactly was wrong with her. They had already ruled out whooping cough. We waited several hours for her test results and once they were completed, they called me back to talk with her doctor.

The nurse asked me to come back by myself without the children. When she asked me to step back into the other room without them I immediately got a sick feeling in my stomach. I had been in this same situation before and feared, having witnessed the same sequence of events, bad news was to follow. One of the nurses out front said she would watch all the girls while I went back to talk with the doctor.

As I waited for the doctor, sitting there by myself, looking at the four walls made me nervous and anxious. I worried about what the doctor was going to tell me about Anneliese. I nervously wrung my hands together, interlacing and twirling my fingers. I assumed from past experience the doctor wouldn't have asked me to come back to talk to him unless it was something serious.

I hoped my imagination was getting the best of me. When Ingeborg had whooping cough, I remembered being fearful. I tried to reassure myself that despite my worries, Ingeborg ended up being fine. I prayed this was the case with Anneliese as well. It was unsettling, however, knowing the doctor had not wished to speak with me privately when he gave me Ingeborg's diagnosis.

When the doctor entered, the empty look on his face made my heart sink. I was afraid of what he was going to tell me next and hoped the news wasn't as bad as I imagined. The doctor rubbed his hands together nervously and the worrisome look on his face made me feel apprehensive. When he told me he didn't have good news I braced myself for his coming words. A sickening numbness settled within me. I could tell the doctor's words didn't come easy and it was difficult for him to deliver the news. As he spoke to me the only word I heard before my ears started ringing was "tuberculosis."

With my head in my hands, and tears from fear and confusion spilling from my eyes, it was hard to make myself listen. Tuberculosis, a word I hoped I would never hear again was once again in my life. It had already destroyed someone I dearly loved.

The doctor told me TB had settled in Anneliese's brain. Unlike her father, it had not moved to her lungs. It progressed much differently when it invaded her body. I tried to make sense of what he told me. I thought TB was a disease of the lungs. My sweet girl, her teacher said she was the smartest child in her first grade class. I didn't know how this could be. I did not want to accept the doctor's words.

I had lost Hinrich to TB in 1944. As much as I willed myself not to think about it, it was to no avail. I knew there was no medicine or a cure available in Europe for this terrible disease. Anneliese's father suffered horribly. I didn't want her to feel the same pain he had. Hearing the news was devastating. I needed to get a hold of myself fast. I didn't want the children to see me so upset or let them know how worried I was for Anneliese.

The girls were in the other room with the nurse while the doctor and I were speaking. I knew I had to pull myself together before I stepped out to speak to the children. I couldn't share this horrible news with them, it was too soon and none of them needed to know the seriousness of Anneliese's condition.

I couldn't help but question if the doctor's diagnosis was right. I couldn't imagine how my little blond-haired beauty, who bounced about like nothing was wrong could have something as serious as TB. I wanted with all my heart to protect her. Yet I knew there was nothing I could do to help cure this disease. How could I proceed and what steps should I take next? I felt useless with nowhere to turn. There were no words to adequately describe how helpless I felt as her mother.

I forced myself to gather up whatever strength I had left and wiped the tears from my eyes. I wasn't about to let my girls know how scared and worried I really was. Not knowing what the future would bring was unnerving. I wondered about the health of the rest of the family. I couldn't get the thought of Hinrich's suffering, the blood pooled around him, and his horrible death out of my head. I was afraid and had images of the same thing happening to Anneliese.

The task of telling my family the news weighed heavily on my mind. The doctor had little comfort to offer us. As far as I knew, there were no known medicines or treatments that would cure this illness. Our treatment options were very limited. The doctor had suggested Anneliese go high up into the mountains to ease her symptoms and potentially cure the disease. The same thing had been told to me once before by the doctors who had treated Hinrich. Their advice was useless and the available remedies were full of empty promises. The mountain air did not prolong his life, although being in the mountains seemed to lift Hinrich's spirits. The doctors for some reason believed the mountain air would help Anneliese breathe easier, be more comfortable, and possibly cure her illness.

I couldn't just stand idle waiting for her illness to progress. I felt compelled to do everything I could to help her. I remained hopeful a remedy would be developed or the mountain air recommended by the doctor would save her life. I needed to believe she had a fighting chance. I had known people in the past, including many children, that had died from

TB. Knowing these children who had died and the memories of Hinrich's dreadful death made me question my own faith.

Before I stepped out of the room, I somehow found the strength to stop crying, put on a fake smile, and walked out the door. I looked down the hallway and there were my girls in the entryway playing without a care in the world. Ingeborg and Anneliese were coloring, both of them busy drawing pictures and sharing stories about their drawings. Ingeborg was telling Anneliese a story about a princess she had drawn. Anneliese tried to listen to her while Krs was busy trying to steal away their things by grabbing and ripping the pictures they had drawn. Anneliese began to cry because her drawing had been ruined, and like any other toddler Krs paid no attention. Krs continued to irritate both of her sisters. Anneliese didn't appear to be gravely ill. Her playfulness and active nature gave me hope she would somehow survive all this.

When the girls noticed me standing in the hallway, they all came running to me. Anneliese, always curious asked, "Mommy do we have to take medicine now or can we go home and play?" Ingeborg had no idea her sister was ill and continued to argue with her about their drawings. I told them both to hush feeling more protective of Anneliese's feelings. In a fog I helped gather up all of our things, left the office, and headed out the door. Before we left the doctor's office, I was told the doctor wanted to monitor Anneliese's condition and see her at least once a month. He told me to call him if she had any difficulties or if I saw any changes in her condition.

On the way home I mentioned the possibility of visiting Oma Agnes in Austria sometime soon. The girls were thrilled to hear we might go back to Austria for a visit. When Djura came home that evening, I told him the terrible news and then we both headed out to tell Oma Engle and Opa Brase. It wasn't easy telling my family about Anneliese as I could barely handle thinking about it myself without breaking down. Oma Engle loved Anneliese so, and Djura had grown very close to all our girls. The news of Anneliese's illness was devastating for both of them. Oma Engle broke down and cried as she remembered Hinrich's cruel death. Djura was their father now and the person they knew as Papa. Eventually we told Anneliese and Ingeborg that Anneliese was ill and may require further treatment without any specific details that would frighten either of them.

The news about Anneliese changed the course of our lives, yet Djura and I continued our wedding plans. Both Ingeborg and Anneliese looked forward to the wedding celebration and wearing pretty new dresses. With the news of Anneliese's illness, Hinrich's family pitched in with wedding preparations without any further rude comments.

## Chapter 74

I remember our wedding day well. We had the ceremony and reception at our small home. Oma Engle and Opa Brase worked hard to get their home ready for visitors and the after celebration to commemorate our special day. Oma Engle and Anne had agreed to come to our house and bake many scrumptious breads and goodies for the festivities.

Djura had five Yugoslavian friends stand up for him as part of the wedding party. All three girls, Ingeborg, Anneliese and Krs dressed in their very best, were part of the wedding party. Ingeborg wore a lovely blue, chiffon dress. It had see-through, sheer lace that covered the entire dress and she wore high top shoes that laced up above the ankles. Her long, sandy blonde hair was done up in *Korken Zier*, (elongated curls) a German word for long loose ringlets. I curled her hair before the wedding. The curls hung down to her mid back and she looked stunning even as a child. I remember Ingeborg hated the shoes I made her wear and begged to wear something different. She argued with me saying, "These high top shoes are made for boys and they are so ugly." She wanted shoes that were more delicate, lady-like, and prettier like other girls wore, but the high top shoes were all she had to wear. After the celebration began she soon forgot about her issues with the shoes and had a lovely time at the wedding.

Anneliese ran around playing and did not listen to Oma Engle at all. Oma Engle told her several times during the ceremony to hush while we said our vows. She wore a matching dress I made for her. It was exactly the same color as Ingeborg's. Her hair was also in curls with a matching blue ribbon tied in a perfect bow. She looked as beautiful as her older sister. Krsmanija was a little over a-year old and was wearing a dress that she would end up getting dirty before the night was over. Krs was such a pretty little girl and looked so cute in her dress. She was still a bit unsteady on her feet, tripped easily and fell if she was running too fast. I worried she

293

would never make it through the entire wedding without falling, spilling food on herself, and getting messy. I felt so proud and privileged to be Ingeborg's, Krs's and Anneliese's mother.

Memories of the entire day are as clear as a bell. Everything began as planned. I looked down the road and saw there were seven horse drawn wagons coming toward the house. All of them were full of people. They all came to greet and congratulate us; all ready to join us in our celebration. Everyone was excited and happy, wanted to drink and be merry, and became part of the planned festivities. The crowd was noisy with conversation. The tables were covered in white cloth. Delicious foods were spread over the top of the linens covering almost every inch of the tables and countertops. There were wonderful cream and fruit-filled decorated cakes and tortes.

Oma Engle, Opa Brase, and Anne had brought and baked a variety of breads, cooked and smoked meats before the ceremony ever began as part of the festivities. Using our small stove, made of stone and bricks, I spent hours preparing food the night before and the morning of our wedding. I rushed around early in the morning to get the girls and myself ready and to make final food preparations for the upcoming events.

I was pleased to have the Brases be part of our special celebration. Helping us prepare for the wedding, cooking such wonderful food, and cleaning was their way of giving us their blessings. Oma Engle and Anne had cooked and cleaned for hours preparing for the wedding feast and they never complained once about me marrying Djura.

Throughout the celebration I feared Oma Engle's impulse to speak out against the marriage. They all helped in the best ways they could, and in their own way showed their support. Or maybe they had just given up on the idea they could talk me out of marrying him.

I could tell Djura was nervous so he had a few drinks with his friends to help him relax. He spent most of his time visiting with his Yugoslavian buddies that had come that day. He enjoyed being able to talk freely, laugh, and salute his marriage with several shots of whiskey and his friends. He acted as if something was bothering him and I realized he was feeling badly about not having much money for the wedding. By the time we paid our bills there wasn't much money left to save for our wedding day. Though he didn't get paid much, working for the British Army guarding the depots was a good job. He wasn't able to afford a real wedding ring for me, but he had promised someday he would buy me a proper ring once we were more financially stable.

I loved him regardless, not having a gold wedding band on my finger made no difference to me. It was just a piece of metal of little importance. A lifetime commitment to one another was more meaningful, and no matter what the ring was made of, the sentiment it held was more important. It represented a circle of everlasting love. Djura made me a homemade ring and hoped I would accept it. The type of ring didn't matter because I thought his promise of love to me was quite romantic and I believed he was sincere. Djura was very creative making me a substitute wedding ring using the metal from a bottle top. He had formed it in a perfect circle so it resembled a real wedding band. I tried it on before the wedding and it fit me just fine.

His blacksmith skills had paid off. He had worked with metals most of his life, bending and fixing things that were broken, or creating tools. This band of metal he had made for me was soon to be placed on my left hand and was the symbol of our love. The belief surrounding the wedding band was that the vein which ran through the ring finger was supposed to lead to the person's heart. I didn't believe the cost of the symbol mattered much, as long as we loved each other. I would be completely happy with whatever was placed on my finger.

There was much celebration the day of our wedding with many drinking and enjoying the festivities long before the wedding ever began. The men Djura had asked to stand up for him could really put down the liquor. Many of the other men that came joined in the celebration, drinking their own whiskeys, beer, and wine.

## Chapter 75

Our wedding ceremony was held outdoors in the yard. The day was bright and warm. Djura wore his British uniform. I wore a white, silk dress that was fitted and draped all the way to the floor. The dress had see-through, white lace chiffon that covered the entire dress and my sleeves were mid-length so my arms showed. My white veil was draped over my dress and hung to the floor. I carried a large bouquet of fresh, deep red roses cut from the garden and given to me by Djura. Following the ceremony, I placed them in a vase so they became part of the decorations. While we repeated our nuptials, I thought how fortunate I was to have found two very special men in my life whom I loved and cherished. They both meant so much to me and I loved them until "death do we part."

I realized at a very, young age one thing I could always count on was change. I couldn't stop it from happening nor could I predict what would happen next. I was never sure how these changes would affect me and where life might take me. We all had hidden talents and strengths and the will to survive. Our will to live kept us going and there was always a new tomorrow to look forward to.

Everyone at the wedding seemed happy and the guests continued to celebrate eating the scrumptious tortes and drinking whisky and wine. I mingled with the crowd and tried to greet all our guests. I didn't want to be rude and leave anyone out because I wanted to make everyone feel welcomed. There were some guests I had a difficult time communicating with because I didn't speak their language. Djura's friends were all speaking Serbian. I knew very little of the language, only what I had picked up from Djura. He was able to speak German fluently so that's what we spoke at home and since we lived in Germany it only made sense to speak it.

There was about an hour before the actual ceremony was to begin and Djura was nowhere in sight. I began looking for him. I searched the yard and was unable to locate him. Moving through the crowd, I noticed some of his friends were also missing. I asked some of the guests if they had seen him or knew where he had gone. I found myself doing most of the entertaining because he was nowhere to be found. I was beginning to feel some frustration. He had left me at our house all alone to visit with everyone.

I knew he was nervous but hoped not nervous enough to do something drastic like changing his mind about marrying me. Maybe he needed to get away from the crowd for a few minutes to collect his thoughts. I knew the minister would soon be ready to gather the wedding party. The last time I had spoken to Djura he seemed to be fine. Moving through the crowd, I asked about his whereabouts. I learned a few of the guests had overheard Djura and a few other guests complaining about the heat. They had talked about going swimming. I worked hard to conceal my frustration. Several people heard them talking about going to a nearby swimming hole to take a quick dip to cool off. I discounted that as a possibility as I could hardly believe he and his friends would leave right before our ceremony to go swimming.

Several of us began searching for him. I knew he and his friends had been drinking for several hours before the ceremony began. I was unsure how much they had actually drank that morning, but maybe it was enough liquor they lost track of time. We looked for him for nearly an hour and I was feeling desperate to find him. Minutes before the ceremony was to start, Djura and his friends, laughing and singing while they staggered arm and arm were spotted walking along the path that led to a nearby pond. Everyone looked relaxed and no one seemed to be in a rush. They had actually gone swimming!

## A picture of some of the infamous swimmers

They wandered into the yard and Djura could tell I was extremely irritated with him. He had been swimming with his buddies; I could hardly believe it. He grinned making up several excuses for their behavior saying the heat was unbearable. He complained of wearing his warm uniform all day long and said they went for a quick dip and had every intention of getting back in time for the wedding. I was not at all amused. Swimming only minutes before our wedding was inexcusable! The alcohol they had drank didn't help matters any.

Nonetheless, we went on with the wedding as planned. I was relieved they all made it back in time. I never would have heard the end of it from my guests, especially Oma Engle and Opa Brase. Djura would have also found himself in big trouble with me if he had not come back in time for our wedding.  It wasn't the best way to start out a marriage, yet all in all things turned out fine.  We were officially married on June 11, 1948.

Djura and I had several conversations about his swimming excursion after the wedding.  Through the years this story has come up many times.  With time I was able to joke and laugh about it with Djura.  My advice to anyone is to avoid swimming minutes before your wedding no matter how hot it is outdoors to avoid future quarrels.

**Djura in his British uniform similar to the one he wore at our wedding.**

## Djura and Karoline's wedding June 11, 1948

## Chapter 76

The distraction of our wedding was welcomed, however after the festivities I focused my energy on Anneliese. We found it difficult to get our lives on track. Djura stayed in the barracks most of the time while our girls and I remained in our house near Oma Engle's. We tried to see each other as often as possible. We would stay at the barracks with Djura for a few days or Djura would come home to stay during a leave from duty. Our lives became more hectic running back and forth between the barracks and home. I became accustomed to Djura being gone for up to week at a time depending on his detail with the British Civil Service. I knew I couldn't always depend on Djura to be home with us when work took him away.

We considered living on the base permanently, however, decided it would be too far to travel to Anneliese's doctor appointments. Anneliese's appointments were now twice a month and Djura usually took her on his bike. She loved riding with him. Ingeborg sometimes rode along with them for fun and even though it was just a trip to the doctor, they always enjoyed a bike ride to town.

**Ingeborg riding her bike while in Germany when she was eight-years-old.**

A few months after our wedding, Anneliese began to show more signs of her illness, although her symptoms were much different than her father's. Because she wasn't coughing intensely, most of the family around us didn't realize how sick she was becoming. She felt restless, tired easily, and at times was too exhausted to play with her sisters.

Sometimes during the night she awoke in a cold sweat, which left her soaking wet. It was as if she had just stepped out of a bath totally drenched from head to toe. She woke up crying out for me. She cried tears of shame. She was embarrassed thinking she had wet the bed. We had to change her clothes and bed linens. I tried my best to comfort her. I held her, rocked her, told her how special she was and how much I loved her. It broke my heart to see her hurting. It took every bit of strength I had not to break down in front of her. After she was taken care of and fell back to sleep, I left her room and wept endlessly praying to God he would not let my baby suffer. I felt useless. The best I could do was to help her to stay comfortable and reassure her she would be alright.

The doctors told me people could have TB living dormant inside of them for a several years before they started showing any symptoms and were diagnosed with active TB. Some of the inflicted died in a short period of time while others recovered and ended up with a dark spot on their lung or elsewhere that was visible on an X-Ray. Others had a persistent cough throughout their lives. The doctor thought that Anneliese's immune system had been weakened, but he was unsure why. Perhaps it was because of the all stress we had gone through during the last five years. I wondered if Anneliese had been infected with TB by her father. That would never be known. She was the only one in the family that had become ill. The rest of us all tested negative for the disease.

Anneliese's illness began to affect her activities and playtime. I felt helpless because there was really little I could do for her. I tended to her in any way I could and gave her all my love. At only six-years-old she didn't understand what was happening to her little body. I tried hard not to think about the future and dealt with life one a day at a time. It was heart-wrenching when I thought too far into the future. Thoughts of terrible things happening to her were overwhelming and discouraging. I could only consider the future in short increments of time.

Every day was becoming a crisis. I was haunted by the image of Hinrich dying, laying on his death bed and vomiting pools of blood towards the end. If I fixated too much on Anneliese's illness I knew I would go crazy. I needed to stay strong for her and our other two daughters. When Anneliese woke up at night, dripping wet and in tears, I went to her and cradled her in my arms, as I did when she was a little baby. I sat and rocked her, holding her close until she drifted back to sleep. Gently I explained the sickness was at fault, not her. It made her body do things she could no longer control. I reassured her she hadn't done a single thing wrong, none of this was her fault and she had done nothing to feel bad or embarrassed about. When she asked questions about her illness, I felt compelled to distort the truth by telling her she would be alright not really knowing if that were true.

When I lay next to Anneliese, I stared at the blank wall. I held her close hoping she felt my warmth and all the love I had for her. Curled up next to her, I held her tight all through the night freeing her of all her fears. When I'd lay with her she just looked at me and smiled, as I tenderly stroked her soft blond hair. She would hold my hand to make sure I was still there and hadn't left her side. I resurrected whatever hope was left inside me telling her all of this would soon pass.

The doctor's only suggestion as Anneliese's illness progressed was to take her to Austria to breathe the mountain air. As the days went by she began to have profound symptoms that left her small body ravished and weakened. The high fevers started and sometimes lasted for days, and her night sweats never seemed to end. Anneliese was no longer the energetic little girl we once knew. She became increasingly tired and frail. I found her standing outside the house many times as she watched her sisters play; too exhausted to join in their fun. She suffered from severe bouts of nausea, which affected her appetite. I tried to persuade her to eat. She told me, "Mommy, I'm just not hungry anymore." Anneliese had lost several pounds and couldn't afford to lose anymore.

Her condition was getting worse and she struggled to get bites of food down during a meal. I could hardly stand watching my little girl slowly withering away right in front of my eyes. Anneliese's stubborn temperament and feisty personality slowly faded, leaving her weakened and more fragile than ever. She was no longer able to battle with her sisters and didn't seem interested in keeping her things to herself and away from them. Her strong will and spirited personality was dwindling fast. My little, feisty child was slowly disappearing.

The doctor said sometimes the disease was worse for young children. It seemed as though the bacteria was spreading more quickly inside her small body, quicker than anyone had thought was possible. I didn't understand why or how this was happening to her. It had taken years for Hinrich to be diagnosed with TB and he had lived quite some time with the illness before he died. She started complaining of having headaches and sometimes found it hard to go to sleep from the pain.

Thankfully even with all of her troubles she still had some good days and was able to enjoy herself. On a good day I would find her happily playing with her sisters, but I noticed her weakened manner. We realized with her rapidly declining condition, we needed to get her to Austria quickly in hopes the mountain air would help her body fight the infection.

At Anneliese's next doctor's appointment, I asked him if he would write a letter of support so that we could get visas to travel legally to Austria. I prayed and hoped that her stay in Austria would help save her life. Her sisters didn't understand how sick she really was especially since she had good days occasionally. When I asked Ingeborg if she thought Anneliese felt ill she would say, "She isn't sick at all." Ingeborg was seven-years-old and it was difficult for her to understand what was going on with Anneliese.

I tried to prepare Anneliese for the trip to Austria. I told her we needed to go there because she was sick, and if we went to the mountains, the air would help her feel much better. I reassured her by telling her the doctor recommended we go, and that Oma Agnes and Opa Valentin would be waiting for us with open arms.

With the letter of support from Anneliese's doctor, our visas were processed quickly. Djura, Krs, and I were granted temporary visas and Anneliese a long-term visa. Djura and I tried to obtain long-term visas, but were denied since we were not the ones who had fallen ill.

Our options were limited so we decided we would leave Anneliese in Austria in the care of her Oma Agnes until she recovered. If we overstayed our visas we would be in Austria illegally, and possibly found and prosecuted. Once approved for our visitor's visa we had to adhere to the European travel protocols and knew the border guards were monitoring travelers closely. There were constant checks and everyone was carefully tracked on the length of time they were gone out of the country. Random checks were done to see if visas were valid or if they had expired once one crossed a border.

With the travel stipulations stated on our visas I would have to leave Anneliese behind with her Oma Agnes. Her doctors recommended she stay until she was cured. We were considered lucky to have been approved for any kind of legal passport to travel with Anneliese.

I tried to explain to Anneliese she would be staying with her Oma Agnes for a while and I would have to leave her in Austria. She didn't understand why I must leave her there all alone. And being the curious child she was, she had a million questions to ask me about her Oma Agnes, Austria, and about how long it would take her to get better so she knew how long we would be separated from each other. She talked about her Oma Agnes and loved her, although did not know her well. Oma Engle was the only other person she stayed alone with overnight. Leaving her sisters would be terribly difficult for her.

I tried to explain to her with words she understood why the officials wouldn't let me stay with her. I told her if I did not follow the rules on my travel papers and return to Germany, I would be arrested and perhaps thrown into prison. Once she knew we were leaving she made me promise over and over many times I would never forget to come back for her. I assured her she didn't need to worry because I loved her with all my heart and would miss her far too much to ever leave her. I consoled her as best I could because I wanted to alleviate all her fears. And mine.

I swore I would visit her as much as possible and made a solemn vow to go back and get her so she could come home once she was feeling better. I assured her the mountain air would help cure her and she never doubted me for a minute. In her mind she knew I would be coming back for her, yet she was terrified to be left alone in Austria without her mother, grandparents, Djura, and her sisters. I felt heartbroken trying to explain the situation to such an innocent soul. She was only six-years-old.

I had many sleepless nights thinking about leaving Anneliese in Austria with my mother. I prayed night and day all would turn out well and she would be cured. I was hopeful and held on to the only thing left; faith. I believed in God. He would surely protect her, only a cruel inhumane God would let her die and take my little girl from me.

I hoped as Anneliese spent time with her Oma Agnes, it would ease the pain of her missing me after I was gone. I was much like my mother and was wishful her surrogate nurturing and love for Anneliese would keep her healthy and happy until I was able to return. I clung to the hope the doctors would be right this time and the mountain air would help my sweet girl recover.

I had written to my mother to let her know about Anneliese's condition and our plan to come to Austria one way or the other. I was glad we would not be trudging by foot over the mountains with a sick child. Oma Engle had already agreed to keep Ingeborg while we were gone. She was worried sick about Anneliese.

Our temporary visas were approved for two weeks. I believed the Processing Agency was afraid if they approved anything other than temporary visas, we may not return to Germany once in Austria. After the war the government seemed concerned about the population of Germany dwindling. If people started leaving the country in masses it would have negatively affected the economy. Granting temporary visas seemed to be the best way to control the flow of traffic coming into and out of the country.

Fortunately, Anneliese was excited about going to visit her grandparents and Aunt Frieda. She happily told the other relatives we were going to Austria. I overheard her tell her sister, "Ingeborg, I'm sick, but I will get better soon, that's why I'm going to go stay with Oma Agnes at her house." She was a brave little girl and didn't seem scared of her illness. Despite her worries about being left in Austria, she somehow managed to stay positive and looked forward to the trip.

We hadn't even left yet, and I couldn't help but think about my separation from Anneliese. I kept reminding myself of the ultimate goal which was to get her well, and I was willing to do whatever it took to make that happen. I tried to stay optimistic, implanting images and thoughts in my head of her becoming healthy, playing, and frolicking as she once had with her sisters. I stayed focused on the idea she wouldn't be in Austria long and we would be together in no time at all. Holding on to those thoughts and picturing her healthy once again was the only way I kept my sanity.

## Chapter 77

It was November of 1948. We learned that Djura would not be coming with us to Austria as we had first planned. He had to report for duty and was denied time off to make the trip. Djura had gone with us to Austria before and was able to meet my mother and father when we visited them.

Travel continued to be difficult for everyone. The borders were closed to travelers without visas and heavily guarded by American and British soldiers. Djura planned to help us catch our first train. There were no passenger trains up and running. With all the travel restrictions and rebuilding taking place in Germany, many of the railways were shut down after being damaged during the war. Anneliese, Krs, and I would have to ride on top of the coal cars all the way to Austria in the cool November air. Opa Valentin would meet us after we crossed over into Austria.

I carried my bag and pushed Krsmanija in her small baby buggy. Djura had come to the train station along with us to help us climb onto the coal cars. Having both children with me made our journey more difficult, and if we wanted to travel by train that meant we rode on top of coal. At the station we found there were many other passengers waiting to get on top of the train. I hoped the baby buggy I had brought for Krs would make our travels much easier. I wouldn't have to constantly carry her in my arms. Djura boosting us up on to the coal cars made my job of getting the girls up on top less difficult.

Riding on top of the cars was very uncomfortable. Black soot was everywhere. The dirty conditions were no surprise to any of us as we had made the same trip before. We knew the journey would be long and unpleasant, but it was the only way we could travel legally to Austria. It would take days before we reached Bleiberg. The trains would take us part of the way, but the rest of the tip would have to be made on foot. This would make it very difficult to carry Krs and care for Anneliese. Our food was in short supply because I could only bring so little with us.

Father would be waiting in Austria with a horse and wagon to take us to Bleiberg. He helped me across the border during every trip I made. I don't know how we would have done it without him.

This trip was more grueling than previous times. I met some kind, dark-skinned strangers along the way that had been traveling on top of the same coal car with me. They offered to help me with the girls and gave us some food to eat. I hadn't seen or known many black people in either Austria or Germany. They were few in number at this time. I had only met two black families the entire time I lived in Europe. The wonderful family I met on the train had been persecuted terribly during the war and had gone through many awful experiences, more than most could imagine. They were fortunate to have survived the war. And I felt fortunate to have their assistance.

This particular black family seemed genuinely concerned for our safety. They helped me carry my things and stayed with us until we made it over the border. I was glad I stumbled upon this caring family during our journey. I met many kind people during my travels and was amazed by their willingness to help a stranger. The only thing most people had left to give was of themselves. Many people had lost their families, homes and friends. Once we were over the border I made sure to thank the family for all their help and kindness. They didn't ask for anything in return and a simple, sincere thank you seemed to be all they expected from me.

My mother and father were elated to see us. Mother's eyes filled with tears as soon as she saw the girls and me pull up in front of the house. As soon as Anneliese saw Oma Agnes, she jumped off and gave her and Aunt Frieda hugs and kisses. I was relieved to be home. My mother's loving presence helped me to relax and take my mind off of our problems. Anneliese did well during most of the trip with only a few small setbacks. She tired easily and needed to stop several times to rest before we reached

Father. I was relieved she was close to the mountains. I knew this was exactly what the doctor ordered and it provided me with a greater sense of hope. I wished our time together would last forever, but I only had two weeks to stay in Austria before I returned to Germany with Krs.

**Picture of Anneliese (on the right), before she was diagnosed with TB.**

Anneliese was a bit restless after the long wagon ride. Totally exhausted she still wanted to run and play with her sister and Aunt Frieda. My mother watched Anneliese romp about while she played with the other children. It was hard for Mother to understand how sick Anneliese really was after watching her with the other children. She was active, playful, and at times full of energy. She seemed too healthy to be sick. Mother didn't realize this was one of her better days. It was only a matter of time before her Oma Agnes witnessed how harshly the infection affected Anneliese.

Our stay with Oma Agnes was filled with happiness. On a good day Anneliese laughed and giggled while she played with her dolls and the other girls. She pushed her baby dolls about in their stroller and rocked them on her hip. Nurturing them as if they were real while whispering and motioning for us to be quiet by putting her finger up to her lips, warning us we'd wake them up. When I heard the girls laughing and playing together it helped take my mind off of her illness.

I thought about the doctor's encouraging words. I tried to distract myself from my most painful thoughts. I hoped with my mother's help Anneliese could win her battle against TB. The time we spent with my mother was a Godsend. She planted an extra dose of hope in all of us. She somehow convinced me things would be fine, given time. Mother promised to stay in close contact and reassured me she would take care of Anneliese until I returned.

The days spent with my family went quickly. My mother's comforting words and her heartfelt promises kept me from falling apart. Her optimism was infectious. I began to think only good things lay ahead for Anneliese and me. Mother constantly reassured me Anneliese and I would only be separated for a short time, she would soon be cured, and before long I would be back in Austria to get her.

I was deeply saddened our time together had gone by so quickly and our visit came to an end far too soon. No matter how much time I spent with Anneliese it didn't seem to be enough to satisfy my hunger to hold her. My desire to keep her close became my own personal demon. I struggled with the idea of leaving her behind. It was almost more than I could stand.

I had thought spending every minute with my daughter over the last two weeks would have made things easier when it came time for me to leave her. Unfortunately, I found when that day came it made no difference. The anguish and emptiness I felt had only intensified. It settled in the pit of my stomach. I wished I could take her away with me. I couldn't get leaving out of my head and pictured her heartbreak when I said goodbye. My heart ached for her and I hadn't even left Austria yet.

How could I leave her behind?  She was in the best possible hands staying with my mother, yet it still didn't make leaving her any easier.  I worried about both Anneliese and my mother.  But staying with an expired visa meant possible imprisonment and being torn away from my entire family.

Mother hadn't had an easy life over the past nine years.  I worried about the toll it would take on her having to care for a sick child.  I didn't want to burden her any more than she already had been, but I believed this was the best place for Anneliese to recover.  It was the only option we had left and our best hope for her recovery.

Oma Agnes's undying love and dedication to Anneliese most certainly made caring for her more difficult.  The constant dread of possibly losing Anneliese weighed heavy on Mother's mind and watching her sweet granddaughter grow weaker day by day was emotionally draining.  Oma Agnes wasn't about to let anyone else take care of her.  Her steadfast wish to help Anneliese recover took precedence over any other consideration.  She felt compelled to care for her.  Her loving devotion to Anneliese was shown in the most heartfelt ways.  Oma Agnes prayed every night for Anneliese's recovery just as I had in the past.  She hoped Anneliese's stay in Austria would remedy all of her weaknesses and she would win the battle against TB.  Oma Agnes's optimism inspired everyone around her and gave me added confidence that Anneliese was in the best of hands.

We spent our last night wishing we had more time left together.  I didn't want morning to come, afraid to face the next day.  I had to leave her, but I did not know if I could walk away.  In our bed I held her close in my arms and sang her favorite lullaby stroking her head gently.  I wanted her to remember the love and the warmth we felt for each other.  I wanted to remember her touch and the smell of her skin.  I held her as tight as I could and never let go.  She needed to feel the warmth from my body and know I would never forget her.  I quietly whispered in her ear that I loved her, hoping she would feel safe, and rid her of all her fears.  I wanted so much to explain why I had to leave her and struggled to articulate each and every word. The words came hard. I couldn't help myself as I felt tears trickling down my face. We then folded our hands to say our traditional bedtime prayer. She looked up at the sky thanking God for everything he had done for us, asked him to keep us in his heart and with him forever.

I prayed silently for Anneliese so she would not hear me ask God to please, please save her life. I didn't know if I could live through losing her. I didn't want her to experience any suffering nor be tortured by the loss of not seeing her mother. I was glad she did not understand how long she would be in Austria or leaving her would have been much harder.

I lay awake for hours thinking about my precious little girl. She snuggled up next to me and slowly drifted off to sleep. Grandma and Grandpa were in their beds. I wondered if Mother was restless and lay awake like me thinking about tomorrow. I didn't want Anneliese to worry about me or be afraid of anything after I was gone. Anneliese would sleep with her Oma Agnes after I left. I hoped this would ease the transition of our separation.

At home in Germany, Anneliese and the other girls could wander into my bedroom when they felt scared and I'd let them crawl into bed with me. When I think back I clearly remember how I felt when I slept next to my mother, protected and safe from all that was bad. When she held me close, my worries magically went away. I hoped Anneliese would feel that same emotional connection with her Oma Agnes. I hated the thought of her waking up frightened and crying out for me.

My mother and father would be left alone to deal with Anneliese's pain. The guilt I felt was unrelenting. Restless and tired, I tossed and turned most of the night. After only sleeping a few hours, I awoke to the sun peering over the horizon. I forced myself to gather up my things. Every few minutes I wandered back over to my bed and gazed at Anneliese. She was the image of a beautiful little angel, lying there peacefully cuddled in her down blanket Oma Agnes made for her. I never wanted to forget her sweet smile, rosy red cheeks and her fine, golden, blonde hair, I gently caressed her cheek.

I couldn't help but stop and stare unable to continue or think about leaving. Her golden hair was draped across her cheek with a soft gentle smile on her lips. I called to Krs to come get ready to leave. Anneliese heard us talking. Within minutes she jumped out of bed, running to see what we were doing, wanting to come with us. It was only a matter of time before we were all dressed, and ready to leave. In the next half-hour we would be on our way back to Germany. Father was outside getting the horses and wagon ready, loading our things. I turned away and tried not to watch him, not wanting to be reminded I was leaving Anneliese. The inevitable was about to happen so I spent my last few minutes surrounded by my family. My mother had started crying over a week ago and had not stopped. Father had finished outside and came back in to see if I was ready for the journey.

I wanted to keep my emotions in check, and tried my best not to cry in front of Anneliese, not wanting her to feel any worse. Fighting back tears and all out sobbing in that moment was one of the hardest things I have ever done in my entire life. I went to the wagon to put one last piece of clothing in my bag. As I walked back to Anneliese, I felt like someone was ripping my heart right out from my chest. I stopped next to her, bent down and whispered in her ear. I told her that I loved her more than she could ever know, that I would be back very soon, that she would be feeling much better by then, and that we would pack up her things and go back to Germany together. She smiled and gave me a big hug and kiss. I tightened my grip around her and she asked, "Mama, when are you coming back to get me? I don't want you to leave me here by myself." I promised her with all my heart I would be back in a few months to see her. I never wanted to let go and held her tight in my arms. I forced myself to loosen my grip, knowing what I had to do in order to save her life, even if it meant destroying a part of mine.

I needed to say goodbye. My heart was breaking and I could barely tear myself away from her. She was holding me tight as tears streamed down her face; she did not want to let go. I pried her little fingers off my dress and handed her, screaming, over to my mother. It took all the strength I had to tear her away from me. Then I turned away hoping she had not seen the stream of tears rolling down my face. Both Mother and Anneliese were sobbing. Anneliese was reaching her arms out for me crying that she wanted to come with me. It was heartbreaking, I couldn't stop my tears. Leaving my little girl was more than I could bear. I had to rip myself away from her for she never would have let me go. This was her last chance to survive. It was the only way to save her.

I wept for my daughter and my mother and myself. None of us should have had to suffer like this, after everything we all had survived. I somehow found the strength to walk away from her flailing arms that were reaching for me. I then turned and waved goodbye while calling out one more time "I love you."

The emptiness I felt was indescribable, I felt hollowed from the inside out. I climbed into the wagon with my father, and as I looked back I saw my mother trying to comfort my Anneliese. I wanted to jump out of the wagon, run back and scoop her into my arms. I needed to have faith, and believe Anneliese would be alright. The mountain air had to help her.

I waved and watched their silhouettes fade until they disappeared from my sight. I felt empty, numbed by my despair. It was as though the rest of the world was turning, yet I was standing still, as I had felt when I stood over Hinrich's grave. Wiping the tears from my eyes, I turned to my father in the wagon. He nodded at me as if to say things would be okay. I noticed he had been crying too and he wiped his own tears away. He said, "Karoline it will be alright, Anneliese is in good hands and she will be with God and her Oma. They will take good care of her while you're gone. You need not worry. We will all pray for her every day and take good care of her." He tried to fill my head and heart with good thoughts. He reassured

317

me I would be able to apply for another visa and come back to visit them soon. By then Anneliese would be feeling better and she could return with me.

## Chapter 78

It took four days before we reached our home in Klenkendorf. I was sure Oma Engle and Djura waited for our safe return home. I had written them one letter on the second day we were in Austria, telling them of my intended date of return and my planned route to Klenkendorf. It was a possibility I would return to Klenkendorf before the letter reached them. They needed to know my route in case something happened to me along the way. If I didn't make it back home to see them again, I wanted them to know how much I loved them. During these uncertain times I never knew if I would make it back home. I could take nothing for granted.

I missed the rest of my family and I so much wanted to see Ingeborg. My feelings were fragmented and torn between my desire to stay in Austria with Anneliese and the deep fear of what would happen to me and my family if I didn't return to Germany by the time my visa expired. The trip back to Germany was the most grueling and exhausting trip I had ever taken. Anneliese weighed heavily on my mind through every leg of our journey.

When we finally arrived in Klenkendorf, Oma Engle, Opa Brase, Djura, and Ingeborg eagerly waited for our return. Ingeborg met Krs and I as soon as we pulled up in front of the house. She ran toward us, jumped up on the wagon, and gave us both a big hug and a kiss before we ever made it to the door. Oma Engle greeted us with a smile, glad to see we had arrived home safely. Djura waited outside the front door, the crestfallen look on his face was obvious. He didn't have to say a word, I knew exactly how he was feeling. Had she returned with us Anneliese would have darted past me yelling, "Papa, Papa," and "Hello!" Her blithe spirit had been left in Austria, distant and unreachable. Our family no longer felt whole. Everyone in the Brase household prayed every night for Anneliese's recovery. We waited impatiently for her to come back home. Peace had not yet come to my family, even though the war had ended several years ago.

The entire family was deeply affected by her illness. Her absence was like a gray cloud hanging over us. The distance between us made it so much harder, and I sensed the same empty feelings I had when I was taken from my own mother. I now knew exactly how Mother must have felt when I was snatched away from her. It wasn't a feeling I wished on anyone.

Mother wrote she had been very busy with Anneliese this last month. They traveled back and forth to Klagenfurt because Anneliese's doctor was located there. He was a specialist and had worked with many other TB patients. We had been told he was a good doctor and knew a great deal about her disease. He had given us additional hope of Anneliese's possible recovery, seeming genuine and positive about her future prognosis. I held on to every reassuring word he told my mother. I played it back over and over in my head.

The map below shows the city Klagenfurt where Anneliese and Hinrich traveled to see their doctors for evaluation and their treatment. Bleiberg is not shown on most map, however is approximately 53 kilometers (33 miles) from Klagenfurt.

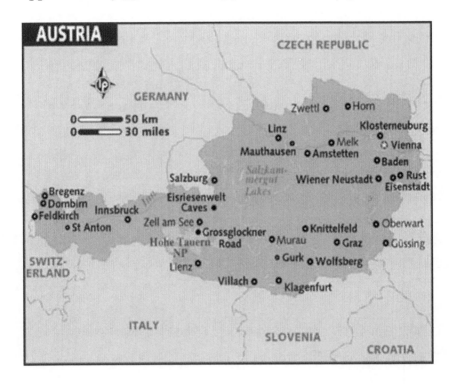

(http://www.mapsofworld.com)

Both Djura and I tried to stay busy, although Anneliese was always on our minds. Mother wrote to me several times after my return. Anneliese wasn't getting any worse, yet she wasn't showing any signs of improvement either. Her letters gradually began to reveal that Anneliese was growing weaker. The doctor in Klagenfurt was not able to offer much help. Anneliese had now been with her Oma Agnes for nearly two months. Mother suggested I try to get another visa and come back to Austria as soon as I could to see Anneliese before she became more ill. Mother was afraid she might take a turn for the worse; her condition was not improving.

My mother struggled and tried to stay strong for Anneliese though she found it more and more difficult to watch as Anneliese became weaker. Mother tried her best to console Anneliese when she cried out for me. Anneliese had drawn pictures of her, me, and the rest of the family. She insisted that mother send her colored pictures along with the letters. She insisted these pictures were only for her mother. The longer she was in Austria the more she missed me.

Mother said she found Anneliese pacing back and forth in front of the house holding on to her doll calling out "Mommy where are you? Please come get me!" She would stop for a moment, then looked down the road to see if I was coming. Her times of sadness became a daily ritual. I wondered why this poor little girl was being punished. The sense of guilt I felt for leaving her overwhelmed me.

I became desperate and tormented by Anneliese's incessant wish for me to come get her. I had no choice but to leave Germany as soon as I could and planned a trip back to Austria. I couldn't imagine how my mother must have felt seeing Anneliese cry out for me day after day. She wanted her mother in the worst way and could not understand why I was not there with her.

I had to secure a visa to travel to Austria and I hoped this trip Djura could come with me. I needed his support now more than ever. Oma Engle was sympathetic and willing to help. All of this was a strain for her too. She missed Anneliese greatly and prayed for her safe return home.

Djura heard conversations at work about giving displaced persons in Germany the opportunity to immigrate legally and permanently to other countries. We spoke about finding Anneliese the best of medical care and seriously considered the possibility of someday moving outside of Germany to start a new life as well as provide her with the medical care she needed.

Hearing from Mother about Anneliese's declining health made us more determined to find a place where she could be cured.

I needed to first secure a visa to travel to Austria because being able to move from Germany was not likely going to happen as quickly as we hoped. I completed several travel requests hoping I would be granted a visa. The processing agency denied request after request. With each rejection, I grew angrier. I emphasized how sick Anneliese was to the processing agency and how important it was for me to get there, although it didn't seem to matter. I was frantic and worried sick something terrible would happen before I could get there. I went to the consulate day after day hoping to persuade them to open up travel to the domestic people of Germany. The workers grew tired of seeing me and listening to my repeated requests. No one cared about my little girl or what was happening to her or that I was not with her.

As a last resort, I contacted Anneliese's local doctor and asked him to write another letter of support hoping he could persuade the agency into giving me a travel visa, but to no avail. My requests were continually denied. I was losing hope I would ever be granted permission to go to Austria so I planned another trip regardless.

Anneliese had been in Austria without me for far too long. The thought of her being in pain and her desperation to see me was driving me insane. I needed to see her as soon as possible no matter what happened to me.

Djura was unable to come with me as he had to work and I decided to leave Ingeborg with Oma Engle. Krs would travel along with me. Everyone worried about me leaving by myself with a two-year-old knowing I was already upset about Anneliese. I couldn't stay in Germany a minute longer and had to see Anneliese before her condition continued to deteriorate and I was too late.

## Chapter 79

It was the end of March 1949. Ingeborg's birthday had come and gone. My things were packed and I was ready to leave for Austria. Within only a few days I would be traveling by train with Krs across Germany. Djura and Oma Engle both understood my strong desire to be with Anneliese, but worried for my safety as I again planned to travel illegally.

Snow would remain higher up in the mountains with the possibility of wet melting snow in the lower elevations. I wanted to protect both Krs and me from illness or frost bite during our travels. I planned on having to carry Krs most of the hike through the mountains.

We would hitch a ride on the train through Germany and hoped to reach the border without complications. At the train station I searched for a safe place where we could hop up on the coal car without being noticed. As expected, the trip was long, cold, and tiring. We stopped at a train station close to the border, and with Krs in my arms I climbed down off the car. I decided to check my suitcase at the baggage claim in the train station. Baggage claim was good about keeping your luggage, sometimes for months until the rightful owner claimed it. I had used the baggage claim service before and knew they didn't inquire about your intentions to cross the border.

Krs and I took a short walk down the road close to the train station. I planned on returning for my suitcase within the next hour. I let Krs run about as we walked paying close attention to any signs of danger. There were a few other people walking in the area where we had gotten off to stretch our legs. Suddenly, a deep stern voice called out, "Stop!" from behind us. I turned around and saw three armed border patrol guards looking directly at us. Frightened I would be arrested, I scooped Krs up and began to run.

Stealing a quick look behind me, the guards pursued me as I fled. I ran as fast as I could, but they closed in quickly and soon surrounded me. Forcibly, they grabbed my arm and asked where I was from and where was I headed. I quickly made up a tale that my husband was close by and he and I were traveling home to Klenkendorf.

Disbelieving my story, they dragged me by the arm and took us toward an old house. Several armed guards were posted around the perimeter of the house. They asked me for my legal travel documents. I told them they had been left on the train and asked to be released so I could get them, hoping to escape. Ignoring my request, they locked Krs and me inside a small room in the old house.

The room was locked up tight with no windows for escape. A metal watering bucket sat in the middle of the room. I was instructed to use it for bathroom needs. The only other item in the room was a small tattered cot pushed next to the wall. Shortly after our arrival, I was interrogated by guards for nearly an hour. I revealed nothing new, sticking to my original story.

We sat in the room for hours with nothing to eat or drink. My thoughts fluctuated between Anneliese and our fate with the guards. We were threatened with being locked up indefinitely if I didn't produce proper travel documents. We fell asleep on the cot that evening and were awakened early for another round of interrogation. I again repeated what had already been said. If I shared my plan to illegally cross the border, I would have been immediately imprisoned.

During our second day in the room we were given a small amount of water and bread. I pleaded with the guards to release us. As day turned into night, I worried how long we would be kept and locked up in the small room. Lying next to Krs on the cot, I thought of Anneliese and my family in Klenkendorf. I was desperate to get out of this situation. I was fearful of the guards, leery of what they could do to us, to me. Knowing what men were capable of intensified my fright.

325

On the third day, I begged one of the guards to release us so I could buy Krs some milk. They had heard her crying the last two days for milk and I hoped they would show mercy. To my surprise, Krs and I were allowed to go to the nearby kiosk and buy some milk and food. I didn't ask questions and left immediately. I ran back to the train station as fast I as my legs could carry me. I'm not sure what precipitated the guard's decision to let us go. Perhaps it was kindness, I'll never know.

Terribly frightened and utterly devastated at my failed attempt to cross the border, I decided to return to Klenkendorf. My decision to return did not come easy. The patrolling guards knew my face and I worried they would be looking for me.

I rushed back to the train station with Krs in my arms, picked up my suitcase, and we fled for safety and home. Overcome with guilt, I questioned my decision to bring Anneliese to Austria. I cried in agony from not being able to fulfill my promise to her. I could only hope I would get back to see her before her condition worsened.

Once back in Klenkendorf, Djura told me he did not want me traveling illegally to Austria again for fear I would be imprisoned. Oma Engle agreed it was too risky. I was shattered by the thought of not seeing Anneliese. The image of her weeping and crying out for me was always in my thoughts. There was nothing I could do to relieve her pain.

## Chapter 80

Mother wrote often hoping to relieve some of my heartbreak. I could tell she tried to protect me with guarded words, but she could not hide the truth from me. Anneliese had grown too weak to climb up the steep mountainside. Mother wrote she carried Anneliese in her arms up the mountain path every day, never giving up hope she would benefit from breathing the mountain air.

I thought constantly about Anneliese. It went against every fiber of my being, every element of my motherhood not being with her while she was scared, sick and wanting me. When Ingeborg would ask when her sister was coming home a raw ache penetrated through me. Every moment I thought about Anneliese, I contemplated ways to bring myself to her. I was braver when I was younger, perhaps because I was more naïve and unwilling to accept harm could really come to me or my children when I had traveled illegally to Austria in the past. Before Krs was born I took some comfort in knowing if something ever happened to me, Oma Engle would have raised Anneliese and Ingeborg as her own. It was obvious now, Krsmanija would not be afforded the same courtesy as Oma Engle's own grandchildren. What would have become of Krs if I would have been imprisoned indefinitely or dealt a worse fate. What if Krs had been injured or harmed in some way? The horrid memory of the mistreatment of children during the war haunted me.

After all I had witnessed and been through in my life I did not trust the British or American forces any more than I had the Germans or the POWs. The fear I had for Krs and myself while detained was indescribable. I carried with me the horrid memory of the soldier flinging the innocent baby against our neighbor's barn, stealing life from him and his family without remorse. The soldier who had somehow allowed his humanity to slip away or had forgotten it at some point during the wretched war. I knew the British and American border patrol were not the Nazis, but they too were men, men in power away from their loved ones, who I knew at any point could also forget their values. I had to think of all my children.

My conflicted thoughts cycled through my mind. The only reprieve I had was knowing my loving mother was the one caring for Anneliese when I could not. Her next letter told of Anneliese's rapidly declining condition. Mother assured me she comforted Anneliese by reading the letters I wrote to her every day. Mother told Anneliese I loved her dearly and would come get her very soon. Mother distorted the truth for good reason. Neither of us wanted our darling child to lose hope. We wanted her to believe her mother was coming back to her soon. There was nothing any of us could do but pray. The borders continued to be shut tight. I did not give up attempts to travel legally, although I felt great disappointment with each denial. The war was over, yet restrictions persisted. I could not understand how anyone could justify keeping a sick child from her mother.

I received a letter from Mother that Anneliese was admitted to the hospital in Klagenfurt and later released to her. Mother stayed with Anneliese in the hospital until she was released. I painstakingly read each word longing to hold my little girl.

At the beginning of May 1949, I received another letter from home. Mother wrote that Anneliese's condition had grown much worse and she had been readmitted to the hospital. Mother was having a difficult time watching Anneliese's deterioration. Anneliese's birthday was in a few days and she lay seriously ill in the hospital. At times, she was non-responsive. Mother tried in the most delicate way to tell me Anneliese was dying, but I denied her words. I was unwilling to accept I may lose her before I could get to her. I lived day by day praying for a miracle.

On May 16, 1949 I received a message from Austria. The message was delivered through the British Civil Service where it had made its way to Djura. We were notified that Anneliese had died at 2:00 pm in the afternoon while she was hospitalized in Klagenfurt. She had taken her last breath with my mother at her side. She passed away one day after her seventh birthday. Mother said she was with Anneliese every second until her final breath.

Hearing the terrible news, I collapsed as Djura held me. I took her picture down from the wall, and held it close to my heart. I wanted to feel her, smell her, and touch her. That picture was all I had left of her to hold in my arms. I couldn't believe she was gone.

A couple of days later, I received a message from my mother and the minister who prayed over Anneliese while she lay dying in her hospital bed. They were planning Anneliese's funeral in the next few days and wondered if I could obtain a visa for her funeral. I felt sad for my parents to have to take care of all of the funeral arrangements. They both grieved for the loss of their granddaughter. Mother had gone through her own hell caring for her dying grandchild. Her strength was amazing.

I received word my application for a visa to attend Anneliese's funeral was denied. I was trapped in Germany, unable to attend my own daughter's funeral. I sat in disbelief and waited to hear some news from Austria.

Mother tried to console me. She wrote towards the end when Anneliese's mind had declined, she would speak of how I was coming to get her. She said there were times Anneliese thought I was there with them, she could see me, and spoke of how I held her in my arms. Mother said in the end Anneliese couldn't remember many things as the disease progressively affected her brain.

Anneliese's funeral took place in the nearby town of Klagenfurt. She was buried in the town cemetery. Mother wrote of her plan to come see me in Germany as soon as we were allowed to travel. She knew what it was like to have your daughter taken away and fear she would never return, that you would never see her again. Mother attempted to obtain a visa, taking a chance it would get approved, however it was denied. I wasn't sure when we would see each other again.

Confused and bewildered I tried to get through the next week, but I could barely function in any kind of capacity. I couldn't focus, and I only thought about Anneliese's memory. Her scampering through the house, pushing her stroller while she played and pretended to be both the mommy and daddy of her babies. I couldn't make sense of it all, questioned everything in life and why God had let her die.

I couldn't imagine my life without her, yet couldn't forget or ignore Ingeborg and Krs. They were also grieving for their sister. I could barely handle my own grief, but I knew I needed to find the strength to help them through this. If it wasn't for Krs and Ingeborg, my life would have seemed meaningless. I found myself going through the motions of living. Everything was a blur. Oma Engle was feeling her own pain and loss and tried her best to help me through that awful time.

I waited anxiously to hear from my mother to find out more about Anneliese's last days. Those written words describing Anneliese's months in Austria almost made her seem alive. I didn't want anyone to stop talking about her or act as if she was gone. I didn't have the strength to let her go.

Another letter had come through the mail and Djura went to pick up the delivery. I could tell by the forlorn look on his face it was more news about Anneliese's death. The letter was a familiar one. The envelope was perfectly shaped, white in color, and was entirely bordered in black. A letter with indisputable markings that were recognizable, exactly like the ones we had received about others who had died in the past. The envelope contained an official message; a heartbreaking note that I didn't want to read. It was a memo about Anneliese's death, the official notice had come telling me of my darling daughter's last day.

Her death had been reduced to a written obituary. I had tried to accept that she no longer walked among us. When Djura walked toward me, my heart stopped. I didn't want the envelope anywhere near me. Thinking if I didn't touch it or tear it open the finality of her death would not become a reality.

The letters below are just like the ones I had received through the post when I was officially notified about Anneliese's death. The envelopes I no longer have, but her certificate of death I was able to save. I protected these documents and kept them close to me through the years. They were a reminder to all of us of her pain and suffering. They helped me keep her in my memory, real and alive. They reminded us that she had once lived and at one time was a vibrant, beautiful, playful little girl. A very special little girl no one wants to forget.

### A rare picture of Anneliese

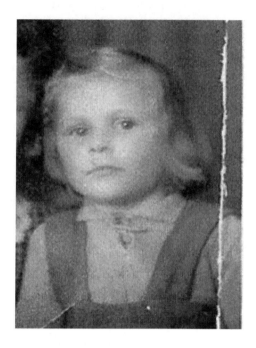

Maybe it was my imagination, but her scent whisked by me at times. It was the smell of the perfumed powder she used to sneak out of my room. I could smell the lavender fragrance that was once in the locks of her golden hair. Her memory was like a mist. There was nowhere left I could go that was untouched by her presence. Her kindred spirit was everywhere. There was nowhere I could hide that didn't remind me of her sweet little face. I needed to know she was somewhere safe and no longer afraid. I was struck with a terrible unease. Fearing she still waited for me.

I carefully unfolded the letter, my face was flushed and on fire. I was barely able to open the envelope as the tears streamed down my face. I somehow found the courage to pull out the documents and caught a glimpse of the death certificate tucked very neatly inside. Shaken by the words, I held the notice in hand and wept endlessly as I read aloud.

**The black framed death notice bearing a cross at the top read:**

Wir geben hiemit tieferschuttert Nachricht daB

*We give you the bad news to the bereaved parents*

Heute unser: _____Liebling_____

*That today your loved one*

Anneliese Brahse

Schuleren

*School girl*

 Fur immer verlassen hat

*Has forever left us*

Die Beisetzung findet:

Giving you the news that she died on:  Motag den 16, Mai 14 uhr im

 Klangenfurter

*@ 2:00pm Monday on May 16ᵗʰ in Klagenfurt*


Six long months had been lost with my precious daughter. Full of hate and blame I cursed everyone in the government for denying me my last chance to see my daughter, especially the department in charge of issuing visas. It was all over and she was gone. I have always carried deep sadness and guilt. I was angered with God for not answering my prayers to save her. My only hope was Heaven existed and someday I would see her again.

## Anneliese's Official Death Notification

I had had enough of Germany after Anneliese's death and wanted to leave the country. I wanted a better life for us all. I didn't associate all of my pain and suffering to Germany, because of course, I met both of my husbands and many other kind people there. But I felt I needed to get out.

Knowing I planned to eventually move from Germany, I thought about where I wanted to call home. I didn't want to live too far away from my home in Austria. We had already lost many years together and as badly as I wanted to get a fresh start, I couldn't imagine leaving my family behind. I wanted to find a place where there was hope, peace, and stability. At that time however, we had to continue living in Germany until we were allowed to leave the country legally.

334

I was 27 years-old when Anneliese died. The day she died my life changed forever. My faith began to waiver. I hoped for an afterlife and a savior, but found myself questioning my own faith in God. Was there nothing left after death, except to be placed in the cold ground? Life's disappointments had hardened my emotions.

We had no choice but to move on with our lives or lose ourselves in a world of sorrow. I gathered up my strength knowing I needed to be there for my family. It would have been much easier to have just given up on life because with every death came more uncertainty.

Nearly a month after Anneliese's death a letter from Mother arrived. As I got the letter opener, I noticed the envelope wasn't flat. It had a small bump in it. I was very curious by this time yet carefully slid the opener along the top, laid the letter opener down, then reached inside. I stopped when I touched the contents and closed my eyes for just a moment. Instantly, my heart skipped a beat. From the envelope I gently pulled out a lock of shiny golden hair held together with a small piece of pink ribbon tied in a neat little bow. Raising the lock toward my face, I brushed Anneliese's soft blonde hair across my cheek. The smell of lavender bound up in the bow took my breath away. A piece of Anneliese that I held in my hand would be with me forever.

## Chapter 81

The next year dragged on and I welcomed the ordinary and monotonous. Life was easier that way and became more predictable. I had had enough of the fighting, death, and destruction in the last ten years so ordinary and dull was just fine with me. I prayed for good health for my remaining family while clinging to Djura, Ingeborg, and Krsmanija. I was not sure how I would have survived without them.

In 1950, Germany and various other countries were discussing a more permanent plan for the many displaced persons that had survived the war. Djura and I wondered if these discussions would lead to an opportunity for us. Our girls and I continued to live off and on at the British barracks with Djura, as well as our small home in Klenkendorf.

Because of Djura's post with the British Civil Service, he was able to get reliable information firsthand about the options government officials were organizing for displaced persons. He learned of refugee camps in Germany and government programs willing to help displaced persons resettle in other countries. The countries willing to take displaced persons were America, Canada, Australia, and England. It seemed there was an actual possibility of our family leaving Germany. These countries were welcoming and willing to give us a fresh start. Djura said eventually we could become legal citizens after being resettled for a few years. Many countries did not want to take on the responsibility of accepting new immigrants. I was relieved there were a few countries willing to help.

After the Second World War there were no formal refugee programs. For those wishing to immigrate to another country, it was necessary to find a sponsor. If we were fortunate enough to be approved to move to another country, an agency or business would have to sponsor us. In most circumstances, the sponsor helped the displaced persons find jobs and secure adequate housing. Some displaced persons were already being sponsored by these welcoming countries, local businesses, and their community churches. The thought of moving thousands of miles from my family in Austria was frightening.

Travel requirements were becoming less restrictive around the country and we were allowed to travel more freely. I had lived in Germany for over ten years; however, I continued to consider Austria my home. I loved the countryside, the small villages tucked neatly away in the Alps and hoped to travel home more often. My family all lived in Austria and Germany while Djura's entire family lived in Yugoslavia. If we considered making such a move to one of the welcoming countries, we knew we may never make it back home.

England was the closest to Europe so we gave living there much consideration. We had little money or resources and facing the unknown terrified me. I could only speak a few words of English and felt quite insecure about learning another language. I didn't want to be made fun of or look stupid if I couldn't speak correctly and knew the English language was difficult to learn. No matter where we moved we knew it would be necessary to learn the language in order to become self-sufficient, employed, fit in with society, and succeed in a new land. In the next six months hundreds of thousands of people would be making plans to leave Europe. We had to decide soon.

When the travel restrictions were lifted, we traveled to Austria. Djura and Krs made the trip with me. The journey to Austria was bittersweet. I was happy to see my family but couldn't help but feel great sadness and disappointment wishing the visit could have taken place sooner when Anneliese was alive and needed me. I was flooded with the emotions and memories of leaving Anneliese behind. However, as we neared Austria on the train I began to feel a sense of peace and I felt Anneliese's presence. I knew she was with me.

I chose not to share with Mother and Father that Djura and I were contemplating immigrating to a sponsor country while we visited them. I knew my mother would be devastated by the news. During the visit I felt more indecisive about our deliberations to move, but knew Djura leaned heavily in the direction of taking the opportunity.

I visited Anneliese's grave during our visit with great difficulty. How I needed the support of Mother and Djura. With my mother and Djura beside me I grieved as I did the first day I found out I had lost her. I grieved for Anneliese, I grieved for my mother, and I allowed myself to finally grieve for my own loss.

We were not able to stay long in Austria because Djura had to return for duty with the Civil Service. The time I spent with my mother was exactly what I needed to restore my sanity. Mother always had a way to comfort me. I missed Anneliese terribly. The trip home gave me a sense of closure.

We returned to Germany and over time I began to feel like I could actually enjoy life again. At first I had to force myself to go on living. I knew it was unfair to Krs and Ingeborg if I completely shut down. I still had very difficult days and nights. Discussing and planning for our family's future with Djura brought back some purpose and meaning to my life that had been lost when Anneliese died.

Djura often played his accordion to entertain us. We'd gather together singing familiar songs. Music was a pleasurable pastime. Ingeborg, Krs and he would sing and harmonize to many traditional tunes. We gathered frequently with family, neighbors, and friends. We played our instruments when company came to visit. We would dance, have sing-a-longs, laugh and joke. We treasured being with friends and family.

Djura usually played traditional Yugoslav and German tunes. His songs lifted our spirits. Occasionally Djura and I went to town to attend the local dances. Many times he jumped up on stage and sang a few customary medleys along with the band. He had an excellent voice and knew many folk songs.

The crowd indulged themselves by drinking homemade ale. There was always lots of liquor, gaiety, and laughter. Everyone's inhibitions became non-existent. I was approached many times by men who had too much to drink. Djura's jealous temperament was revealed when men made advances towards me. At times his jealousy was uncontrollable and unwarranted. When we would go out I had to be aware and in control of my surroundings to guard against any misunderstandings that would arise from talking or enjoying time with others. Fortunately, most of the time we had fun without much conflict.

The more the men drank, the more offers the band received from the audience to get up on stage and sing a song. Some were too drunk to carry a tune and I saw more than a few men fall off the stage. Surprisingly enough the entertainment was generally quite delightful. It was all in fun and everyone had a good time.

It was traditional in Germany, Austria, and Yugoslavia to gather in large groups and join in music, singing, and dancing. An abundance of good food was always involved when we gathered. Even during wartime, we shared whatever we had with family and friends. If you didn't offer your guest's food and drinks, it was considered very rude.

We loved to spend time with Ingeborg and Krs playing outdoors. Djura or I would push them on the tree swing or they played in their sandbox building a sandcastle. If it happened to be cold and rainy, the girls played indoors with their dolls.

Even though we had little money to spend on entertainment we found ways to have fun together as a family. We found things to do that didn't cost much money and enjoyed the simple things in life. We took a few trips to see the sites in Germany that hadn't been damaged or destroyed during the war.

Family was always one of the most important things Djura and I valued and enjoyed. Our family's encouragement, support, and strength helped get us through many hard times. Their unconditional love made life bearable. I don't know what I would have done without my family.

We had so much to be thankful for even with the sad events that had transpired in our lives. Life had its good moments and we did not take them for granted. I gave thanks for waking up alive every morning with my family by my side and counted my blessings.

**Below is a picture of Djura playing with Krs at age four in the snow and Karoline having a rest in the meadow after a day's picnic. Krs sitting with me at about age three.**

## Chapter 82

Unfortunately the economy continued to be unstable and didn't follow suit with the new optimism of the people in Germany. Employment opportunities were scarce and many individuals lived in poverty. Making ends meet and surviving from day to day proved to be a job in itself.

Once Djura's services were no longer needed by the British Civil Service he would have to look for another job. There were not many jobs available for someone like him. The unfair and undeserved stigma associated with being an ex-war prisoner certainly impacted his employment opportunities. Djura was a hard worker and took on two and three jobs to make ends meet. He could never sit idle for any length of time because he needed and wanted to be the provider for his family.

He might have worked for Oma and Opa Brase on the farm, but they didn't have much money for wages. While they had enough to cover their own basic living expenses, they didn't have any to spare for additional farm laborers. Farm hands that worked there were paid by a bartering system. They received free room and board and food for their labor. If they were paid at all they received only a small wage. Djura and I hoped for better opportunities.

Our living space in the barracks was located in a large, long, narrow, wood building. There was a long hallway that ran through the entire interior separating each individual living quarter. We had our own key to our apartment and the building accommodated ten families. Our apartments were equipped with modern electricity and plumbing. Almost everything in the barracks was free, including our rent. Since many of our expenses were paid for, we were able to save a little money for our future.

With all that had happened during and after the war, Djura and my relationship was sometimes stressed. We found ourselves fighting and arguing about unimportant and petty things. I blurted out things

341

unintentionally and we both said hurtful things we later wished we would not have said.  Dealing with all the instability and habitual trauma in our lives had affected the way we reacted to life and each other.

One argument we had was more serious.  I was concerned about Djura's card playing and gambling while he was in the barracks when he was away from me and our girls.  There was a time he had gambled his whole paycheck away and because of that incident we battled.  He never apologized, but he eventually stopped.  I hoped gambling would never become a habit.

Djura's childhood disciplines were much different than mine. Being raised so differently put a strain on how we raised our children, dealt with household problems, and how it was thought I should conduct myself in public.  Djura was a controlling man, he expected complete and total control over every aspect of our marriage.  It was also difficult to get used to his jealous nature.

When I was married to Hinrich, I had all the freedom in the world because he was a very trusting man.  He didn't care who I talked to or spent time with, and didn't think anything if I had a short dance or conversation with another man.  I was free to make my own choices and he consulted with me before we made any important decisions regarding family matters. I felt unrestricted and free to make my own choices.  I was able to laugh with and plan outings with others.  Hinrich never made me feel like I had done anything wrong when I enjoyed myself with friends and family.

With Djura, however, things were different.  He did not like me giving anyone else my attention.  I wasn't allowed to talk, laugh or dance with any other men.  It seemed to anger him if he thought I was having fun without him, especially if I laughed while having a conversation with another man.  I had never done anything inappropriate to make him distrust me.  Yet for some reason he was very doubting and I wasn't sure why he felt that way.  If he didn't like what I was doing, I would get an unmistakable glare.  He didn't have to say a single word.  It was something

I didn't necessarily like about him. His father and uncles were also jealous men. Maybe his distrust was an inherited trait.

I found as time went on I had to change myself for he wasn't about to change his jealous ways. If I wanted to keep the peace in our marriage I had to change my personality, and not act carefree. I sometimes felt like I was walking on eggshells. I was unsure if he would get angry about something that most men considered silly or trivial. It got to the point where I didn't dare glance at another man because I wondered if it would make him angry. He didn't fight fairly, would shut me out and not talk to me for three days at a time. His destructive behaviors that came along with his wild jealousy were at times detrimental to our marriage.

There was an incident where I had talked to a male friend. Djura became so angry he struck me across the face. I let him know I would not tolerate this type of behavior from him, and he never did lay a hand on me after that incident. However, I ended up altering my behavior around others, especially other men, rather than Djura changing his mistrustful nature.

Even though I had to change to keep the peace in our marriage, I was willing to make the compromise. I loved Djura with all my heart and knew he loved me. We had been through so much together and had created our own new traditions and knew each other's histories. Even with his jealous bouts he was a good man and husband who cared deeply for our family and me. Djura was always able to keep humor in our lives and there were many times his lightheartedness was a distraction. He worked very hard to provide for us. I knew he would always do whatever he could do to make sure we were taken care of and safe.

Djura had shown incredible courage through the years and had saved our daughters and me from many perils. He had proven many times his willingness to sacrifice his own life for ours and at times was a most compassionate companion. I wished he could have been more like Hinrich in some ways, but Djura was his own man. It was unrealistic for me to think I could ever change him. Djura had many positive qualities and I came to the conclusion it was unfair to compare the two men.

I loved them each deeply. Djura was very intelligent and could think quickly on his feet. He was a wonderful family man and loved both Ingeborg and Anneliese as if they were his own children. I'm not sure I would have found anyone else that was as loyal to my daughters and me. Djura's love for our children was evident. He always made time for them when he wasn't working. I never doubted he loved me, although sometimes he had a difficult time showing his feelings. His positive traits far outweighed his short-comings.

Most men in Germany, Yugoslavia, and many other countries during this time period were considered the kings of their households. They made most of the important family decisions without ever considering or consulting with their wives. I went along with the views of society and conformed to what was thought a woman and a wife should look and act like. I struggled changing some of my own personality traits, but I never stopped loving Djura because of his own imperfections. Most of the time we had a great relationship, and he was a caring man. I loved Djura and I never regretted my decision to marry him.

Below is a picture of Djura and me in 1950 enjoying a walk close to the British base; the other picture is of me and the girls on a separate occasion strolling through Germany taking in the beautiful weather and sites that day.

## Chapter 83

Time never stood still. It was Ingeborg's tenth birthday on March 17th of 1951. Amid the celebration Djura and I came to a final decision about our plan to leave Germany. After much discussion we decided to begin the process of moving to America. The first step was to seek approval through the government sponsored displaced person's program. We then had the responsibility of finding a sponsor in America willing to help us find a place to live and future employment. We heard many wonderful things about England and Australia, however, we heard many more astonishing stories about the United States of America. The U.S. was known to many people in Europe as the land where anything was possible. A place where hopes and dreams come true. We had hopes our family would thrive there and we wanted to provide our children with the best opportunities.

Djura and I had come in contact with the United States Red Cross toward the end of the war. We had witnessed firsthand the help they had given so many people in war-torn Germany. They had distributed ten pound care packages full of food and supplies in Germany after the war, especially where people had suffered the most. Watching so many care packages fall from the sky had been an amazing sight. Their generous, kind, and humanitarian gestures were welcomed by those who had been held in the prison camps. The individuals who had been released from these places had been discharged with little or nothing. The Red Cross had attempted to fulfill some of their basic needs. America's compassion for humanity had influenced our decision greatly. The United States seemed like the best place for us to start a new life for our family.

We didn't know much about the US, but we had seen many pictures of the cities and the countryside. We imagined America as a land of wealth and opportunity. A nonviolent place, where all ethnic groups were welcome and could live together without war. In America we would be able to raise our children in peace with ample opportunities for their future. We could pursue our dreams and nothing we hoped for seemed out of our reach. It seemed like the perfect place for us to get a fresh start and begin building a new life with our children.

The thought of having a new beginning in America was very exciting yet intensely nerve-racking; more so for me it seemed than for Djura. He wasn't as worried as I was about moving an ocean away from our families. He focused more on the opportunities that were possible in the United States. Besides leaving our families, I fretted over learning to speak English and making new friends. I feared people might treat us badly if we were unable to speak or understand the language. When I heard many people in America spoke German, I was a bit less anxious. I worried there would be few people I could talk to or that would understand me.

I wondered about the challenges I would face doing simple things like going to the store on my own or taking our girls to the doctor. Would I be able to take walks or ride my bike to town like we had done in Austria and Germany? Would there be a nearby post office to mail my letters home? Would there be a park or a meadow where our girls could go outside and play? Would we live close to the mountains like I had in Austria when I was a child?

I had many unanswered questions about America. From the pictures we had seen it looked as though everyone owned their own car. I rode my bike pretty much everywhere I needed to go. Djura would need to find employment as soon as we arrived and it sounded as though jobs were plentiful. I would stay home with the children at least until I learned the language.

Both of us had seen propaganda in Germany promoting America as a wondrous land. The pamphlets showed a place where everything seemed to come easy. There were many jobs to fill and images showed widespread employment, an abundance of adequate housing and food, clothing, and higher education prospects for all. The United States was described as a place where everything was good and anything was possible, with opportunities waiting for anyone who dared take the challenge. It sounded like a paradise. We imagined the people living there with ample chances to get what they needed or wanted without having to work very hard to get them. It seemed most people were rich, lived in fine houses and drove fancy cars. A person could get whatever they wished for; it resembled a fairytale land.

We heard stories of immigrants who resettled there before the war who had become rich and successful. Some greatly prospered achieving limitless goals and now were managing their own businesses. They had all the finer things in life. The images and stories were like nothing we had ever heard of or known. We thought once we arrived in the United States we would never be poor again. I pictured everyone having fancy clothes, and more food on the table than anyone could ever eat. The land of opportunity awaited us and we gladly welcomed it.

Even with all the excitement and wonderful things I heard about, I remained hesitant and afraid to leave my family. Money had little importance during the war. We found family far more valuable than the German mark and material goods. I learned early in life that family and good health were the keys to my happiness. I knew it would be difficult to be so far away from my family, but knowing our small family would be in a strong yet peaceful land, gave me peace of mind.

Once our decision was final to move to America, we began the legal immigration process. We would have to move from our home in Klenkendorf and live in the barracks in Hamburg to complete our displaced person's processing. The British and American Barracks scattered throughout the country served as refugee camps for those planning to leave Germany. Before we were allowed to travel, we would have to pass routine medical screenings and meet several other requirements. The medical results were needed to prove we were disease free, healthy and physically able to make the long journey. If we failed the processing requirements we would be forced to remain in Germany.

Djura and I needed to produce official birth certificates to prove our nationality. Djura had never received a notarized birth certificate because he was born at home in Yugoslavia. His birth was not officially recorded nor documented by any legal entity. He had to find a few individuals to bear witness for and sign an affidavit saying he was indeed born in Kormant, Yugoslavia on April, 26th of 1917. His own mother was unsure of the exact date he was born. No midwives were present during his birth and none of his relatives had any memory or knowledge of the specifics surrounding his birth.

Djura eventually found a few old friends who offered to swear on a written affidavit he was indeed born in Yugoslavia. He soon discovered the testimony of his friends alone wouldn't suffice and had to look for a second supporting entity. The Serbian Orthodox Church in Germany agreed to give testimony of his birth and baptism. On April 16th of 1951 he secured an official birth certificate from the church.

Moving to America was becoming a reality. The Refugee Resettlement Processing Center housed in the British Barracks had already begun some routine refugee screenings in Hamburg. Many other displaced persons among various nationalities planned to move out of the country along with us. Most of us would move to the refugee holding camp within a few months.

We were to be housed in the refugee camp for a few months along with hundreds of other families in the same complex waiting to leave for America. Most of the displaced persons in our group had to move to the refugee holding camp by mid-July of 1951. The camp in Hamburg was located 185 kilometers (115 miles) from Bremerhaven, Germany. Bremerhaven was a local port in Germany with access to waterways for shipping. It was approximately 48 kilometers (30 miles) from

Klenkendorf.  Cargo ships routinely docked at the Bremerhaven port and various types of freight were shipped in and out of the country.

We would be traveling by ship to America and leaving off the coast of Bremerhaven after we were approved for travel.  I thought I was emotionally ready for this new venture, but found as the specific details of our journey became known, I began to doubt my decision to leave Germany.  There was very little time left to reconsider the move.  Djura was not experiencing any second thoughts, fully confident in our plan.  He insisted there was no future left for us in Germany and he was determined to leave with our daughters and me.  I also wanted to leave Germany to make a fresh start, but my fears of being far from Austria and my family overwhelmed me.  No matter my reservations, fate seemed to keep pushing me in the direction of moving to the United States.

In the midst of planning to leave Klenkendorf, I found out I was pregnant with my fourth child.  I worried about having a baby in a new unknown land.  Neither Mother nor Oma Engle would be with me when the baby was born.  None of my relatives had any money or desire to move.  They would never consider coming to America to be near us.

Oma and Opa and the rest of the Brase family had no desire to leave Germany.  My mother and father, although only in their late forties, said they were far too old to move and start a new life anywhere else.  They wanted to stay and live the rest of their lives in Austria.  Both of them felt too afraid to venture off and start a new life in an unfamiliar place.  I would only have contact with my family through letters.

I had no idea if and when we would ever be able to return to Austria or Germany to visit and the thought of traveling across the entire Atlantic Ocean was distressing.  One of the reasons Djura and I decided to move to America as opposed to Australia was because we felt Australia was a greater distance away limiting our chance to return to visit our families.  He tried to reassure me that when we had saved enough money in America, we would return to Europe to visit family.

Regardless of my reservations we proceeded with the immigration process. We shared our intentions with our girls. Ingeborg was ten-years-old and Krs was four. They were very curious and asked many questions. How long would the trip take? Were we going by boat? Why weren't Oma Engle and Opa Brase coming with us? Ingeborg would miss her grandparents dearly and worried about when she would see them again. The transition would be more difficult for her than Krs. Ingeborg struggled with some of her own fears, yet showed excitement about our new venture as well. I remember Djura kidded Ingeborg about meeting the President of the United States, Harry Truman, one day. Djura heard great things about the President and admired how he loved the people and despised Hitler. Djura hoped maybe someday we would have the chance to meet him.

Our girls and Djura looked forward to traveling across the Atlantic. They looked at it as a great adventure. Oma Agnes and Oma Engle felt otherwise. They feared losing us forever and they both struggled greatly with us leaving. The thought of having a massive barrier like the Atlantic Ocean separating us weighed heavily on their minds.

I stayed busy with the tasks of packing and preparing for our departure trying not to think too much about actually leaving. Djura continued to remind me of the benefits we would realize once we were in America. His optimism prevented me from succumbing completely to my fears, however, I wasn't able to shake them entirely.

The time approached for us to say goodbye to Oma and Opa Brase and move to the refugee camp in Hamburg. Even though Oma Engle and I did not agree on many things, she was Hinrich's mother and Ingeborg and Anneliese's grandmother, and had been a significant part of my life since I was 17-years-old. I felt badly for Ingeborg having to say goodbye to her beloved grandmother. I also felt sadness for Oma Engle because she had already lost two sons and a granddaughter, and I knew she would miss Ingeborg greatly. It was a very emotional time.

I found it strange that Ingeborg's Aunt Anne was suddenly uncharacteristically kind to both of us. At one time she was unable to conceal her jealousy of Ingeborg and her hatred of me. I wasn't sure what to credit her newfound kindness towards us. Was she hoping we would gain riches in America that she would profit from? Or had she realized her past behavior was misguided and desired to make amends before we left? Or was she just glad to be rid of us so she would have Oma Engle and Opa Brase all to herself?

## Chapter 84

The unguarded refugee camp in Hamburg was run by the British. We had to live in the barracks until we left for Bremerhaven. Once in Hamburg we received our medical exams and vaccinations in the holding camp before moving into the barracks. All of our vaccinations and medical tests would be completed in the holding camp where the medical personnel were housed.

There were over nine hundred refugees on the roster waiting for medical screenings and vaccinations. Everyone waited patiently in a giant line formed in front of the medical compound. All hoping for their names to be called so they could be the next ones to get their vaccinations. While waiting for our vaccinations, I heard at least seven different languages being spoken. I wasn't able to understand many of them, although some were speaking German. I hadn't learned as many languages as Djura had during the war. He was able to communicate with pretty much anyone in our compound. Because I spoke the German language, I was able to communicate with the doctors when it was our turn.

Everyone was required to get immunized. Prior to receiving my vaccinations, I discussed my pregnancy with the camp doctors hoping it would not interfere with our travel plans and to determine if the shots would endanger my baby or myself. The doctor assured me the vaccinations would pose minimal to no risk and it was necessary to receive the vaccines to leave Germany. I was inoculated just like everyone else. It took one day for everyone to make it through the medical exam and vaccination process. We wouldn't know the results from most of our medical tests until the first part of August.

Once in the barracks, the British Civil Service workers greeted us and showed us where we would be staying. The staff was kind and helped us get settled into our own individual living quarters. Djura had become familiar with this type of living arrangement while working for the British Civil Service. He lived at the base off and on near Klenkendorf for two years.

The camp put together a makeshift classroom in one of the buildings with all the children placed together in the same room. Krs went along with Ingeborg. It was her first educational experience up to this point because she had not yet been enrolled in a German public school. Ingeborg had done well academically while attending school in Germany and I was grateful for the opportunity so she would not fall behind in her studies.

The nearly one thousand refugees housed in our same area made conditions overcrowded. Many of the amenities and facilities on the grounds had to be shared with others. We had our own personal family living quarters and were somewhat secluded from the others if we stayed indoors. Having hundreds of other people placed in the huge apartment like complexes along with us made it difficult to find privacy. Personal cares were sometimes done out in the open; some used little discretion. Because of the lack of space and crowded conditions, people sometimes went off outdoors to find privacy. We caught people in the open going to the bathroom, washing up, and sometimes having sex. For the most part everyone used good judgment, especially with the many children in the camp.

The units in the camp were constructed simply and inexpensively. The modern indoor plumbing and electricity made the units somewhat comfortable. Fortunately, it was summertime so we could go outside and enjoy the good weather.

Most of the time we were free to come and go as we pleased once we moved into the barracks including trips to town or to see family. Visiting our family was not a likely option for us since we were close to 160 kilometers (100 miles) from Klenkendorf. The Refugee Resettlement

Agency kept certain groups together in the camp to make it easier to track everyone during the processing steps.

I had yet to experience morning sickness and I worried how I would react journeying across the open sea. I had never been on a big ship before and the idea of the long voyage on the ocean excited me. I was looking forward to the ride and couldn't wait to see the Statue of Liberty once we reached the U.S. We heard much about the statue and admired pictures of the crowned sculpture.

The longer we were held in the camp the more restless we became. My fears of leaving creeped up on me and intensified with each passing day. I had a lot of time to think about leaving my homeland and my family. Though it had only been a few weeks since we entered the camp, I already felt completely isolated from the rest of my family. I cried often during our time in the camp. The notion of moving thousands of miles away from home no longer seemed like such a good idea. Djura, unlike me, was bound and determined to leave Germany.

With us we brought two large suitcases, a few handbags, and a small wooden box that held my family pictures. It was difficult to choose what was most important to bring with me. I packed some of our personal belongings, keepsakes and mementos that were the most meaningful and precious. I had some finely detailed pillow cases hand embroidered by my mother. Handmade tablecloths and doilies Oma Engle and Oma Agnes had made for us were carefully packed along with a beautiful glass *koogal* (paperweight) that sat on my buffet at home. I could not bear to leave them behind. I filled our suitcases with clothing and a few nice dresses for both the girls so we would look presentable when we departed off the ship. Most of my jewelry had been stolen except for a finely made silver bracelet Hinrich had given me. I had my wedding rings and a few other trinkets that held more meaningful memories. I packed many family pictures and the prayer book given to me by my Oma Margarette. We sold some of our belongings before we moved to the camp hoping to make a few extra dollars for living expenses when we arrived in the United States. We sold our bedroom dressers, kitchen table, and chairs. We gave a majority of our possessions away to close family members and friends. Once again I was forced to choose what I valued most amongst my possessions from my home. It was not an easy task.

Djura and I were hopeful the Orthodox Church in America would sponsor us as they had already taken on sponsorship for many other Yugoslavian families. The Orthodox Church paid for travel expenses, found additional supports once refugees arrived in the U.S., sponsored employment, and gave substantial financial contributions to each of its sponsored families.

We learned the Orthodox Church was unwilling to sponsor our family. The church rejected our family since they were unwilling to recognize our marriage as a legitimate union because of my Lutheran faith and desire not to convert to the Orthodox religion. Djura blamed me for our lack of sponsorship and our now desperate need to find an individual, agency, or organization willing to sponsor our family. We were being punished for my Lutheran faith.

During the early 1950's it seemed that churches, non-profit organizations, or private individuals were the only outlets available to us to help us become settled once in America. It would be important for Djura to find work as soon as we arrived in the United States. We certainly did not want to find ourselves homeless. Djura was a very proud man, and was driven to support his family.

Uneventful days and constant boredom in the camp reinforced feelings of uncertainty. There were a few activities which helped distract us from the nervous anticipation widely evident in the camp. Each morning the camp leader blew reveille sparking most kids in the camp to run out and watch the soldiers go through morning drills. Many of the American and British soldiers gave the children chocolate candy bars, piggy back rides, and many sang the song "Frere Jacques." We were awakened at 7:00 am every morning to do exercises before we could eat our breakfast.

**Once we were settled in the camp we took a few photos. The picture below is an image of Krs and some of the other children in the holding camp in Hamburg. Krs is the little girl standing in front of the adult furthest to the left. She has dark short hair and is wearing a black short sleeved dress. Her arm is raised holding a flag.**

Pictured below is Djura, Krs, Ingeborg and me in the refugee camp in Hamburg.

The pictures below are of Krs and Ingeborg in our room at the camp, passing the time playing with their dolls. Krs is in the photo on the left sitting in the window with her dolls. She wore a headscarf that day because she was suffering from a cold with a terrible cough and an earache.

Krs had always been a very slender little girl, and never had much of an appetite. We didn't have good wholesome food to give the children for many years during the war so her thinness and dark circles under her eyes sometimes made her look a bit sickly. It was rare to see anyone overweight in the camp mostly due to the unavailability of nutritious food during and after the war. In the camp children were fed nutritious meals regularly; they had not gone hungry once since arriving at the camp. The children were given milk to drink, which was not normally in their daily diet. It was much appreciated. Many had not been so lucky during the war because they were not able to afford such things.

We completed several applications and continued to look for possible sponsors. Leaving Germany depended on us securing sponsorship. We finally heard from an individual willing to sponsor our family.  His name was Gerald Wetlaufer.  He and his wife, Betty, were owners of a small laundry business in a small town in Northeast Iowa.

Gerald and his wife lived and ran their business in Oelwein, Iowa.  Djura and I had never heard of Oelwein or Iowa for that matter.  I wondered about the local people and the landscape.  Were there mountains that would remind me of home?  After we made initial contact with the Wetlaufers, we learned that City Laundry and the Zion Lutheran Church in Oelwein had become our sponsors.

The small laundry business was family owned.  The company and its owners had been part of the rural Oelwein community for many years.  We understood the business itself was well established and the owners and their family were committed to helping displaced persons like us.  The Wetlaufer's, the minister, and members of Zion Lutheran Church would provide us with much needed support, help us find employment, and locate an apartment for us to live in until we were more established.  They would pay for our travel expenses to the United States.  The Wetlaufer family and the Oelwein community seemed eager to help us.  City Laundry promised to give Djura a job as soon as we arrived in Oelwein.

We were very thankful for the Wetlaufers and the community's act of kindness.  We were one step closer to coming to the U.S. and now awaited our medical results.  With great excitement, we found out everyone in the family had passed the physical part of the exam.  Our blood tests and x-ray results were the only barrier left in leaving Germany.

The very next day we were approached by the medical staff.  Everyone received a clean bill of health except for Ingeborg.  Her chest x-ray revealed a small spot on her lung, which raised concerns about past exposure to TB and the possibility of spreading the disease.  I was dumbfounded since she had not exhibited any symptoms of the disease.  Ingeborg had suffered from pertussis and diphtheria, but she never had any indication of TB.  The thought of her possibly becoming ill like

Anneliese unsettled me.  Both Djura and I were worried sick.  We needed to find out more information.

The Refugee Processing Center's medical team told us Ingeborg would not be allowed to travel.  The rest of us were cleared to go to America.  It made no sense to me.  I had been exposed to TB for at least nine years and had never contracted it or had any symptoms or signs of the disease.  Both Hinrich and Anneliese suffered from symptoms before being diagnosed with the disease.

It was only a few weeks before we were scheduled to leave for America and the bad news devastated the entire family.  Our dreams of going to America were crushed in a matter of seconds.  We were told by the World Health Organization that Ingeborg would not be allowed to leave Germany with us.  I was surprised when the Processing Center told us we could leave Ingeborg behind in Germany with family if we desired to continue on to America.  I was appalled they would suggest such a thing.  Without any hesitation, Djura and I both refused their offer and told them we would never leave Germany without her.  I was very concerned about her health and possible prognosis.  I wanted to get her tested a second time.

Ingeborg's Oma Engle would have gladly kept her in Germany, but neither Djura nor I were willing to leave her behind.  We would stay together as a family in Germany if necessary and would never consider being separated.  I requested that Ingeborg be retested.  I did not believe she was ill.  The World Health Organization was sympathetic toward our situation and wanted to help us since we had our hearts set on going to America.

The doctors agreed to take another look at her and repeated her chest x-ray.  They would consult after reading her new results and make a final decision about her ability to travel from Germany.  While we waited for the new results we were approached by another Refugee Resettlement Center official.  This person came to us with another barrier that could prevent us from resettling in the United States.  Ingeborg would not only need to be cleared medically, but Djura would have to adopt her as his own before she could obtain a legal passport.

We feared the test results and now also feared that the paperwork for the adoption process may take too long to be finalized before we could board the ship.  Djura had no reservations concerning adopting Ingeborg since he already considered her his daughter.  Given our current dilemmas, our plans to leave Germany seemed hopeless.  We couldn't catch a break and we had to deal with one serious problem after another.

The ship would soon be prepared to leave the Bremerhaven port. We came to terms with the possibility of staying in Germany if Ingeborg wasn't cleared to travel.  While awaiting the Processing Center's final decision, Djura went through the court system and completed the adoption paperwork relatively quickly.  Everything was approved in an expedited manner and the adoption was officially sanctioned by the courts.  In less than a week Ingeborg was legally adopted and her last name was changed to Stefanovic.

Waiting for the doctors to review her x-rays and make a final decision was grueling.  Once they reviewed her new x-rays and compared them to her previous image, a team of physicians disproved her initial results.  They concluded Ingeborg did not have active TB or any type of communicable disease.  There remained a small area about the size of a quarter on her lung, however they did not credit it to active tuberculosis.  I was overjoyed to learn my daughter was healthy.  She was given an authorized health certificate clearing her for travel.  At that moment migrating to America became a certainty for our family.

Going through the immigration process had been a rollercoaster. Our plans at times totally changed and being patient and flexible was key to surviving the process itself.  Everyone was happy learning our plan was in definite motion.  Djura joked with Ingeborg that now she would indeed meet President Truman.

We were thrilled and overjoyed our family was finally approved to travel to the US. We imagined what our new lives would look like in America. Djura and I both looked forward to meeting our sponsors, Mr. and Mrs. Gerald Wetlaufer. Djura was excited about having a job waiting for him once we arrived.

Our approval documents from World Health Organization
Refugee Resettlement Center certifying good health and
approval for International travel.  Pictures of Djura and Krs
below.

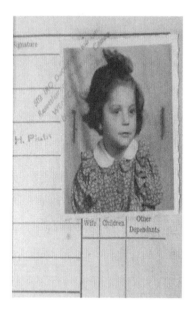

## Karoline and Ingeborg

Anxiously we waited to hear news from the refugee resettlement officials regarding our official departure date to America. We were taken by surprise one day by an unexpected announcement over the loudspeaker at the camp. We were told all refugees in our barracks would be immediately transferred to another location. We would be moving to larger units in a nearby barracks operated by Americans. We were not informed of the reason for changing locations, which created widespread speculation and worry among those in the camp.

We eventually learned we were moving because the British camp was heavily infested with bedbugs and many people contracted head lice while in the camp. The overcrowded conditions made the plague of bed bugs and lice spread quickly invading unit after unit. The thought of having head lice and bedbugs thoroughly disgusted me making my skin feel like it was crawling. I felt dirty and happily moved to another site.

Hundreds of us traveled in jeeps to the nearby American camp. We didn't have to travel far to get there. It was less than 15 minutes away from our initial placement. The entire camp had to be deloused and all were required to wash their heads in gasoline to get rid of the infectious bugs. Once poured on our heads, the gasoline burned our scalps and our heads felt on fire. The odor of the fuel was so strong our hair carried the scent for days. Even after a thorough cleansing, I continued to itch worried there were bugs on me.

When we moved to the new compound I checked all of our mattresses and looked for bugs in all of our belongings. Piece by piece, I went through our belongings hoping we hadn't brought any with us. The entire grounds were sprayed with insecticide and disinfectant. Our old compound was sterilized for the next group of refugees that would be coming to the camp. Djura helped carry out the infested mattresses. They were piled up high and were all burned. We were more than ever ready to leave and badly wanted out of the camps.

We were told we were within a week of our departure and would only be in the new barracks for a few more days. Djura was asked by the Americans if he wanted to work as a MP (military police) on the ship during the ten day voyage across the Atlantic. He graciously accepted the position and was happy to make a little extra money. He was paid a small stipend and would collect his wages when we landed.

His duties included helping passengers board when it was time to load the ship and to keep peace on the ship once we started the journey. Djura would assist in ensuring eating schedules were observed and proper ship etiquette was followed. He was available to answer any questions and break up fights if necessary. The ultimate goal was to maintain order on his assigned deck. He was familiar with this type of work and had performed similar duties when he worked for the British Civil Service. Djura's ability to speak many different languages allowed him to effectively deal with problematic situations.

## Chapter 85

September 11th, 1951 arrived and became one of the most important days in our lives. We were leaving shortly to America on the USS General Muir. Oma and Opa Brase came to the camp in Hamburg to visit us one last time before we left for America. From Hamburg, they accompanied us to Bremerhaven and were present as we boarded the ship.

Our last farewell was filled with much heartache and tears. Everyone was deeply saddened by the thought of us leaving. They worried our absence would be permanent and we would never return. The planned separation became too much for both girls and Oma Engle to handle especially when they realized we were finally leaving for good. Saying goodbye wasn't easy.

I knew what it was like to say goodbye to someone you deeply love. The uncertainty of our return was discouraging. Oma Engle struggled intensely with our departure. With tears streaming down her face, she hugged the girls as if she would never let them go. Oma Engle and I had our problems in the past, but it was heartbreaking to watch her suffer. The best we could do was hope someday we would return to see them since they had no intentions of ever coming to the United States. No promises could be made to Oma Engle; our future was unpredictable.

**Photo taken during the visit, Klaus (Oma's son), Karoline, Ingeborg, and Oma. Opa was also there to see us off but was absent from the picture.**

I wished my parents could have been there as well to wish us farewell. Letters from my mother during this time were difficult to read because her own suffering was evident in them. She was tormented by the thought she might never see us again. I felt great sadness for my mother and wished her no pain. It seemed in the last ten years she had suffered one heartache after another. I would in turn write her and Father as often as possible filling our exchanges with heartfelt words that would hopefully set her mind at ease. I wanted to leave her with hope we would someday return and see her once again.

Djura and I were ready to set out and seek our fortune in the United States. With hard work and time, I knew in my heart we would someday return to Europe to see our families. I also knew Djura would do whatever he could to make a return trip possible.

Our Ship, the USS General Muir was an army transport ship that would bring thousands of European refugees to the United States of

America over the next few years. Many nationalities boarded the USS General Muir as it departed off the coast of Bremerhaven.

Each person had their own reasons for leaving Germany; some were similar to mine. Each had recollections of how they had suffered during the war with stories of their own victimization while under Hitler's madness. There were Jews, Poles, Czechs, Serbs, Croats, and Slovenians who had been released from concentration or slave labor prison camps. Some were Lithuanians, Latvians, and Estonians who had fled their countries in front of the Russian advance into Germany. Many Serbs, Croatians, and Slovenians feared persecution related to their religious and political beliefs. Many of the Yugoslavian's shared Djura's views and feared retribution by the Yugoslav leader, Josip Tito. They had no desire to live under Tito's form of communism. We all looked to America with such hope in our hearts; all of us very grateful for this opportunity.

**The picture below is from the archives of the USS General Muir:**
(http://en.wikipedia.org/wiki/File:USS_General_C._H._Muir_(AP-142).jpg)

      The Displaced Person's Relief Program was slotted to end around 1957. If Mother or Oma Engle changed their minds about joining us in America, they would need to do so within the next six years. When the program ended, refugee travel through this mechanism was terminated. After the allotted time frame anyone migrating elsewhere had to go through mainstream immigration channels, which were much more time consuming. The Refugee Resettlement Agency predicted approximately 600,000 refugees would choose to go to the United States by 1957. (http://www.unhcr.org)

## Chapter 86

The final moment arrived and we prepared to board the ship.  The entire camp lined up to board the USS General Muir.  Once on the ship we were organized by families and escorted to our designated sleeping quarters.  Next we were given a tour of the ship and shown the mess hall and the areas we could gather.  We were told important safety procedures in case of an emergency.  I was terrified of the water because I had never learned to swim.  The thought of falling overboard scared me to death.  Many lifeboats hung off the side of the ship.  Seeing them actually frightened me more, facing the possibility we may need to use them if the ship sank.

Djura and the other MPs were busy keeping order of the huge crowd that waited to step on board.  We were very excited and overjoyed to finally leave the camp.  This made it difficult for all of us to stay patient.  Djura helped answer questions and direct those unable to find their way.

Our voyage across the sea would take ten days once the journey began.  Over nine hundred refugees boarded the ship and we all lined up facing the dock.  Everyone wanted to catch one last glimpse of their loved ones and wave goodbye to their family and friends back on land.

I struggled with my mixed feelings when we set out to sea and cried while waving goodbye.  Friends and relatives stood on the shore watching and waving farewell as we slowly drifted out to sea.  We made it aboard and were on our way to America on the biggest ship I had ever seen.  I hugged the girls as we waved goodbye knowing there was no turning back.

The ship drifted smoothly over the soft flowing waves as we pulled away from the harbor.  I watched the silhouettes of families waving goodbye slowly fade away into the distant horizon.  Once on our way the men were directed to the top levels of the ship.  The women and children were guided below into the belly of the ship. There were no windows in our sleeping quarters.

We climbed several sections of steel ladders to get from one deck to the other. Climbing up and down the ladders provided plenty of exercise for the girls and me. We were permitted to come up on the top deck anytime we wanted to feel the sunlight and to get a bit of fresh air. I spent much of my time on the upper deck in hopes the fresh air would help with the seasickness I was experiencing. The crashing waves slammed into the side of the boat constantly rocking the ship.

Djura was on duty most of the time working as a temporary MP. I found myself crying some every day for my home and family. Our girls ran about the ship as if it were a playground. Ingeborg marveled excitedly at the enormity of the ship. She had noticed a tiny bird resembling a brown wren that kept flying about the top deck of the vessel. The wren had built a tiny nest in the middle of a large iron support that rose up high from the middle of the deck. The bird completely aroused her childlike curiosity and she watched for the nesting wren on a daily basis. The wren would fly off and Ingeborg would await its return, watchful of the bird's busy schedule. Every time the bird flew away, sometimes for days, Ingeborg feared it wouldn't come back, yet it always returned.

The ship was crowded and there wasn't much room. It was difficult for us to find any privacy. There was very little room in our sleeping quarters, just enough space for our bunk beds and a small closet to hang a few of our clothes. If I remember correctly the ship had five different levels.

The many different languages spoken made it difficult for many of us to communicate with one another though we tried our best. The language barrier and cramped quarters on the ship created a breeding ground for arguments between passengers. It was easy to become irritated and lose patience, plus the crowded conditions seemed to bring out the worst in some of the passengers. On occasion there was yelling and

372

physical altercations, drawing the attention of the military police who intervened to settle disputes. As a temporary MP, Djura became involved when necessary. Fortunately most of us tried to help one another realizing we were all in the same uncomfortable predicament. Patience became a virtue and comradery was welcomed.

I was simply amazed by the meals we were served. The amount was enormous and the meals were both delicious and nutritious. We had never had such luxuries before other than in the barracks. Second helpings were unheard of at home, but on the ship you could eat until you burst. We were given more helpings than any one person could eat. No one ever went hungry while aboard, and during the first few days everyone stuffed their stomachs full.

Occasionally a fight broke out when someone tried to cut in front of the meal line. Mostly the arguments started among adults. Full grown men sometimes trampled over children to get to the front of the line. Djura was involved in a few scuffles where he had to threaten men to stop or they'd be placed in confinement.

Most of the time Djura was able to settle conflicts quickly. He was a physically strong man and very charismatic. He was almost always able to talk people down and could deescalate most conflicts. It was a rare occasion when he had to call in reinforcements. Following the incident of bullying children in the mess hall, a new rule was immediately enforced. The meal line was patrolled and all women and children were served first, followed by the men.

A natural remedy also helped squash trouble in the meal lines. After a few days out to sea we hit rough waters. By the time we reached England, many aboard suffered from severe seasickness. There wasn't a soul left on the ship rushing to the table to eat. It seemed the only ones managing to enjoy the food were the sailors who manned the ship.

Part of Djura's duties consisted of making daily rounds. He would determine if anyone was in need of assistance or medical attention, especially with so many stricken with seasickness. The number of people that had fallen ill far outnumbered the crew members and MP's. Because Djura's time was desperately needed, we didn't see him for most of the day.

On the fourth day out to sea while making his rounds, Djura came across a woman on deck who appeared fatally ill. She lay on the deck incapacitated. She lay moaning and groaning flat on her back, and cried out as if she was dying. The poor woman spewed vomit and it shot straight upward like a fountain. The vomit splashed back down on her completely soiling her neck and her face. Too sick to move or roll out of the way, her body was totally covered in vomit within minutes. As Djura tended to the woman, hundreds of people lay close by, sprawled every which way holding their own painfully churning stomachs. Everyone silently begged the swaying to stop.

Raging thunder storms swept across the open seas and heavy rains often darkened skies. Thick fog crept across the deck making visibility so poor at times, we could barely see. Giant waves crashed against the steel walls of the vessel rocking it so violently, I feared we might tip over.

When the huge waves bombarded the ship, massive amounts of salt water spilled over onto the deck. The ship's crew was armed with brooms. They swept the rivers of salt water off the deck floor where it had pooled from the heavy rain storms. Those left on the upper deck during a storm were drenched from head to toe. Until then, I never knew the oceans were salt water.

There were thick braided ropes tied to the insides of the decks. They were uniformly spaced and scattered about the ship. If we happened to be topside when the boat began to sway we grabbed onto the ropes to steady ourselves so we wouldn't topple overboard. If we weren't hanging on, the thrust from the strong waves knocked us to the deck. Sometimes we were thrown right out of our beds. Krs was tossed from her bed countless times during the trip.

Once both girls were thrown right out of their bunks in the middle of the night. Ingeborg was on the top bunk and had fallen to the floor. She woke up screaming, still half asleep. After being thrown out of our bunks a few times, we started strapping ourselves into our beds. We weren't always sure when a severe storm was approaching and often got caught off guard.

The dangerous waves reached up to 50 feet high and did inflict some damage to the ship. A raging storm once caused a main support to crack. In the midst of the storm some of the crew shimmied up the pole to weld the break in the steel. They had to fight the blustering wind and the driving rain. They feverishly worked to repair the damage while the wind almost blew them right off the metal support. The metal beam swayed dangerously in the wind. If it had caused the metal beam to break and fall, one or all of the repair detail would certainly have been killed.

We learned very early on the ship of the necessity of hanging on for dear life. If things weren't nailed down everything would end up on the deck. There were times as we were eating in the mess hall when the waves began crashing. Within a matter of seconds the water spilled over the top deck. We were unprepared for the big wave so everything slid off of our tables. Our food, plates, and silverware were ruined and dirty on the floor.

Everyone hung on so they didn't fall out of their chairs. After it calmed, if we weren't too sick to eat from the swaying, we went back for second helpings. At times just as we were ready to take a bite of food, our plates would fly right off the table. It was like being in a cartoon where the shipmate kept trying to eat, but with every attempt, the ship rocked and his food sprung off the plate. The sea was unforgiving and we were stuck in rough waters for days.

There really wasn't much to do while we were on the ship. We ate, took short strolls on the deck, smoked cigarettes, played cards, or we slept. Our girls were afraid to stray too far from me. Ingeborg stayed close by and feared some of the passengers. A strange acting lady wandered about the ship. She sat on a bench in a fetal position and constantly rocked herself back and forth. I never heard her speak and she never said a single word to anyone on the ship that I recall. She just stared out at the sea as if she was in some sort of trance. Ingeborg was frightened the lady might scream or grab hold of her. I felt sorry for the poor woman and thought something terrible must have happened to her during the war. Why would she distance herself from other people this way? She was in a world of her own, totally disconnected from reality. I wondered how she would survive and live once we landed in America. I hoped she had family waiting for her in New York. I told Ingeborg and Krs to be kind to her and not be afraid, yet both girls were too scared to go near her.

We had been at sea for several days and most of the passengers continued to be seasick. The ship was clean and well maintained. The crew members were responsible for keeping it tidy. If we felt ill we were supposed to use the paper bags they had distributed or we had to get to the side of the ship and empty our stomach contents overboard. The unrelenting waves kept pounding the ship while we were at sea. It wasn't unusual for people to have their paper bag in one hand while holding their food and silverware in the other. A Polish woman became so ill they came to get her and flew her back to Germany by helicopter. No one knew for sure what exactly was wrong with her, but she was sick enough she could no longer stay on the ship.

Being pregnant made the trip all the more miserable for me. I wished every day I could get off and be back on land. I stayed sick throughout the entire journey. There were days I felt so ill I wondered if it would ever end. We were completely surrounded by water so there was nowhere to run or escape the crashing waves.

When together, Djura spent much of his time trying to console me and lift my spirits. I became depressed and my nerves were on edge. I was trapped and felt like I was suffocating. I thought for sure I had made one of the biggest mistakes in my life. I would have turned around and gone back home if someone could have taken me. I lashed out at Djura and cried. I pleaded with him to go back to Germany with me after we landed. I blamed him for my current misery as he was the one that encouraged me to leave Germany.

In the belly of the ship where we roomed there was little fresh air flowing. The air that circulated came through big open steel vents, which led to our sleeping quarters. There were fans inside the vents to blow fresh air into our rooms; they circulated the air most of the day. The girls and I were stuck rooming close to a heavy set woman who didn't have the best personal hygiene. She washed her dirty underwear and her other clothes in a sink near the open vents. Then she would hang them in front of the opening to blow them dry. Her heavy body odor made us all want to run. I'll never forget her oversized stained underwear blowing back and forth in front of the fan. Many times we were trapped in our quarters and we had to breathe the same air that was circulating through her drying laundry. It blew directly into our sleeping quarters. The strong odor was disgusting. Complaining wouldn't have helped, and I didn't want to start any arguments so we just suffered quietly but not happily.

Below are pictures of us on the USS General Muir in September of 1951. Ingeborg, Krs, and Karoline are in the picture below along with a man lying on deck in the bottom of the photo cleverly wearing a paper bag as a hat. Because of frequent use, most kept their bags close by.

**Picture of Ingeborg, Krs, and other children gathered on the ship**

**Ingeborg and Krs on the deck on the USS General Muir**

## Chapter 87

On September 21st of 1951 the crew began to maneuver the General Muir into the New York harbor. Everyone on the ship eagerly watched as the captain and his crew prepared to dock the large cruiser. I grabbed the girls and hurried to get topside. We didn't want to miss the crew maneuvering the ship inland. Most of all we wanted to catch a glimpse of the Statue of Liberty. We were only a quarter of a mile out from the port when we made it to the top deck. I could see her silhouette through the mist settling over the harbor.

Many others pushed ahead of us to watch the boat approach the dock. The General Muir had slowed considerably inching our way closer and closer. The crew was busy making sure the ship came in straight. It didn't take the crew long to get the ship turned just right and before we knew it we were floating alongside the Statue of Liberty. She welcomed the General Muir and everyone on the ship that had made the long arduous journey. The enormous statue towered over the bay. Her torch pointed toward the open skies and touched all of our hearts, for she represented peace, opportunity, freedom, and a fresh start in this new land. The Statue of Liberty represented the manifestation of hope, which was evident to all who stood on the deck.

Admiring the wondrous statue, I noticed the wren flying above the ship. Nudging Ingeborg, I drew her attention to the bird. She now bid farewell to the wren which had kept her company throughout the entire journey flying thousands of miles across the Atlantic Ocean.

We were thrilled to have reached our final destination after traveling so far, for so long. We were soon towed into the dock by another smaller boat. The ship's crew busily worked to get the ship anchored and tied so we wouldn't float back out to sea. The MP's were doing their best to assist all passengers giving instructions on gathering their luggage and how we would be exiting the vessel. Long lines of passengers formed on the top deck. The crew took a head count to make sure no one had been lost at sea.

Suddenly we were given orders to unhand our luggage and throw it all over the side of the ship into the water. I asked crew members why we had to dump all of our belongings overboard, however, my questions were ignored. Completely confused and angered by the order, I refused to toss my most precious mementos into the New York Harbor. My defiance made no difference because we were not going to be allowed off the ship unless we followed their orders.

One by one I watched our suitcases tumble over the side of the ship into water. As they plunged into the water I somehow lost the grip on my prayer book. It had slipped out of my hand, and dropped into the water when I hurled my suitcases over the side. I had tucked many of my official travel documents inside the pages of the prayer book to keep them safe during the trip.

When I saw the book plummet into the water I was frantic. I spotted a crew member and stopped him. I begged him to jump into the water and try to save it for me explaining what the book meant to me. I didn't realize the man was a professional diver. He understood my dilemma and was sympathetic. Within moments after we spoke he jumped over the side diving into the water. He searched the murky waters until he found it, then he climbed back aboard the ship and handed it to me. I expressed my most sincere gratitude and thanked him for saving one of my most valued possessions. Once more I met a kind hearted stranger willing to help me. I never learned the diver's name and wished I could have had the opportunity to thank him and show my appreciation once we were on land.

To this day, I have no idea why we had to throw most of our belongings overboard. No one was ever able to explain why we needed to discard our suitcases into the water. I had lost many of my most meaningful keepsakes including the hand embroidered pillowcases and blankets my mother made me. The few nice dresses I had packed for the girls along with other keepsakes now lay under water sinking to the bottom of the harbor. It was heartbreaking for all to throw their last remaining possessions away as if they were garbage.

For some reason we were allowed to keep our small carryon bags. My wedding ring from Hinrich, a bracelet and watch he had given me, and most importantly the pictures of my family had been saved. It was very important to me for our family to look respectable and presentable when we met with our new sponsors for the first time. But unfortunately our nice clothing was gone having been thrown overboard.

It took a few hours before we were finally able to get off the ship and onto land. Once everyone was organized and accounted for, we were allowed to exit the ship. Our paperwork was already in order, but we needed to be processed through customs. My emotions were scattered; my guilt for leaving my family behind was unrelenting. I considered myself selfish for coming to the U.S. I struggled with my desire to return to Germany and blamed Djura for convincing me to take this direction. These emotions were contradicting because I knew deep in my heart coming to America was the right thing for us to do if we wanted a better life. We wanted to build a bright future for ourselves and our children and there were no other alternatives, but to live in America.

Emotionally broken I gathered up what strength I had left and glanced back at the 'Lady' one last time. We had made it to the United States safe and sound. Walking in line with what was left of our possessions, we headed off the ship. When I set foot on land, I was overcome with a sudden burst of happiness and relief.

Djura wrestled with some of his own demonizing thoughts. He never had the opportunity to say goodbye to his own mother, sisters, and extended family. The last time Djura was home was in 1936 when he was 18-years-old. He had returned home once in the midst of his military service in Yugoslavia while on a short medical leave to nurse his sick kidney back to health. Not being able to give his mother and the rest of his family a proper goodbye haunted him. When he left Yugoslavia he said a quick goodbye to his family and headed out the door. Now thinking back he was saddened and felt guilty for never taking the time to give his mother or sisters one last farewell hug. He was 34-years-old and hadn't seen any of them in 15 years. To keep our sanity we had to put much of our past behind us. We had to look toward the future and move on with our lives.

While in customs, I was awestruck we were sharing a similar experience to the thousands of other immigrants that had been processed and provided legal passage into the United States. I felt so thankful for the opportunity. It was hard to believe Djura and I would be part of the immigration history of America.

While we waited to get through customs it was wonderful feeling the earth beneath our feet. We had been trapped on a ship for days and now felt like we had been released from prison. I wanted to lay in the soft grass, touch the ground and hug the trees, but the weather was chilly and unexpectedly cold for September. Frost was on the ground everywhere, yet our girls didn't mind. Ingeborg stopped happily to touch the chilly white frost covering the blades of grass.

We waited in several different long lines before customs allowed us to leave the grounds. We weren't supposed to bring anything across the border except for our pre-approved checked luggage. We waited in one line to show proof of our identity and to make known our country of origin. In another line our remaining bags were searched. Once we completed the entire process, we were allowed to leave the grounds.

Many American women worked in the Processing Center had volunteered their time. They helped direct refugees, translate if they could, and fed many of the displaced persons. Some of the refugees' sponsors had already shown up in New York to pick up the families they sponsored. Most of the women volunteering were unable to speak German. They had good intentions, and although we were not able to understand each other, everyone seemed to be moving successfully through customs. We were offered food by the volunteers, and since my nausea had yet to lift, I regretfully turned down the delicious desserts being offered.

We were happy to have Djura alongside us to help since he had completed his duties with the military police. Going through customs with our girls wasn't easy. Djura spotted some vending machines in the building filled with various candies, chips, and other delicious snacks. Djura wanted to buy a snack for the girls so he pulled out the change in his pocket. We both tried to figure out how to operate them. We pushed buttons and pulled levers to no avail. We were unable to figure out how to make them work. Neither of us could read, write, nor speak English. Djura had learned a few conversational words. Neither Djura nor I wanted to ask anyone for help. We felt ashamed and stupid for our inability to use a simple candy machine. We left it at that, and both of us walked away frustrated with ourselves for not knowing the language or how to operate a vending machine.

Some of the refugees' families were already in New York and had arrived at the Center to help translate for their relatives. We had no family or friends living in the United States and were on our own to figure out how to proceed with the rest of our journey. We eventually made it through customs and were soon on our way to Oelwein, Iowa.

## Chapter 88

After going through customs, we were gathered in a large group. A lead person split us up into groups to be ferried across the bay. Once across the bay, a train was waiting for us. The processing staff, family, and friends of others helped us find our connecting trains to take us to our final destination. The group who had come on our ship would be traveling to many different cities. Some intended to live in New York, while others had found a place to live in Chicago. Some would be living with relatives while others would have to make it on their own. Djura had several Yugoslavian friends heading for Chicago. They told Djura big cities offered much opportunity and they had big hopes of someday starting their own businesses. Our destiny would be much different than most. We would be traveling to a small town in Iowa with a population of about 7,850 people.

It took about a half a day to get everyone off the ship, across the harbor and transferred to their connecting trains. Djura, our girls and I traveled by train from New York to Chicago. When we arrived in Chicago, we waited a few hours before boarding the train headed to Oelwein. We eagerly looked forward to meeting our new sponsors and seeing our new home. A kind young man from Maynard, Iowa was on the train. He took the time to introduce himself. He welcomed us to the country and tried to talk to Djura and the girls during the ride. I remember exactly what his face looked like, but cannot remember his name. I wished I could have properly thanked him for being so kind to us.

The train from Chicago was quite comfortable. We were bundled up in our sweaters and scarfs. The girls sat next to the window though we were all seated together. We watched out the window with excitement as we whizzed by the Iowa countryside. The vast open farmland was like nothing I had seen before and it was colder than any of us had expected.

The kind young man assured us the cold day wasn't normal September weather and the area was experiencing an early frost.

The girls were thrilled to be riding in a comfortable train, neither of them wanted to miss a thing. I kept waiting to see if we would pass by any mountains. All of us were curious about where we'd be living. We wondered about the American cuisine. What kinds of food did they raise and serve?

When we looked out the windows, we were surprised to see the ground was frozen and the garden goods, field corn, and bean fields were covered in white from the early frost. Frozen ears of corn hung from the corn stalks and garden tomatoes were blackened and ruined. Djura watched out the window to see if he could spot any potato fields, but he was unable to find one. He had been forced to work in the potato fields for many years while he was a war prisoner. In Germany potatoes were abundant and large fields of vegetables were a common sight. A primary source of our family's diet were vegetables, especially potatoes. We wondered if there would be any potatoes to eat. We hoped they would be plentiful.

It was like being a child seeing many wonderful things for the very first time. I was amazed by the hundreds of cars we passed on our way to Oelwein. We saw so many cars driving on the roads we assumed everyone living in America was rich. Most people in Germany did not own their own vehicles. For the most part we rode bikes everywhere and didn't travel far.

Watching the new scenery along the way made the train ride go quickly and we arrived in Oelwein on September 23rd at 1:00 a.m. The Wetlaufers and a few members from the Zion Lutheran Church met us at the train station. A German speaking member came along with them to help translate our first meeting and help communicate our needs. The Wetlaufers had already rented a small motel apartment for us, but we would only be staying there for a few days as it was too small for a family of four. They had secured a larger apartment for us, which was located in the upstairs of their home.  We planned to move into the upstairs apartment once it was furnished.  It wouldn't take Djura too long to learn the language as he easily picked up new languages much quicker than I.

We were told by the Wetlaufers of an article written about our struggles and planned arrival.  It had been published in the Oelwein paper.  The article told the story of our family's dilemma, our intentions to resettle in the Oelwein community and Djura's plan to work for City Laundry.  Mr. Wetlaufer had the paper with him and offered it to us.

**The article written in the Oelwein Daily Register below.**

The Wetlaufers and the Zion Lutheran Church had worked in partnership together to help people like us resettle in the United States. We felt blessed Djura had a job waiting for him the minute we arrived. He was paid 18 dollars per week, which seemed like a livable wage to us.

After staying a few days in the motel rooms we moved into an upstairs apartment above the Wetlaufer's. They owned a beautiful two-story brick home located on North Frederick Avenue in Oelwein. The Wetlaufers lived on the lower level of the house and they shared the upstairs with us. Mr. Wetlaufer and his wife were such kind people. They had prepared the entire upstairs for our family before we arrived. We had our own bathroom and kitchen facilities to use, and there was plenty of privacy for Djura and me. The backyard was gorgeous with plenty of plush grass and mature trees, and enough room for our girls to play.

The Wetlaufers and the Zion Lutheran Church, had welcomed us to Oelwein with open arms and unselfishly placed us in their own home. Gerald and Betty became our good friends, church family, and Djura's employer. They were like family to us. They bought our girls birthday and Christmas presents every single year. The Wetlaufers treated Ingeborg and Krs as if they were their own grandchildren and helped them in many ways. They helped me learn about American culture, traditions, and cared for the girls if we needed to leave home.

Djura began working one week after we landed in the New York Harbor and worked for City Laundry over the next year and a half. Later, when we were more settled, he found a job in a feed mill where he made more money. Even though Djura was no longer employed by the Wetlaufers, they extended their kindness to us for the next several years.

Djura never sat idle and worked much of the time. He was driven to provide for his family, and find better opportunities for our girls. He worked hard and long hours for days on end. Sometimes he worked two jobs to make ends meet. Life could be hard in the United States. Unlike the propaganda we had heard in Germany, we found wealth didn't come so easy. You had to work hard to get what you wanted, but the opportunities were far greater than in Germany.

A few others spoke German in the community and they were willing to help us learn the English language. The whole town wanted to help us and the community's extreme kindness along with help from the church became crucial in helping us get established. The entire community played a major role in our lives. We expressed our sincere gratitude and thanks to these individuals and organizations who made such a difference in our lives.

Of course there were challenges that came with moving to a new country. The language barrier was difficult for me. It took me several years before I felt comfortable speaking English because I was always fearful I'd make a mistake. I continued to speak German in our home for many years to come. To this day I don't feel confident when I speak English.

I missed my family terribly. However, the people in Oelwein and the state of Iowa were friendly and accepting, and it was easier to cope. It seemed as though our neighbors and friends wanted us to succeed and they helped us feel like we belonged and were part of the community. I wanted to make the best out of the opportunities we were so graciously given.

I decided it was time for us to create new memories and traditions of our own. I made a promise to say a prayer every night and thank God for all he had done for us. Honoring a part of my past, while creating a new future for us, I picked out a prayer from my grandmother's prayer book and read one each night to my girls. I will never forget the kind faces of those who helped me through my life's journey both in Europe and in America.

Our long journey to America was over and we settled into our new life in Oelwein. I prayed for God to bless America for providing us with the opportunity to start over and thanked Him for placing us in a small friendly community where we could raise our family. A place where we felt safe. We were lucky to have been placed in a town and country with such caring people.

I remember crying every day for three months straight when we arrived in the U.S. From the moment we left Europe I hoped and prayed someday both Djura and I would be able to go back to Austria, Germany, and Yugoslavia. I wished with all my heart to see our families once again and be able to tell them face to face how much we loved them. Although, I continued to miss my family, I cried tears of joy 11 years later on the day I received my citizenship. One of the proudest days of my life was the day I became an American citizen. I was so appreciative to be a citizen of and live in a nation where hope and opportunity were a reality.

Djura and I have felt blessed over the years to have been able to see our children, grandchildren, and great-grandchildren thrive and grow in our new home. We continued to face challenges even in America as that is the way of life. There are many more stories left to tell of Djura's and my past. Some I've probably forgotten, some I want to forget, and others I'll always remember. I have had tragedy, but also many blessings in my life and continue to be thankful for everything in my life.

Thinking back it is hard to believe all that transpired in my lifelong journey. My children have asked me how I survived. I honestly have no good answers. I simply had to push it all from my mind. That was the only way I could move on and free myself from the grip of sorrow. I have to force myself not to think of all the tragedy or it would consume me. There are moments when this isn't possible and I am flooded with emotion, but I try my best for Djura and for my children. So many had had it much worse than I during and after the war. I hope they were able to find some peace, prosperity and meaning in their lives as I have today.

I continue to contemplate my faith and destiny and the role each has played in my life as well as the lives of my loved ones. I believe destiny played a part in bringing Djura and me together and in bringing us to America. So many times our lives could have taken different paths. At times it seemed as if we were destined for a life of difficulty and sadness, yet when times were at their worst we found a way to persevere. We refused to forfeit our faith entirely even though there were moments when it was irrevocably challenged. We never relinquished our belief there was good in the world and we could find happiness for ourselves and our children.

*I believe in the sun even when it's not shining,*
*In love even when I'm alone,*
*And in God even when he is silent.*
**By: Unknown Author**

**A quote found scratched into a cellar wall in Germany by someone hiding from the Nazis.**

# Author's Note

The events that took place in my mother's life are not unique to WWII. Horrible atrocities have occurred in all wars and conflicts past and present. There are casualties on all sides during war. War is nondiscriminatory. It affects everyone young and old from the unborn to soldiers fighting on the front lines.

Innocent civilians are caught in the midst of war battling to survive, often not supporting the political agendas driving initiatives to obtain power or financial gains. War can force people to abandon their values and morals. Choices are made for the preservation of oneself and one's family. It's unimaginable how someone could lose their humanity and inflict such cruelty on others when making these choices. Equally unimaginable are those that carry within themselves the ability to act selflessly and risk their own lives trying to help others while clinging to their own humanity. It is my belief that there are more courageous people in the world who are willing to sacrifice to help their fellowman than those few who choose ignorance, supremacy and revenge.

Below is a picture of Djura and Karoline's descendants,
(children, grandchildren, in-laws and significant others) taken
in 2004. Missing from the picture is daughter Angelina
Stefanovic. I would like to honor those who have passed: The
late Djura Stefanovic, Kosta Stefanovic, Dobrina Stefanovic-
Folsom, Monika Stefanovic-Roepke, Les Folsom and John G.
Woodson.

# Notes and References

**Edelweiss**

Normally a white flower sometimes called the snow flower. One of the major interactions that Edelweiss is a part of is the relationship it has with humans. The people who reside in the mountainous regions where Edelweiss is found have been fascinated by it for centuries. "It is said that more people have lost their lives trying to collect it than climbing the high peaks of the Alps." The fascination with this plant is due to the medicinal qualities that Edelweiss has. It has been used as an anti-diarrhea and dysentery cure for many generations. However, there are studies that show most of the health qualities of the plant arise due to "the presence and spectrum of polyphenolic secondary metabolites." These polyphenols have antibacterial and anti-inflammatory properties. The polyphenols are found in the leaves of the plant, but also in the root systems. *Leontopodium alpinum* has the ability to absorb ultraviolet rays, scavenge "free radicals", and antioxidant properties when used for medicinal purposes. These properties are all very helpful to humans for a variety of conditions. From skin diseases to stomach conditions, Edelweiss has been helpful in more ways than one would think.

(http://bioweb.uwlax.edu/bio203/s2014/wlodyga_eliz/interactions.htm)

## The Anschluss

The Anschluss violated Article 80 of the "Treaty of Versailles", the terms of which had been drawn up by the victorious Allies without the participation of the Germans after WWI. At the insistence of France and Great Britain, the "Treaty of Versailles", which Germany was forced to sign, included the following words, "Germany acknowledges and will respect the independence of Austria within the frontier which may be fixed in a treaty between the State and the principal Allied and Associated Powers; she agrees that this independence shall be inalienable. America did not sign the "Treaty of Versailles" because the U.S. Congress, dominated by the Republican Party refused to ratify it. This was not because of any disagreement with the harsh terms of the Treaty, but because signing the Treaty would have automatically included America in the new world government called the League of Nations. Our Congress voted against it, although it had been proposed by President Woodrow Wilson, a Democrat, and was included in Wilson's Fourteen Points which formed the basis of the Armistice that had ended WWI.

(http: www.scrapbookpages.com/Austria/anschluss01.html).

# Hermann Göring Biography

Warrior, General (1893–1946)

Hermann Göring was a leader of the Nazi Party. He was condemned to hang as a war criminal in 1946 but took his own life instead.

## Synopsis

Born in Germany in 1893, Hermann Göring was a leader of the Nazi Party. He played a prominent role in organizing the Nazi police state in Germany and established concentration camps for the "corrective treatment" of individuals. Indicted by the International Military Tribunal at Nuremberg in 1946, Göring was condemned to hang as a war criminal, but he took cyanide the night he was to be executed. (http://www.biography.com/)

## Rudolf Hess Biography

Adolf Hitler appointed Rudolf Hess deputy of the Nazi party in 1939. Following World War II, Hess was convicted at the Nuremberg Trials and sentenced to life in prison.

### Synopsis

Rudolf Hess was born on April 26, 1894, in Alexandria, Egypt. In 1920, he became the 16th member of Nazi party. Hitler appointed him deputy in 1939. After staging a coup in 1941, he became a prisoner of war in England and was ousted from the Nazi party. Following World War II, he was convicted at the Nuremberg Trials and sentenced to life in prison. He committed suicide on August 17, 1987, at the Spandau Prison in West Berlin, Germany. (http://www.biography.com/)

**Adolf Hitler Biography**

(https://www.google.com/search?q=hitler+adolf+wikipedia&tbm=isch&imgil=Hitler%)

Military Leader, Dictator (1889–1945)

Adolf Hitler - Mini Biography (TV-14; 04:54) Adolf Hitler was leader of the Nazi Party and became Chancellor of Germany in 1933. As leader of the Third Reich, he invaded Poland, which started World War II. He orchestrated the Holocaust, which resulted in the death of 6 million Jews.

**Synopsis**

Born in Austria in 1889, Adolf Hitler rose to power in German politics as leader of the National Socialist German Workers Party, also known as the Nazi Party. Hitler was chancellor of Germany from 1933 to 1945, and served as dictator from 1934 to 1945. His policies precipitated World War II and the Holocaust. Hitler committed suicide with wife Eva Braun on April 30, 1945, in his Berlin bunker. (http://www.biography.com/)

## Sandbostel

Dokumentations Und

Gedenkstätte Lager Sandbostel

Greftstraße 3

(http://www.stiftung-lager-sandbostel.de/pdf-
dateien/flyer/sandbostel_infoflyer_x_eng_zoll.pdf)

**Jill Woodson's sketch of her grandparents:**

**Oil painting of Djura, Karoline, Ingeborg and Krsmanija riding on the coal car**
**Painted by: Krsmanija Craig**

# Acknowledgements

I would like to thank the many people who contributed to the writing of *Triumph Over Destiny* and those who inspired me to write the book. With much gratitude I want to thank my parents. Their eternal inspiration influenced me to write about their life long journey. It's difficult to find adequate words to completely describe their high degree of integrity, strength, courage, and compassion they instilled in all their children through the years. With much respect and great honor I want to acknowledge my parents as being the most influential people in my life. I admired their willingness to share their compelling story with others.

A big thank you goes to my two daughters Jeannie and Joni, who put up with me as we all struggled through the writing process of the book. I appreciated their drive, insistence on quality and willingness to assist me with editing, spell checking and rewriting while trying to find a proper flow to make *Triumph Over Destiny* a more enjoyable read. They patiently listened to my constant nagging insisting *Triumph Over Destiny* be completed and published by December 2014." Thank you Jeannie and Joni for spending your weekends, days off, and the many nights you worked after midnight and beyond to accomplish and meet the December deadline. I could not have completed this four year project without Joni and Jeannie's constant support and assistance.

A sincere thank you goes to my son Wallace John, who jumped in to help the team during the tail end of the project. His honesty, constructive criticism and his support was greatly appreciated. Thank you for being our fresh set of eyes and carefully reading the almost finished book while checking for proper flow and any other necessary revisions.

Thanks to Trishia, my niece, for helping me make revisions, deletions, cuts, and simply making sense of many of the stories and paragraphs I thought already made perfect sense.

Thank you to my daughter Jill and her artistic skills. I thank you for drawing the sketch of your grandparents standing by the Statue of Liberty. It will be a keepsake for many years to come.

A big thank you goes to my sister Krsmanija who was instrumental in helping me remember details that were included in some of the various stories. I appreciate your artistry and the brushed oil painting where you captured the emotions and images of our mother, father, Ingeborg and yourself as you rode hundreds of miles across Germany on top of a coal car when trying to reach the border of Austria. Thank you for being a survivor and sharing your love and kindness through the years.

A sincere thank you goes to Eugene Craig who was our expert historian and helped us answer and confirm various historical questions during the writing process.

I can't forget to thank my sister Ingeborg, for putting up with my persistent phone calls during the past four years and for asking her numerous questions about her own past. I am grateful for her agreeing to be voice recorded and for the many times she called relatives in Germany and Austria for more needed information to complete the book. I mostly want to thank her for her courage and resilience and for surviving the war so that I have a wonderful sister I can love and who loves me.

I would like to thank Audrey Besler the initial editor of *Triumph Over Destiny*. A sincere thank you goes to her for the heartfelt compassion she has expressed associated with my family's story after learning about their struggles. I am grateful for her willingness to work with me, her editing skills, and competence when completing the editing process. Your patience was greatly appreciated and your professionalism valued during the process. Thanks for respectfully listening to all my suggestions and considering my thoughts and judgment during the rewrites.

Kudos to all the others, Tracy Deutmeyer who should have received a gold medal for her incredible lightning speed word processing skills. To Amy Lickiss, Melissa Hamilton, and Hatidza Mujakic whom helped with many other miscellaneous details, such as editing, translation, organization, referencing, word processing, and research. I would like to acknowledge their support and confidentiality during the writing of the *Triumph Over Destiny*.

And to my many Bosnian friends, Semso Beganovic and his wife Saliha, Budo Kajtezovic, Edin Ardnaut, Amela Mehic, Hatidza Mujakic, Suljo Dizdarevic, Nedjad Jusovic, Omer Bajramovic, Alma Beganovic, Denis Kuduzovic, and Sakib Rizvic who through telling their own stories of their experiences during the Bosnian War inspired me to write *Triumph Over Destiny*. Their stories were inspirational and they helped me further understand how terribly war affects one's homeland, their future, and their own personal lives.

Most of all a great big thank you to all of the individuals who will read *Triumph Over Destiny* and gain insight and understanding about war in general and how it changes every aspect in one's life and interferes with their fate and destiny.

Made in the USA
Columbia, SC
25 November 2018